Dickens, Money, and Society

Dickens, Money, And Society

By Grahame Smith

UNIVERSITY OF CALIFORNIA PRESS
Berkeley and Los Angeles 1968

University of California Press
Berkeley and Los Angeles, California

Cambridge University Press
London, England

Designed by Douglas Nicholson
Printed in the United States of America

To my wife Angela

Contents

In a community regulated only by the laws of supply, but protected from open violence, the persons who become rich are, generally speaking, industrious, resolute, proud, covetous, prompt, methodical, sensible, unimaginative, insensitive, and ignorant. The persons who remain poor are the entirely foolish, the entirely wise, the idle, the reckless, the humble, the thoughtful, the dull, the imaginative, the sensitive, the well-informed, the improvident, the irregularly and impulsively wicked, the clumsy knave, the open thief, and the entirely merciful, just, and goodly person.

JOHN RUSKIN

The Problem of Form

In all my writings, I hope I have taken every available opportunity
of showing the want of sanitary improvements in the neglected
dwellings of the poor. Mrs. Sarah Gamp was, four-and-twenty years
ago, a fair representation of the hired attendant on the poor in
sickness. The Hospitals of London were, in many respects, noble
Institutions; in others, very defective. I think it is not the least
among their instances of mismanagement, that Mrs. Betsey Prig
was a fair specimen of a Hospital Nurse; and that the Hospitals,
with their means and funds, should have left it to private humanity
and enterprise to enter on an attempt to improve that class of persons—since, greatly improved through the agency of good women.
                                    (Preface to *Martin Chuzzlewit*)

In this way, in a passage that begins with the flatness of a
sanitary inspector's report and ends with a compliment to a
"class of persons" at the farthest possible remove from the
coarse vitality of Mrs. Gamp herself, Dickens introduces one
of the great characters of fiction. Almost all critics have suc-
cumbed to the overwhelming pressure of her presence, which
continually explodes the tidy and seemingly secure fortifications of literary theory with an irresistible force. Any view of
characterization must take her into account, and one can sense
the nerveless despair with which the theorists anxiously peer
out at her advancing bulk. Nearer and nearer she looms until,
with one sweep of her umbrella, the whole flimsy edifice is
sent skyward, and when the dust has settled, nothing is to be
seen but the broken remains of limited categories: "flat" and
"round" characters, "types" and "individuals" scattered in hopeless confusion.

It seems generally agreed that she is a character who belongs
to the highest realms of artistic creation. To find the defining
comparison we must go to Shakespeare. And yet it becomes
clear that in placing Mrs. Gamp side by side with Falstaff, for
example, the comparison limits as well as defines. Certainly
she has, as Orwell says of all Dickens' characters, no "mental

life,"[1] no moral complexity. Anecdote and obsessive monologue encompass the range of her metaphysical universe, while Falstaff can rise to the level of generalizing insight into the nature of the world he inhabits. His speech on honor is a devasting critique of the weaknesses of the knightly code as exemplified by Hotspur. Mrs. Gamp remains blissfully unaware of the possibility of criticizing the life she finds around her. Again, she is incapable of love or even affection: Mrs. Prig is nothing but a sounding board for her endless imaginary dialogue with Mrs. Harris. Insulated in her own private world, she knows nothing of the joy to be found in other people, such as that expressed in Falstaff's affection for Hal and his delight in Bardolph's "salamander" face. And with the lack of self-knowledge of the utterly self-absorbed, she remains unconscious of her own evil. Falstaff's claims of imminent reformation are never serious, but they are part of the self-awareness of the man who feels himself to be in some kind of relation with his external world. There may be an essence of joyous anarchy at the heart of his character, but its surface shifts and glimmers with the possibility of change and amendment. Mrs. Gamp is a totally fixed character and so lacks all pathos.

And yet these figures do have enough in common to make it possible to speak of them in the same breath. The liberating laughter they arouse in us is quite without malice, for their creators communicate the delight they felt both in contemplating them and in the act of embodying their vision. Keats's understanding of the nature of the artistic process is as relevant to Dickens as it is to Shakespeare. For him, the artist "has as much delight in conceiving an Iago as an Imogen";[2] and "the excellence of every art is its intensity, capable of making all disagreeables evaporate from their being in close relationship with beauty and truth."[3] Mrs. Gamp must be condemned in the preface and in the novel's conventional conclusion, but in Dickens' imagination she is accepted without reservation and she emerges from that fire purged of viciousness. The duality of her nature is conveyed, symbolically, by her function as both deathbed nurse and midwife: her evil incompetence in this first

---

[1] "Charles Dickens," in *A Collection of Essays* (New York: Doubleday Anchor Books, 1954), p. 106.

[2] Letter to Richard Woodhouse, Tues., Oct. 27, 1818, in *The Letters of John Keats*, ed. Maurice Buxton Forman (London: Oxford University Press, 1960), p. 227.

[3] To George Thomas Keats, Sun., Dec. 21, 1819, *ibid.* p. 70.

occupation ensures that we see her as a harbinger of death, while the second forces us to recognize that she is at the same time, however parodoxically, an affirmer of life. No matter how reprehensible she may be from a moral point of view, as an artistic creation her final effect is one of life-enhancing vitality. Similarly, we frequently see Falstaff disporting himself among the very dregs of London's whores and villains, but his own enjoyment is presented with such gusto that the elements of evil are dissolved in life-giving laughter. Another basis for comparison between them is that Falstaff and Mrs. Gamp share, to an almost hallucinatory degree, an absolute physical reality. Every wrinkle and crease in Falstaff's heroic body is present in a single phrase: "He hath a monstrous beauty, like the hindquarters of an elephant." And the wheezing, rustling, and creaking of Mrs. Gamp are as obtrusive as the sounds of a next-door neighbor. The minutiae of her dress, gestures, and mannerisms are set out in complete detail, but never simply with the effect of a Defoe-like catalog. The selection is always controlled by creative imagination, and so the details achieve an inner cohesion.

She was a fat old woman, this Mrs. Gamp, with a husky voice and a moist eye, which she had a remarkable power of turning up, and only showing the white of it. Having a very little neck, it cost her some trouble to look over herself, if one may say so, at those to whom she talked. She wore a very rusty black gown, rather the worse for snuff, and a shawl and bonnet to correspond. In these dilapidated articles of dress she had, on principle, arrayed herself, time out of mind, on such occasions as the present; for this at once expressed a decent amount of veneration for the deceased, and invited the next of kin to present her with a fresher suit of weeds: an appeal so frequently successful, that the very fetch and ghost of Mrs. Gamp, bonnet and all, might be seen hanging up, any hour in the day, in at least a dozen of the second-hand clothes shops about Holborn. The face of Mrs. Gamp—the nose in particular—was somewhat red and swollen, and it was difficult to enjoy her society without becoming conscious of a smell of spirits. Like most persons who have attained to great eminence in their profession, she took to hers very kindly; insomuch, that setting aside her natural predilections as a woman, she went to a lying-in or a laying-out with equal zest and relish. (XIX)

Like Falstaff, Mrs. Gamp is one of the great facts of English literature: she may not be liked, but she cannot be ignored.

Emboldened by the conviction that so secure an edifice of fact as Mrs. Gamp could never be explained away, one may attempt some elucidation of what it is that constitutes her greatness as a character. Many of the attempts to do this have centered on that most elusive of critical terms "realism." I myself have already pointed out her extraordinary physical reality, but at the same time have been compelled to admit that she lacks human complexity when compared with Falstaff. And so, from one angle of vision she is just as "realistic" as Sir John, from another, less so. Again, K. J. Fielding claims that she and Pecksniff were founded on actual people and so, he seems to imply, are "real" because of this;[4] while Dickens appears to regard her as a characteristic type, "a fair representation of the hired attendant on the poor in sickness" of twenty-four years earlier. At first sight, this last view seems the most unconvincing of all. The notion of that intransigent and gin-soaked individualist as a kind of Platonic form of inefficient midwifery, constructed to fulfill the most narrowly didactic of social aims, seems to indicate an almost willful blindness to the power of her achieved life on the part of the very man who called that life into being.

The necessary clue to the riddle of her triumphant vitality may be found if we return to the comparison with Falstaff. When we listen with breathless delight to him promising self-improvement, disclaiming knowledge of his own wickedness, and, best of all, exaggerating the number of those who attacked him on Gad's Hill, we feel that he leaves behind the raffish realism of the medieval London underworld and moves into the only fit world for such a monstrous and genial liar—that of poetry. Falstaff's evasions and subterfuges never serve the merely utilitarian purpose of saving his skin; he elaborates them beyond what is strictly necessary because he enjoys his lies for their own sake. They are the comic poetry of a man profoundly but resignedly aware of the vast gulf that exists between human aspiration and achievement. Surely it is true that Mrs. Gamp also belongs in this rarefied atmosphere; and there is a sense in which Dickens' achievement is even greater than Shakespeare's at this point (or, if not greater, at least "purer"). The fun of *Henry IV* is compounded of all the elements of drama: language, plot and situation, character. All of these are displayed in the Boar's Head scene, for example, and they constitute an essentially social comedy; not in being a Jonsonian criticism of society, but because they make for the clash of character and the exposure of observable human idiosyncrasy. It is this last point that accounts for the fact that even Falstaff's wildest

---

[4] *Charles Dickens* (London: Longmans, 1958), p. 77.

flights belong to a recognizable world. The comedy of Mrs. Gamp is pure fantasy because it is stripped of all social reference and exists self-sufficiently in and for itself. It is, above all, a construction of language. On our first meeting she is described to us with masterly force and compression, and from then on she simply speaks.

We can find the contrast I am attempting to elucidate within Dickens himself if we return, for a moment, to *The Pickwick Papers*. Monroe Engel claims that language and "particularly spoken language—is the major distinction *The Pickwick Papers* has over its predecessors."[5] But it remains true that a great deal of its humor springs from what may be called situation comedy: Mr. Pickwick entering the wrong bedroom, the military parade, the first ride to Dingley Dell. This is the humor of social observation rather than comic imagination. The most important example of the second is to be found, of course, in the great trial scene. Here the laughter represents, as Edmund Wilson says, "like the laughter of Aristophanes, a real escape from institutions."[6] It has the wildness and inconsequentiality of fantasy. Yet even here we still find a strong sense of social reference, in the direct attack on the law, for example, and the implicit condemnation of unjust trials. The very richness of the comedy stems partly from the exaggerations by means of which a recognizable social reality is inflated into a grotesque parody of itself. Language plays its part in all of this, but it is a language that reflects, in however distorted a manner, the everyday world. But with Mrs. Gamp things are very different.

When Gamp was summoned to his long home, and I see him a-lying in Guy's Hospital with a penny-piece on each eye, and his wooden leg under his left arm, I thought I should have fainted away. But I bore up. (XLX)

The final thrust of genius in this bizarre picture lies in the nightmarish exactness of detail—"his wooden leg under his *left* arm"—and with it we recognize that we are enclosed in a magic circle of pure comedy from which it is impossible to break out with explanations of satirical intent or didactic purpose. This is even more true of the tea party with Betsey Prig, which moves from the rhythmical lyricism of

"Betsey . . . I will now propoge a toast. My frequent pardner, Betsey Prig!

[5] *The Maturity of Dickens* (Oxford: University Press, 1959), p. 84.
[6] "Dickens: The Two Scrooges," in *The Wound and the Bow* (Boston: Houghton Mifflin, 1941), p. 13.

"Which, altering the name to Sairah Gamp; I drink . . . with love and tenderness,"

through the terror of Mrs. Prig's "memorable and tremendous words" concerning Mrs. Harris—"I don't believe there's no sich a person!"—and her equally awful irony:

"And *you* was a-goin' to take me under you! . . . *You* was, was you? Oh, how kind! Why, deuce take your imperence," said Mrs. Prig, with a rapid change from banter to ferocity, "what do you mean?"

to the coda of sublime nonsense: "the words she spoke of Mrs. Harris, lambs could not forgive. No Betsey! . . . nor worms forget!" (XLIX)

Mrs. Gamp, then, is a creation of the comic imagination in its purest form. It can be argued, of course, that she is representative in the sense that she embodies, in a comic vision, a kind of alienation from society and a consequent "inner emigration"[7] that are held to be peculiarly characteristic of the modern world. But if this is true in general terms, it obviously is not so at the level of didactic or even thematic purpose This modern sense of isolation is clearly neither the "message" nor the theme of *Martin Chuzzlewit*. I later try to show that parts of this novel do have a significant relationship to the nineteenth century as a whole, but the attempt to demonstrate that it possesses an overall unity, and that Mrs. Gamp has a meaningful role to play within such a unity, is doomed to failure. Mrs. Gamp is representative in the same sense as Don Quixote; that is, by virtue of the power with which she is forced upon our imagination, and because she is a figure created on the grand scale, she is irresistibly linked to the whole sweep of our common humanity. But there is, ultimately, no incompatibility between a character's echoes of the universally human and our view that, in purely literary terms, its deepest interest is to be found in and for itself. If all this is accurate, what are we to make of Dickens' own words in describing Mrs. Gamp as "a fair representation of the hired attendant on the poor in sickness"? This is the question toward which my whole discussion has been tending, for it brings us face to face with one of the most difficult problems with which Dickens presents us: the relation in him between realist and poet; in his work, between didacticism and pure creativity.

[7] Oswald Schwarz, *The Psychology of Sex* (Penguin Books, 1949), p. 145 n. 1.

Facing, and attempting to account for, this strange duality gives one, I think, a means of understanding both the isolated fictional moment and the overall pattern of Dickens' career. And it is a way of understanding that is doubly meaningful in that it can help to elucidate the weakness as well as the strength of Dickens' work. Dickens is a didactic writer with social concerns that range from the superficial to the profound, and he is a poet who can create characters and worlds with the huge implications of myth. These facts have been so long recognized that such a statement has an air of banality. But I think it is salutary to remember what an amazing, perhaps even unique, combination of qualities this makes for. Ours is the writer who can move from the absurd propaganda of Mr. Bevan's farewell words to young Martin Chuzzlewit:

"If you ever become a rich man, or a powerful one . . . you shall try to make your Government more careful of its subjects when they roam abroad to live. Tell it what you know of emigration in your own case, and impress upon it how much suffering may be prevented with a little pains!" (XXXIV)

through the freely achieved life of a Mr. Micawber, to the wonderfully subtle mixture of social meaning and human reality in William Dorrit. With this in mind, it seems false to the richness of Dickens' vision to concentrate only on the social or the "poetic" side of his genius. Coming to terms with his greatness involves bringing these two aspects of his work together.

In attempting to do this, I have begun by raising the problem of a duality that makes itself felt in every area of Dickens' fiction. I found it convenient to open with characterization because there this duality can be seen in a particularly heightened form, but it is possible to pose many other questions that are intimately connected with it. What, for example, is the relationship between Dickens' total fictional form—complexity of plot, characterization, symbolism, use of language—and social criticism? Again, what is the connection between his development as an artist and the social concerns that continue to be of consuming interest to him throughout his career? I have already suggested that Dickens' mixture of didacticism and poetry is one of the basic facts of his work which has never been satisfactorily explained. It is clearly recognized today that an earlier approach to Dickens such as that of T. A. Jackson in his *Charles Dickens: The Progress of a Radical* fails because of an almost absurd concentration on Dickens as social propagandist, even as revolutionary. But it can be argued that more modern studies are equally eccentric in their insistence on the primacy of a sometimes morbid psychologizing or of the use of myth in understanding the great novels of Dickens' later period. Such critics often seem to forget that Dickens' complexities of personality are those of genius, not sickness, and that the roots of myth lie in the world of external reality as much as in the mind of the creative artist. To raise a second major point, although the increasing darkness of Dickens' vision has been a constant critical preoccupation for many years, the complexity of structure that accompanied this darkening vision has been noticed rather than elucidated.

In my view, the Dickens problem presents itself essentially as a question of fictional form which is related to the analysis of society. As with any other great writer, there are several crucial strands of personality in Dickens from the interaction of which the body of his work emerges, and any coherent account of his fiction must consider all of them. I think it is possible to isolate in Dickens an aesthetic interest, a social concern, and a psychological pressure. Concerning the first, it is a commonplace to point out that Dickens never indulged in any extended theorizing about the novel, but the burden of the evidence that we possess points to an intense preoccupation with the form of fiction. Scattered remarks in letters and articles, his deep-seated professionalism (Dickens regarded himself preeminently as a man "who is content to rest his station and claims quietly on literature, and to make no feint of living by anything else"[8]), the intensity of his creative agony, the significance of the work sheets so ably brought out by Butt and Tillotson,[9] and above all the testimony of the novels themselves, with their ceaseless development toward greater complexity—all of this justifies the anger Dickens expressed in a letter of December, 1852, to Wilkie Collins in writing of "the conceited idiots who suppose that volumes are to be tossed off like pancakes, and that any writing can be done without the utmost application, the greatest patience, and the steadiest energy of which the writer is capable."[10] Second, both life and art testify to a concern with society which is part of the very

[8] Letter to John Forster, April 22, 1843, in *Letters*, ed. Walter Dexter (London: Nonesuch Press, 1938), II, 83.

[9] John Butt and Kathleen Tillotson, *Dickens at Work* (London: Methuen, 1957).

[10] *Letters*, II, 436.

lifeblood of Dickens' being. We can see the artistic proof of this in the fact that, in his greatest work, social criticism is never merely a part of the subject matter competing with other elements for our interest, but a thematic force that informs character, plot, and language with its unifying presence. Last, working sometimes at a less conscious level are the various psychological pressures that contribute to the richness of Dickens' work: the violence, the sadness of deprived childhood, the transmutation of adult problems into the material of art.

And so, bearing these three strands of personality in mind, it might be possible to see Dickens as an ivory-towered aesthetician, a social propagandist, or a treasure house of unconscious Freudian symbolism. But each of these approaches limits the complexity of his greatness. The increasing richness of Dickens' fictional structure is not an end in itself, but the necessary form for his increasing understanding and mastery of society. Similarly, the most interesting psychological pressures have a meaning beyond the purely personal. The almost hysterical power of the mob scenes in *Barnaby Rudge* may convey a repressed strain of anarchy in Dickens' character and express something of the early-Victorian fear of revolution, but they remain isolated pieces essentially unrelated to a story of almost childish melodrama. The possibly unconscious elements of interest in a character such as Arthur Clennam, however, are part of an artistically unified density of texture. The judgment underlying these remarks is, of course, a conviction that any great work of art is significantly a creation of the conscious mind and will. The psychological interest of the great artist lies not so much in the almost, by definition, unchartable regions of his unconscious mind, but in the fascinating link that often seems to exist between his consciously held purposes and the more hidden layers of his personality. Whatever fragmentation may exist on the surface, it seems characteristic of the great artist that emotion and will should finally be fused in him. At any rate, it appears to be this fusion of intellectual purpose, richness of feeling, and echoes from the depths of the human personality that we are talking about when we discuss artistic greatness. Those mysterious father and daughter relationships in Shakespeare's last plays add a powerful vibrancy to their meaning, but we remain convinced that they are part of a coherent and consistent unity of purpose. The choice of a daughter as the symbol of forgiveness and regeneration *may* have been of personal significance to Shakespeare, but this is not a factor of overriding value as far as our response is concerned. In *The Tempest*, for example, Ferdinand seems eventually to have a function similar to that of Miranda, at least with regard to his own father. The choice of a daughter for the symbolic role calls up a series of meaningful responses in us—to the idea of the Virgin, for example, and the healing and reconciling force of the universal feminine—but this choice could be as much a matter of artistic understanding as psychological pressure.

In the same way, it seems to me that Dickens is not a subject for psychoanalysis, but a creative writer who is to be understood by means of literary criticism. My contention is for the importance and for the unity, in his greatest work, of these three elements: the aesthetic, the social, and the psychological. The resolution of these elements into the relationship between didacticism and creative autonomy seems to me crucial, and my major aim is to show that this relationship, again in the greatest work, is indissoluble and is at least one key to the understanding of Dickens' development and the meaning of his later work.

CHAPTER TWO

The Early Novels:
From *Pickwick* to
Barnaby Rudge

The relationship between didacticism and creative autonomy provides one way of viewing Dickens' early novels; and I would here stress "viewing" rather than "understanding" as the appropriate word. The understanding of a novel seems to me the process whereby one reaches the end of grasping some sense of its total meaning; that is, the connection in it between content and its embodying form. Dickens' early work does not appear to be open to understanding in this sense. The connection between content and form may exist in isolated passages—the workhouse scenes in *Oliver Twist*, for example, and the wanderings of Nell and her grandfather—but it does not operate within the structure of any of these novels as a whole. Such passages have their own specific tone and feeling, but we find them side by side with those of a totally different character, and the connection between them is fortuitous rather than significant. The possible exception is *Pickwick*, but there the general unity of tone is maintained by a balance of content and form that is too straightforward to need critical discussion.

In considering these early novels, the despised word "appreciation" would seem to be for more appropriate than "understanding." Understanding engages itself with the whole, appreciation can be content with the part. The Chestertonian function of taking us back into their glorious comedy is worthwhile in that it makes us want to return to these great moments eagerly and with a heightened awareness of the details that go to make up the comic effects. The dangers of misplaced modern criticism have been amply demonstrated in the treatment of Milton, whose "dislodgement . . . after his two centuries of predominance, was affected with remarkably little fuss,"[1] as Dr. Leavis claims, but by means of criteria that are quite inapplicable to the intentions and achievement of *Paradise Lost*. Similarly, the modern fictional criteria of thematic unity, symbolic richness, and total form should simply not be brought to bear on Dickens' early novels. The serious modern respect for Dickens is wholly admirable, but it is bound to fail, and even to become ridiculous, if it seeks to apply Jamesian criteria to such works as *Nicholas Nickleby* and *The Old Curiosity Shop*. The formal anarchy of these novels bears no relation to the critical principles that can be drawn from *The Ambassadors* or *The Wings of the Dove*. The modern concept of myth can find more on which to sharpen its critical perceptions, and few would deny that Mr. Pickwick is a figure with universal overtones of benevolence and goodwill, and that his England is, until toward the end of the novel, paradisal in its disconnection from harsh reality.

If *Oliver Twist* and *The Old Curiosity Shop* are to be seen as fable or fairy tale, however, the critical task is not merely to expend ingenuity in disentangling their meaning, but to point out that they are rather tawdry and vulgar examples of the genre. Both can be shown to be concerned with situations of primitive force, and so of great interest to humanity—the lost and fatherless child who in finding a father finds himself, and the symbolic primacy of innocent good over aged evil. These are, certainly, themes that possess a resonance for all men, a fact proved by their presence in Shakespeare's last plays and in Victorian melodrama. But their very ubiquity should be a warning against finding their simple occurrence a sign of greatness. This is surely to be concerned with only one half of the equation of total artistic meaning, content at the expense of its embodying form. It may be possible, perhaps Dickens even intended, that Oliver's received standard English should be a sign of his angelic purity—for Steven Marcus, Oliver is "very much an angel, and so speaks the language of angels. . . . it is Dickens's way of showing that grace has descended upon him"[2]—although it would seem wise to notice that Nancy's speech is also rather far removed from what we would expect of her background. But does this point find any kind of sanction in the

[1] F. R. Leavis, *Revaluation* (Penguin Books, 1964), p. 42.
[2] *Dickens: From Pickwick to Dombey* (London: Chatto and Windus, 1965), p. 80.

impression actually made upon our imagination by Oliver as a character? It seems mere eccentricity to dissociate oneself from the general opinion here, that in so far as Oliver impresses us at all, it is as a humorless little prig. There is simply nothing in the delineation of Mr. Brownlow as the representative of mature, and Oliver of innocent, goodness, or in their relationship, to interest the adult mind. And so we must convict Dickens either of artistic failure in the embodiment of his literary creation, or of a failure of nerve. Since so much of this novel is avowedly didactic, and brilliantly so in its opening chapters, it seems valid to argue that Dickens lacks the courage to treat Oliver realistically in terms of his environment and so attempt to convince his audience that good could in fact exist in an illegitimate workhouse boy. Oliver's perfect English represents a failure that is at once social and literary. It places him firmly within the spirit, if not the letter (although he conveniently turns out to belong to both) of middle-class values. This is not merely a violation of the social reality from which Oliver has emerged; it is also one of the factors that weaken the formal brilliance of the novel's consistently ironic opening.

To raise the cry of fable at any aspect of Dickens' work which is unattractive to the modern sensibility seems an evasion of critical responsibility. Much of the melodramatic crudity with which Dickens was charged in the past has been shown to be unfounded by sensitive modern criticism, but respect for critical standards demands that this kind of reassessment should not be taken too far. If it is true that *Oliver Twist*, for example, "is connected with a tradition of parabolic writing that has always commanded an important place in English literature . . . the tradition of Bunyan, the morality play, and the homiletic tale,"[3] then it is part of the critic's responsibility to point out just how far this tradition had declined in the nineteenth century. The very lack of originality of the primitive theme should make us demand the finest possible degree of artistic embodiment if we are to find it convincing and interesting. Unlike Rose Maylie, the perfect purity of Shakespeare's Perdita and Miranda is achieved with an absence of sentimentality, and unlike Dickens' often weak use of melodramatic coincidence, the high contrivance of such a work as *The Winter's Tale* gives a keen pleasure in its contrast between primitive theme and sophisticated treatment. Dickens himself, in *Hard Times*, pro-

[3] *Ibid.*, pp. 67–68.

vides a fine example of how fable can be embodied in a successful artistic form.

In my view, we must face the fact that at the beginning of
his career, Dickens' imagination contained elements of vulgarity and sentimentality, in common with those of his age. The
balance between thought and emotion held by the great Romantic poets was a precarious one, as the excesses of Wordsworth's "Idiot Boy" and Keats's self-indulgent "luxuries" can
show. We cannot imagine Pope writing in this way, a fact that
tells us something about his age as well as his own genius. And
once the moment of Romantic equilibrium had passed, the
enormous sanction given to emotion in reaction against the
seemingly rigid disciplines of thought in eighteenth-century
Europe was ready to reinforce the specific pressures of the
nineteenth century and spill over into the sentimentalities characteristic of so much of Victorian life and literature. I consider
these Victorian pressures in more detail in another chapter, but
the sentimental tradition that had been developing throughout
the second half of the eighteenth century can be indicated here
by a quotation from Adam Smith's *Theory of Moral Sentiments*,
in which he describes how the unfortunate "by relating their
misfortunes . . . in some measure renew their grief. Their tears
accordingly flow faster than before. . . . They take pleasure,
however, in all this, and it is evident are sensibly relieved by it,
because the sweetness of the bystander's sympathy more than
compensates the bitterness of their sorrow."[4] Dickens' literary
heritage was one with especial dangers from this point of view.
The combination of extrovert comic action and an extreme degree of personal feeling is characteristic of the eighteenth-
century novel that formed the staple of Dickens' childhood
reading and provided the outline, the characters, and sometimes the situations of his early novels. Of relevance here are
Tom Jones's words to his friend Nightingale, after his desertion
of his young mistress:

"View the poor, helpless, orphan infant; and . . . consider yourself
as the cause of all the ruin of this poor, little, worthy, defenceless
family . . . . Think with what joy, with what transports that lovely
creature will fly to your arms. See her blood returning to her pale
cheeks, her fire to her languid eyes, and rapture to her tortured
heart." (Vol. II, Bk. XIV, chap. vii)

[4] Quoted in A. R. Humphreys, *The Augustan World* (New York: Harper Torchbooks, 1963), p. 201.

And reinforcing this was Dickens' youthful dependence on the theater for much of his imaginative sustenance, a theater composed of vulgar patriotism, absurd melodrama, and odious sentimentality; in fact, a theater that in Allardyce Nicoll's judgment was in these years at "almost its lowest ebb."[5] With this background in mind, it should not surprise us that we find qualities in Dickens which strike us as meretricious, but our admiration should, rather, be increased at the extent to which he was able to exorcise them in his later work.

It seems best, then, to face the essentially fragmentary nature of Dickens' early achievement; and in doing so one does not necessarily wish that it were otherwise. In *Nicholas Nickleby*, for example, the nauseating Smike seems a small price to pay for the glorious Mantalini, the Snevelliccis, and the wonderfully seedy comedy of its theatrical scenes. Taken in and for themselves, these works give us a wealth of humor and incidental satire unparalleled in English literature. My purpose, however, is not to attempt an evocation of these comic marvels, but to see what part the early novels play in the overall pattern of Dickens' development. And in approaching them from what seems the most significant angle for this purpose, one can observe within them a frequent dichotomy between didacticism and creative autonomy.

It would be easy to illustrate this point in a random manner, but coherence is better served by beginning with examples of the extremes of this dichotomy. One extreme is to be found in *Pickwick*, which appears ready to burst under the pressure of Dickens' comic imagination. It seems invidious to select one incident from that richness, but it might fairly be done with what I think is one of the great comic scenes in all literature— Bob Sawyer's bachelor party for Mr. Pickwick and his friends. The pathetic attempts of masculine gaiety to maintain its independence are ruthlessly defeated by Bob's landlady, Mrs. Raddle:

"My good soul," interposed Mr. Benjamin Allen, soothingly.
"Have the goodness to keep your observashuns to yourself, sir, I beg," said Mrs. Raddle, suddenly arresting the rapid torrent of her speech, and addressing the third party with impressive slowness and solemnity. "I am not aweer, sir, that you have any right to address your conversation to me. I don't think I let these apartments to you, sir."

[5] *A History of Early Nineteenth Century Drama, 1800–1850* (Cambridge: University Press, 1930), I, 211.

"No, you certainly did not," said Mr. Benjamin Allen.

"Very good, sir," responded Mrs. Raddle, with lofty politeness. "Then p'raps, sir, you'll confine yourself to breaking the arms and legs of the poor people in the hospitals, and keep yourself *to* yourself, sir, or there may be some persons here as will make you, sir."

"But you are such an unreasonable woman," remonstrated Mr. Benjamin Allen.

"I beg your parding, young man," said Mrs. Raddle, in a cold perspiration of anger. "But will you have the goodness just to call me that again, sir?"

"I didn't make use of the word in any invidious sense, ma'am," replied Mr. Benjamin Allen, growing somewhat uneasy on his own account.

"I beg your parding, young man," demanded Mrs. Raddle in a louder and more imperative tone. "But who do you call a woman? Did you make that remark to me, sir?" . . .

"Why, of course I did," replied Mr. Benjamin Allen.

"Yes, of course you did," said Mrs. Raddle, backing gradually to the door, and raising her voice to its loudest pitch, for the special behoof of Mr. Raddle in the kitchen. "Yes, of course you did! And everybody knows that they may safely insult me in my own 'ouse while my husband sits sleeping down-stairs, and taking no more notice than if I were a dog in the streets." . . . there came a loud double knock at the street door: whereupon she burst into an hysterical fit of weeping, accompanied with dismal moans, which was prolonged until the knock had been repeated six times, when, in an uncontrollable burst of mental agony, she threw down all the umbrellas, and disappeared into the back parlour, closing the door after her with an awful crash. "Does Mr. Sawyer live here?" said Mr. Pickwick, when the door was opened. (XXXII)

After such a beginning, the chances of conviviality getting successfully under way would seem to be very slight, but the initial embarrassment is dispelled by Mr. Jack Hopkins' story of the little boy who swallowed his sister's necklace, bead by bead. This misdemeanor is discovered a few day's later at dinner—the "baked shoulder of mutton, and potatoes under it" that Orwell singled out as such a brilliant example of Dickens' use of the "unnecessary detail"[6]—when the child was running about playing and making a noise "like a small hailstorm." As Mr. Hopkins concludes, "He's in the hospital now . . . and he makes such a devil of a noise when he walks about, that they're obliged to muffle him in a watchman's coat, for fear he should wake the patients!" From then on bachelor freedom gets into

[6] "Charles Dickens," in *A Collection of Essays* (New York: Doubleday Anchor Books, 1954), p. 99.

its stride and is able to overcome even such difficulties as waiting for the establishment's own, and the public-house's bor-
rowed, glasses to be washed before the punch and spirits can
be drunk. But eventually Mrs. Raddle, triumphant in the knowledge of how much rent is owed her, returns to the fray accompanied by her reluctant husband ("they've the advantage of
me in numbers, my dear"):

"Now, Mr. Sawyer!" screamed the shrill voice of Mrs. Raddle,
"*are* them brutes going?"
"They're only looking for their hats, Mrs. Raddle," said Bob; "they
are going directly."
"Going! . . . Going! what did they ever come for?"
"My dear ma'am," remonstrated Mr. Pickwick, looking up.
"Get along with you, you old wretch!" replied Mrs. Raddle, hastily
withdrawing the nightcap. "Old enough to be his grandfather, you
willin! You're worse than any of 'em." (XXXII)

With one necessary reservation, passages such as these represent the acme of Dickens' comic creativity, totally divorced as
they are from any kind of didactic aim. We find here a freedom
of the comic spirit rivaled only by that of Shakespeare and
Chaucer. The reservation I wish to make is that in these moments Dickens is working in the Shakespearian mode, not in
the vein of "pure," almost surrealist comedy we saw him using
in depicting Mrs. Gamp. Bob Sawyer's party is Dickens' Boar's
Head scene, modified by his own genius, lacking the final
comic greatness of Hal and Falstaff's wild insults, and toned
down for early Victorian consumption, but with basically the
same ingredients: the humor arising, as I observed earlier,
"from the clash of character and the exposure of observable
human idiosyncrasy."[7] For many people this remains the "real"
Dickens, but it is difficult to maintain that he ever again recap-
tured quite this magnificently easy flow of comic invention. In
any event, Dickens was too great an artist to be content with
repeating effects that had been taken to their highest point of
development. Throughout his entire career one can find examples of the freely created moment, but increasingly Dickens
sought to fuse creativity and significance within the thematic
texture of the novel as a whole.
    At the opposite extreme is the mechanical didacticism that
disfigures so much of Dickens' early work for the modern reader. An example of this absurdly flat propagandizing is Dickens'

[7] See p. 4.

frequent manipulation of Dennis the Hangman in *Barnaby Rudge*. In the following passage Dennis has been talking of George III:

"Sometimes he throws me in one over that I don't expect, as he did three years ago, when I got Mary Jones, a young woman of nineteen who come up to Tyburn with an infant at her breast, and was worked off for taking a piece of cloth off the counter of a shop in Ludgate Hill, and putting it down again when the shopman see her: and who never done any harm before, and only tried to do that, in consequence of her husband having been pressed three weeks previous, and she being left to beg, with two young children— as was proved upon the trial. Ha ha!—Well! That being the law and the practice of England, is the glory of England, an't it, Muster Gashford?" (XXXVII)

It is obvious that only one level of Dickens' mind is engaged here, an admirable one no doubt, but far removed from the level of creative imagination. Dickens displays a sometimes damaging eye to the main chance of social reform in these early novels. He seems unwilling to miss any opportunity of thrusting in some propaganda no matter how artistically inappropriate it may be. The breathless quality of the lines I have just quoted gives one the sense that Dickens is desperately working the point in while the going is good and his hurried attempt to pass this off as a piece of savage irony by returning to Dennis' "character" with its melodramatic laughter and snarling is transparently unsuccessful. In other parts of the novel, Dennis' black humor is validly used as the vehicle of social criticism because it stays within the bounds of what he, with inherent probability, would say and do. In this instance, it is clear that Dickens has sacrificed the character's autonomy in order to use him as a mouthpiece, and in doing so has failed completely. Because we do not believe in Dennis at this point, we can neither believe in nor, consequently, care about Mary Jones. In fact, her terrible story is much more affecting in the flatly circumstantial language of a speech made in Parliament by Sir William Meredith which Dickens quotes in the novel's preface.

I have claimed that the fusion of didacticism and creative autonomy is characteristic of Dickens' later style, but examples can be found in his earlier work, although these constitute isolated passages and sections rather than the unified structure of an entire novel. One of his more extended, and certainly one of his most brilliant, early successes in this fusion is the masterly irony of the workhouse and thieves' kitchen scenes of *Oliver Twist*. Irony is, of course, a literary technique of particular value to the artist whose social concerns are more than merely propagandist. Characters and situations of the most lifelike vitality can be created within a generally ironic frame of reference, as the work of Jane Austen proves, and in doing so the writer is able to convey his social insight without encroachment upon the freedom of his creation. In *Persuasion*, for example, Sir Walter Elliot's functions as a target of irony and a living character are wholly merged into a creative unity. He is believable and amusing both as a kind of minor and aristocratic Mr. Micawber and as the representative of the faults of a specific social class. In the same way, in *Oliver Twist* Dickens is able to create a sense of life and to achieve a social criticism that is universal in its implications by means of the bitingly effective irony of its best chapters. Dickens' superb handling of this device in the workhouse section is perhaps too well appreciated to need any general discussion here, although it will be necessary that I return later to one or two related points. From the first chapter, Dickens uses a style that combines the maximum degree of indignation for the sufferings of humanity under the "insolence of office," with a complete lack of sentimentality. At this stage, Oliver is a genuinely representative figure, a successful mean between the pasteboard aridities of allegory and rounded, "lifelike" characterization. He is *a* child, whom it is entirely possible to see as the representative of all children:

What an excellent example of the power of dress, young Oliver Twist was! Wrapped in the blanket which had hitherto formed his only covering, he might have been the child of a nobleman or a beggar; it would have been hard for the haughtiest stranger to have assigned him his proper station in society. But now that he was enveloped in the old calico robes which had grown yellow in the same service, he was badged and ticketed, and fell into his place at once— the humble, half-starved drudge—to be cuffed and buffeted through the world—despised by all, and pitied by none. (I)

Of a piece with the language is the rapid forward movement of the narrative itself, pared to the bone, with not an unnecessary or wasted incident in the unfolding of the story. Every element of form is characterized by an incisiveness that is an essential part of Dickens' vision at this point in the novel.

After this wonderful beginning, the book splits in two: Oliver, Mr. Brownlow, and the Maylies form one center of interest, the thieves' kitchen another. If we approach them with the tools of literary criticism, instead of the blinkers of myth and psychoanalysis, it is surely obvious which of the parts is more artistically successful. With the first we struggle and, ultimately, drown in a sea of melodrama and sentimentality; with the second we find the vitality and amusement of life, however reprehensible it may be. The commitment of Dickens' creative imagination to the second is shown by the control with which he keeps these scenes within an artistic discipline. The governing principle at work here is ironic inversion, the presentation of the criminal world in terms of conventional morality. There is nothing strikingly original in this conception; Fielding had used it in *Jonathan Wild*. But Dickens embodies his version of it with an unflagging wit and gaiety.

When this game had been played many times [the game is pickpocket practice, of course], a couple of young ladies called to see the young gentlemen; one of whom was named Bet, and the other Nancy. They wore a good deal of hair, not very neatly turned up behind, and were rather untidy about the shoes and stockings. They were not exactly pretty, perhaps; but they had a great deal of colour in their faces, and looked quite stout and hearty. Being remarkably free and agreeable in their manners, Oliver thought them very nice girls indeed. As there is no doubt they were. (IX)

The fun of all this is infectious because behind it seems to lie a conspiracy between Dickens and the adult reader. His inverted vision is maintained with total consistency, even at fairly unimportant moments in the narrative.

While these, and many other encomiums, were being passed on the accomplished Nancy, that young lady made the best of her way to the police-officer; whither, notwithstanding a little natural timidity consequent upon walking through the streets alone and unprotected, she arrived in perfect safety shortly afterwards. (XIII)

It is impossible to miss the sense of why she is really timid being conveyed by a wink of the creative eye. I do not think it is going too far to see Nancy as a kind of ironic parody of Rose Maylie, and it certainly seems true that Fagin is an ironic complement to Mr. Brownlow. He is constantly the "merry old gentleman," and the "games" that he organizes in the kitchen provide the first real enjoyment Oliver has ever known in his life. The parodoxes involved here have caused some recent critics to plumb the depths of Dickens' unconscious in an attempt to account for Fagin's mixture of evil and rather endearing roguery (he is the epitome of twinkling-eyed ill will, as Mr. Pickwick is the epitome of twinkling-eyed benevolence). Steven Marcus, for example, sees him as connected with Dickens' own experience of "what Freud called the primal scene, to either a memory or fantasy of it: the child asleep, or just waking, or feigning sleep while observing sexual intercourse between his parents, and, frightened by what he sees or imagines, is either then noticed by his parents or has a fantasy of what would occur if he were noticed."[8] I am not primarily concerned with the validity of such an interpretation, but even if it is accepted, there are still aspects of Fagin that can be dealt with by criticism. There is a perfectly adequate social and artistic reason why Dickens should present Fagin's world in terms of the world of bourgeois conventionality. In the vision of the best parts of this novel there is no real difference between them. In artistic terms, they are conveyed to us by their treatment of Oliver. And the inhumanity of a society that can permit institutions such as the workhouse is mirrored by the brutal manipulation of innocence by the thieves. In fact, Dickens' imaginative judgment appears to be on the side of the criminals. They at least enjoy a fellowship and gaiety—admittedly of a highly suspect kind, as Fagin's mixture of qualities makes clear—which is quite denied the inhabitants of the legal workhouse.

The point I am trying to prove in this discussion is the general importance of my concept of didacticism and creative autonomy as a key to the understanding of Dickens' early work. Thus I believe that one meaningful way of interpreting the early novels as a whole is as an attempt, as part of Dickens' consistent social concern, to unify these two elements of his work. The following detailed examination of certain aspects of these books concentrates on Dickens' struggle to achieve that unity.

Benefactors, Benevolence, and Charity

In *Nicholas Nickleby*, Dickens tell us that charity is "the one great cardinal virtue, which, properly nourished and exercised, leads to, if it does not necessarily include, all the others" (XVIII). This statement seems straightforward enough, but when we consider the ways in which charity is brought into play in other novels we are forced to realize that it cannot be accepted at face value. In *Martin Chuzzlewit*, for example, we find "Want, colder than Charity, shivering at the street corners"

[8] *Dickens: From Pickwick to Dombey,* p. 373.

(XV). We will be assured, however, that the clue here lies in
the use of the capital letter. Here, of course, Dickens means
the word to stand for organized almsgiving rather than private
kindness. Whatever may be said of the later work, it is usually
accepted unquestioningly that there is in the earlier novels
a simple opposition between organized and therefore cold-
hearted "Charity" on the one hand, and private generosity on
the other.

But in a novel as early as *Oliver Twist*, written between
1837 and 1839, we find Bill Sikes inveighing against the work
of the Juvenile Delinquent Society: "And so they go on . . .
and, if they'd got money enough (which it's Providence they
haven't), we shouldn't have half-a-dozen boys left in the whole
trade, in a year or two" (XIX). Here we have Dickens in the
late thirties acknowledging the fact that some social problems
are simply too large and too pressing to be solved by the
unorganized kindness of private individuals. Mr. Brownlow
may be a satisfactory deus ex machina for the rescue of Oliver,
but there are too many potential Olivers in existence for such
a solution to be practicable. That the problem of how best to
help the needy was a real one for Dickens can be seen in a
quotation from *The Chimes*:

She mingled with an abject crowd, who tarried in the snow, until
it pleased some officer appointed to dispense the public charity (the
lawful charity; not that once preached upon a Mount), to call them
in, and question them, and say to this one, "Go to such a place", to
that one, "Come next week"; to make a football of another wretch.
(Fourth Quarter)

This is a powerful expression of the hatred Dickens never
ceased to feel for the tendency of organizations to treat those
with whom they deal as units of some statistical table which
are to be manipulated solely by the criterion of expediency.
And yet the central problem remained. People had to be helped
—Dickens' childhood experiences, his warm-hearted nature, and
the horrors of contemporary life all made that unquestionable—
no matter what the difficulties were.

Dickens cared too wholeheartedly for the sufferings of the
poor to raise prim objections to some of the ways used to
collect money for their assistance. Although he had satirized
the custom of holding public dinners in the *Sketches*,[9] he was

[9] In the sketch "Public Dinners," chap. xix of "Scenes," in *Sketches by
Boz*.

personally prepared to suffer them frequently for the sake of the good they could do. That they were sometimes a cause of real suffering to him can be seen from the amazingly violent tone of a letter he wrote to Douglas Jerrold in 1843. He talks of "your City aristocracy" at a hospital dinner as "Sleek, slobbering, bow-paunched, over-fed, apoplectic, snorting cattle."[10] In life Dickens was prepared to accept the snobbery and self-display of such people because of the good that resulted from it. The basic necessity here was to secure some of "those little screws of existence—pounds, shillings, and pence,"[11] by whatever means presented themselves. But Dickens' idealized conception of charity was something other than this. In its finest form it was a relationship, of however short a duration, which was as morally purifying to the giver as it was practically beneficial to the receiver. Thus the challenge presented by charity to Dickens' art was concerned essentially with the depiction of human relationships. The patronizing familiarity that is a denial of such a relation is shown brilliantly in Alderman Cute's treatment of Trotty Veck, the old ticket porter, in *The Chimes*: "I have tasted your tripe, you know, and you can't 'chaff' me. You understand what 'chaff' means, eh? That's the right word, isn't it? Ha, ha, ha!" (First Quarter). Instead of the humanity of one man speaking to another, we have here the abstraction of tone that stems from having an *idea* of how an inferior should be addressed.

There remains, however, the problem of how successful Dickens is in presenting the act of charity in personal terms. For Humphry House, "a film of hopeless gratitude is spread upon the cash nexus between man and man."[12] Can this really be said, though, of Mr. Pickwick's charity, with its air of unpremeditated practicality? When he meets Job Trotter once again he gives him not "a sound, hearty cuff" but something from his waistcoat pocket which "chinked as it was given into Job's hand" (XLII). It is easy enough to sneer at the constant chinking of money changing hands which we find in Dickens, or to rage at a society in which such chinking is necessary; but the fact remains that when confronted with the actual problems of life, this often is a very sweet sound to the ears of the receiver. Moreover, apart from a few very mild

[10] May 3, in *Letters*, ed. Walter Dexter, (London: Nonesuch Press, 1938), I, 517–518.

[11] Letter to Henry Austin, Jan., 1835, in *Letters*, I, 42.

[12] *The Dickens World* (London: Oxford Paperbacks, 1960), p. 66.

words to Jingle, Mr. Pickwick never takes advantage of the helplessness of those whom he aids in order to force impertinent advice upon them. He hopes for, but never expects, a return of his kindness, and humanity is maintained by the fact that Job, for example, at our last sight of him still has "a cunning look just lurking in the corners of his eyes" (LIII). Mr. Pickwick's approach to charity is best summed up by the words of Perker, his solicitor:

"Whether that species of benevolence which is so very cautious and long-sighted that it is seldom exercised at all, lest its owner should be imposed upon, and so wounded in his self-love, be real charity or a worldly counterfeit, I leave to wiser heads than mine to determine." (LIII)

There is a godlike openhandedness in Mr. Pickwick's acts of generosity which is quite in keeping with the spirit of joyous inconsequentiality that pervades most of the book. It is as far removed as possible from the world of prudence and foresight. Yet only two years later we find Dickens, in *Nicholas Nickleby*, introducing these very considerations into his portrayal of the beneficence of the Cheeryble Brothers. Before helping Nicholas, Charles points out: "We must make proper inquiries into his statements in justice to him as well as to ourselves, and if they are confirmed—as I feel assured they will be—we must assist him" (XXXV). This is no doubt an eminently sane way of dispensing charity, but in terms of human response it compares rather unfavorably with Mr. Pickwick's lack of method. The intention behind such a passage is clear. Dickens is attempting both to dignify the Cheerybles' charity by introducing an element of systemization, and to take proper account of the human worth of the person who is to be helped. And yet what is the effect of this organized kindness?

It is no disparagement to Nicholas to say that before he had been closeted with the two brothers ten minutes, he could only wave his hand at every fresh expression of kindness and sympathy, and sob like a little child. (XXXV)

Mr. Pickwick may have brought a tear to the eye of Alfred Jingle, but he never reduced anyone to this condition of imbecility. One can only imagine what forty-odd years of this kind of thing would have done to Tim Linkinwater if, that is, he had borne any resemblance to a real human being. The Cheerybles do, in House's phrase, induce a feeling of "helpless gratitude" in all those who come in contact with them. The relationships they enter into are as inhuman as that between Alderman Cute and old Trotty.

In a speech of 1844, Dickens called for benefits rather than charity, for "a just right which honest pride may claim without a blush."[13] At the time of these early novels the social, political, and economic situation presented him with a perplexing dichotomy. He found a huge mass of human misery which was treated with a very large measure of indifference. Government action was either nonexistent or permeated, as in the new Poor Law, with a spirit of cold and hateful utilitarianism; while private charity, as Dickens knew only too well from bitter experience, was often given from the worst of motives. In transforming these problems of suffering and need into the material of art Dickens was attempting to order them into some kind of pattern that would be both practical and humane. This didactic impulse, the desire to "shame the cruel and the canting"[14] into the realization that a different spirit is attainable in personal relations, remained a constant in Dickens' artistic process. I have already indicated that his attempts to do this in these early novels are not entirely successful. Some lack of conviction, as well as of a fully thought-out response to a complex situation, makes itself felt in the sentimentality of many of the personal relationships depicted.

This uneasiness and imprecision emerge even more strongly when we consider the degree of success Dickens achieved in the realization of the benefactors themselves in these early books. Dickens' benevolent characters are often supposed to be fundamentally alike; however, although Mr. Pickwick, Mr. Brownlow, and the Cheerybles are all plump men, this is only an outward sign of resemblance. The basic difference between them lies, surely, in the conviction and vitality with which they are created. To talk of exaggeration in connection with such a creature as Mr. Pickwick seems an irrelevance. He is impressed upon our imagination with such a wealth of physical detail and in such a variety of situations that he must be accepted. His tights and gaiters, his trotting, his beaming eyes and noble forehead, are all intensely real to us. So also with Mr. Pickwick chasing his hat, Mr. Pickwick in the strange lady's bedroom, and perhaps best of all, Mr. Pickwick drunk,

---

[13] June 4, on behalf of the Sanitorium; in *The Speeches of Charles Dickens*, K. J. Fielding, ed. (Oxford: Clarendon Press, 1960), p. 69.
[14] Letter to John Forster, Oct., 1844, in *Letters*, I, 631.

"with his hands in his pockets and his hat cocked completely over his left eye . . . leaning against the dresser, shaking his head from side to side, and producing a constant succession of the blandest and most benevolent smiles without being moved thereunto by any discernible cause or pretence whatsoever" (VIII). As Stefan Zweig points out, the "rotundity of a Pickwick is an outward and visible sign of his psychical plumpness."[15] There is an organic connection between his warm generosity and physical appearance. Set against this, Mr. Brownlow and the Cheerybles appear thin, not to say emaciated. They have, of course, to fulfill rather different functions in the novels in which they appear, and they do not have the luck to be involved in such adventures as those of Mr. Pickwick. But Dickens clearly wishes us to respond to them in a similar way. From one point of view they are all attempts to solve in art the problems that Dickens found in the life about him. Each is a standard-bearer in his constant struggle against puritanical repression and cold-hearted philanthropy, but it is obvious that these later characters perform both their artistic and their social function poorly. Mr. Brownlow's benevolence may be acceptable, but is it possible, even in the course of reading the book, to remember anything at all about him? So much stress has been laid on Dickens' power of creating a sense of physical immediacy in his characters that it comes as a shock when we consider what an utter lack of impact Mr. Brownlow has on our imagination. Although, as I have tried to show, the humanitarianism of the Cheerybles is nauseating in its personal implications, they do seem to possess a greater degree of presence than Mr. Brownlow, but it is a presence that has roused a universal roar of disgust. Much has been made of the fact that they were based on real people, the Grant brothers of Manchester, but once again the biographical detail obscures as much as it clarifies. The fact remains that as literary creations they come very close to being Aldous Huxley's "gruesome old Peter Pans."[16]

What I wish to suggest is that Dickens' concern with questions of charity and benevolence in these early novels shows an artistic uncertainty that is linked with an uncertainty as to the nature of the social problems with which he found himself

[15] *Three Masters* (English trans.; London, 1919), p. 77.
[16] *Vulgarity in Literature* (London: Chatto and Windus, 1930), pp. 54–55.

surrounded. The creation of Brownlows and Cheerybles cannot be regarded purely in the light of the aesthetics of characterization. They figure among Dickens' first attempts at the artistic embodiment of the pressures of the age in which he lived. With the new Poor Law, government was making its first large-scale effort to deal with the huge amount of suffering that existed in early Victorian England. To many this solution appeared harsh in its lack of concern for individual dignity; and yet all men of goodwill recognized that the situation could not simply be left to solve itself, a fact proved by the plethora of charitable institutions in the nineteenth century. Some idea of their numbers can be gained from Dickens' satire "The Ladies' Societies" in the "Our Parish" section of *Sketches by Boz*:

In winter, when wet feet are common, and colds not scarce, we have the ladies' soup distribution society, the ladies' coal distribution society, and the ladies' blanket distribution society; in summer, when stone fruits flourish and stomach aches prevail, we have the ladies' dispensary, and the ladies' sick visitation committee; and all the year round we have the ladies' child's examination society, the ladies' bible and prayer-book circulation society, and the ladies' childbed-linen monthly loan society. (VI)

It was natural that Dickens, with his delight in human variety, should try to find a personal rather than an institutional solution, although, as we have seen, he was prepared to consider collective action. But at this stage he was as baffled as the contemporaries of whom he made gentle fun, and his confusion is shown in the artistic falsity of the benefactors who succeed Mr. Pickwick. The success of Pickwick's gay and youthful-seeming generosity, on the other hand, has the inevitability of a character perfectly in harmony with his idealized social setting. For one brief, sunny moment it seemed to Dickens that personal kindness could be enough to solve the ills of the world. As Mr. Pickwick left the prison "he saw not one [face] which was not the happier for his sympathy and charity." But even here the warning note of the reality that is to destroy this solution is sounded: "Alas! how many sad and unhappy beings he left behind!" (XLVII).

Character and Environment

In a speech of 1844, Dickens stated clearly one of the major subjects of his early novels, a subject that raises important aspects of the problem of didacticism and creativity. He warned that "there is a spirit of great power, the Spirit of Ignorance, long shut up in a vessel of Obstinate Neglect" whose "blind revenge at last will be destruction"[17] if it continues to be disregarded. These words call to mind the powerful personifications of Ignorance and Want from *A Christmas Carol*: a boy and girl who were "yellow, meagre, ragged, scowling, wolfish; but prostrate, too, in their humility" (Stave III). We find the evil environmental effects of poverty being stressed again and again, from *Sketches by Boz*, which describes a mother whom "misery had changed . . . to a devil," to *Martin Chuzzlewit*, which asks whether "any hopeful plant [can] spring up in air so foul that it extinguishes the soul's bright torch as fast as it is kindled!" (XIII).

Such quotations might seem to suggest, not unnaturally, that Dickens took a materialist and determinist view of the relationship between character and environment. A closer examination of the novels reveals that this is not so. Consider the example of Little Nell. The sentimental horrors of *The Old Curiosity Shop* have been dealt with often enough, and yet its comedy is not the only memorable aspect of the book. The wanderings of Nell and her grandfather do, from time to time, quite genuinely have the beauty and mystery of a fairy tale in the contrast between the delicate young child and the old man, whose natural roles of guide and protector are gradually reversed. The strange and sudden alternation of the loveliness of the countryside with the horrors of the industrial town, and the slow approach of autumn which reflects the waning of life from the child, help to create an atmosphere of sad yet idyllic beauty which is unique in Dickens. But the most important cause of this atmosphere is our feeling of Nell's isolation, the sense of her being unsullied by her environment. Dickens tells us that he wished to "surround the lonely figure of the child with grotesque and wild, but not impossible companions,"[18] and part of his success in doing this can be seen in the moving passage at the end of the first chapter:

I had ever before me the old dark murky rooms— the gaunt suits of mail with their ghostly silent air—the faces all awry, grinning from wood and stone—the dust and rust and worm that lives in wood

[17] Feb. 28, at the Conversazione of the Polytechnic Institute of Birmingham; in *The Speeches of Charles Dickens*, p. 61.
[18] Preface to 1848 ed.

—and alone in the midst of all this lumber and decay and ugly age, the beautiful child in her gentle slumber, smiling through her light and sunny dreams.

The horrors of her death scene have convinced many people that Little Nell is nothing but a sentimental caricature of goodness, but it would be unfair to Dickens to accept this as the whole truth. At her most successful, as in the wanderings in the countryside, Nell attains a certain validity because we feel that she is in harmony with the story of which she is a part. The form that Dickens is struggling toward here is the romance, which, in Hawthorne's definition, is concerned with the truth of the human heart and "presents that truth under circumstances . . . of the writer's own choosing or creation."[19] In such a work, questions of credibility and reality are subordinated to those of imaginative truth. Although their specific characteristics make them very different, Nell would possess more credibility if she were regarded as the same literary type as Hawthorne's Pearl. Her inferiority to Hawthorne's creation is due to the fact that Dickens is unable to discipline his exuberant genius into the pallid brilliance of allegory. In *The Scarlet Letter*, Pearl is not juxtaposed with characters and situations of a more fundamentally realistic kind than she herself. But Dickens cannot resist indulging in this formal weakness, and as a result, Nell is thrust into circumstances that make her appear ridiculous. The same fate would have overtaken Hester Prynne herself if she had been forced to exist within the covers of the same book as, say, Dick Swiveller. At this stage in his career, Dickens is unable to create a form that will permit the cohabitation of these opposite poles of his genius. It is this fact, coupled with the sentimentality that Dickens eventually allows to pervade her, which accounts for the comparative failure of Little Nell, rather than any basic contradictions within her conception.

A concentration upon realistic criteria alone would also be an error in any approach to *Oliver Twist*. Many passages of that novel obviously operate in terms of symbol, romance, or fable. As I have previously tried to show, Oliver himself is a representative figure, but his role is played out in a fictional world that is at once nonnaturalistic and yet bitterly satirical of nineteenth-century society (the nonnaturalistic elements of *The Old Curiosity Shop*, on the other hand, are often expressed in terms

---

[19] Preface to *The House of the Seven Gables*.

of pure fairy tale). This point may help to clarify certain fundamental contradictions that appear in Dickens' presentation of Oliver as the novel progresses. After he has left the workhouse, Oliver is given, on his first evening at the Sowerberrys, what is probably the best meal he has ever had in his life, and we have this picture of him eating: "I wish some well-fed philosopher . . . could have seen Oliver Twist clutching at the dainty viands that the dog had neglected. I wish he could have witnessed the horrible avidity with which Oliver tore the bits asunder with all the ferocity of famine" (IV). In the novel's opening chapters, Dickens conveys with concise irony the misery of the conditions under which Oliver grew up. On the basis of this description, we are justified in forming certain expectations as to Oliver's behavior and character, and these are fulfilled in a striking way by the sight of him tearing his food like a little savage. But when, at a later stage in his adventures, he is taken on Sikes's housebreaking expedition he behaves rather differently: "He clasped his hands together . . . and he sank upon his knees. . . . 'Oh! pray have mercy on me, and do not make me steal. For the love of all the bright Angels that rest in Heaven, have mercy upon me!'" (XXII). His heroic words occur, admittedly, after his rescue by Mr. Brownlow, but there is no evidence that this event did anything to improve either his grammar or his morality, if only because they already left nothing to be desired, as we discovered at his meeting with the Artful. Such a gross dichotomy between character—and, on a more superficial level, speech—and environment is even harder to understand when we remember that the relationship between the two was clearly of great interest to Dickens at this period. In the character of Nancy, for example, Dickens can swiftly and convincingly indicate a background of "cold and hunger, and riot and drunkenness, and—and—something worse than all" (XL), from which we feel that it was almost inevitable that evil should have sprung.

Even here, however, we have to face the problems both of her kindness to Oliver and of the fact that, under the stress of emotion, she also can assume the accents of the middle class. These problems are closely connected with the question of Dickens' prudery, of whether he attempted to glide round controversial matters in a way that was morally as well as artistically reprehensible. It seems worthwhile to spend a little time on this question, particularly with regard to his treatment of prostitution and poverty in *Oliver Twist*. Much has been made of the fact that Dickens nowhere in the novel itself uses the word "prostitute" in connection with Nancy, and this reticence has been traced to an acquiescence in suspect moral standards. But if we bear in mind that Dickens wrote with the certain knowledge that his novel would be read in the family circle, then it might fairly be described as outspoken. There is more than one passage in the book, such as the following, in which Nancy's occupation is suggested in terms that would be understood by an adult at any period.

This allusion to Nancy's doubtful character, raised a vast quantity of chaste wrath in the bosoms of four housemaids, who remarked, with great fervour, that the creature was a disgrace to her sex; and strongly advocated her being thrown, ruthlessly, into the kennel. (XXXIX)

This is an example of the great popular artist's capacity to satisfy public pressures and the demands of his art at one and the same time. Shakespeare preeminently displays this kind of genius in the Porter's scene from *Macbeth*, for example, where the groundlings are given their comic relief in a way that only adds density to the play's tragic texture. Dickens capitalizes on his inability to call Nancy a prostitute by means of the irony that is such a marked feature of the novel's best passages. We can all see unmistakably what Nancy is, and the "vast" quantity of "chaste" wrath aroused in the housemaids easily prompts the thought that they are protesting too much. Dickens suggests to us the universal truth that the condemning world, personified by these paragons of virtue, may be no "better" than Nancy herself. In such passages, Dickens is communicating a moral attitude as part of his narrative. We know what Nancy is and we know that she loves Sikes and lives with him. The horror of her life is brought home to us by suggestion rather than in physical terms.

The same is true of Dickens' treatment of poverty. For Humphry House, "his descriptions of the filth of the slums are quite inadequate to the truth."[20] But consider this description of a street from *Oliver Twist*: "The kennel was stagnant and filthy. The very rats, which here and there lay putrifying in its rottenness, were hideous with famine"(V). Such passages still seem capable of producing a shock of revulsion, but House argues that they lack the concrete detail demanded by Dickens' didactic purpose; that "the cure could only come if they [the

[20] *Dickens World*, p. 217.

foul things] were exposed in their full foulness, about which
dainty delicacy did not like to hear."[21] Such a point raises questions beyond that of the prudery of a particular historical
period. Artistic reticence should never be confused with moral
cowardice. Matters suitable for a work of history or sociology,
and acceptable within such a context, may produce a purely
visceral reaction if they are obtruded onto the body of a work
of art. It is a common experience to find oneself exhausted by
the indiscriminate piling-up of horrific details, so that one's
moral indignation is no longer capable of functioning. And
there is an arrogance in the argument that Dickens should have
included matter that he no doubt knew would make his books
unacceptable to the public. But, as I have indicated earlier, I
do not think that Dickens went to the opposite extreme of
keeping timorously to what his public would allow. One of the
minor subjects of *Oliver Twist* is Dickens' belief in the innocence of the victims of illicit liaisons. We can see this in Mrs.
Maylie's explanation to her son of why Rose should not marry
him: "If an enthusiastic, ardent, and ambitious man marry a
wife on whose name there is a stain, which, though it originate
in no fault of hers, may be visited by cold and sordid people
upon her, and upon his children . . . he may . . . one day repent
of the connexion he formed in early life" (XXXIV). Again,
when Monks refers to his half-brother as a "bastard," Mr.
Brownlow replies: "The term you use . . . is a reproach to those
who long since passed beyond the feeble censure of the world.
It reflects disgrace on no one living, except you who use it"
(LI). There is no reason to believe that these sentiments were
received with rapturous acquiescence by Dickens' middle-class
audience or, for that matter, those words in his author's preface
to the edition of 1867 which show his understanding of the
morality of those who think of poverty as a moral evil: "It is
wonderful how Virtue turns from dirty stockings; and how
Vice married to ribbons and a little gay attire, changes her
name, as wedded ladies do, and becomes Romance." The same
preface contains the famous parenthesis that has been pounced
on as evidence of Dickens' fear of offending his public: "I saw
no reason . . . why the dregs of life (so long as their speech did
not offend the ear) should not serve the purpose of a moral, as
well as its froth and cream." But, as I have shown, Dickens does
not need to use four-letter words to convince us of the squalor

[21] *Ibid.*, p. 219.

and degradation of his scene. As Kathleen Tillotson remarks, "the reticence on which Dickens prides himself is only verbal."[22]

I have pointed out earlier, however, that Dickens must be blamed for the speech he puts into the mouths of Oliver and, to a lesser extent, Nancy. Here he *is* succumbing to the damaging pressure of a conventional idea of what it was permissible for a novelist to do. In the person of Nancy this is surely a minor blemish in a fine piece of characterization, the power of which has never been sufficiently appreciated. Her reckless courage, her moods of hysterical rage and equally hysterical gaiety, her pathetic devotion to the brutal Sikes, even that kindness to Oliver which might at first sight seem difficult to accept—all combine to make her one of the most successful portraits of a prostitute in fiction.

Oliver, of course, presents greater difficulties; the contradictions in Dickens' conception of his character cause him, ultimately, to disintegrate. This is not, however, because of any prudish reticence on Dickens' part. It stems from his unwillingness or inability, at this stage in his development, to pursue his ideas about the individual and society to their conclusion. At an early point in the book, Oliver is asked if he says his "prayers every night . . . like a Christian!" Dickens remarks that "it would have been *very* like a Christian . . . if Oliver had prayed for the people who fed and took care of *him*. But he hadn't, because nobody had taught him" (II). Yet only seventy pages later, we find that this distressing state of affairs has somehow mysteriously changed. On recovering from his illness in Mr. Brownlow's house, Oliver thinks "that death had been hovering there, for many days and nights, and might yet still fill it with the gloom and dread of his awful presence," and so "he turned his face upon the pillow, and fervently prayed to Heaven" (XII). Such an abrupt change would seem to be beyond the powers of even the master of self-instruction that Oliver has so often proved himself to be. Carelessness of this kind is surely the result of a sheer lack of intellectual grip; it marks an escape into sentimental evasion to avoid the harsh gaze of uncompromising fact. The artistic sign of this is the self-indulgent emotionalism with which Dickens himself obviously views Oliver's character. And this self-indulgence can be observed in the lessening role assigned to irony in the

22 *Novels of the Eighteen-Forties* (London: Oxford Paperbacks, 1961), p. 66.

creation of Oliver. The writer who is fully in control of his ironic vision is capable of maintaining a unity of tone even when dealing with his "good" characters. The example of Jane Austen is again relevant here. The irony of *Persuasion* is so deeply organic to the novel's purposes that we feel no depreciation of Anne Elliot's fundamental goodness when she, too, is touched by it. We find this moving heroine being described as an "elegant little woman" and her moral judgments presented with the lightest hint of mockery: "She saw that there had been bad habits, that Sunday travelling had been a common thing" (XVII). And her happiness is conveyed to us in this way:

Prettier musings of high-wrought love and eternal constancy could never have passed along the streets of Bath than Anne was sporting with from Camden Place to Westgate Buildings. It was almost enough to spread purification and perfume all the way. (XXI)

These details serve to reassure us that Anne, with all her fineness of perception, belongs to this world. Her goodness is that of a woman, not a saint. Similarly, there is no doubt of the amusement lurking behind Dickens' agreement with Oliver Twist's view of Bet and Nancy: "Oliver thought them very nice girls indeed. As there is no doubt they were" (IX). This smile at Oliver's childish innocence helps to give him an interest that is gradually lost as Dickens' control of his ironic viewpoint weakens. His surrender to Oliver's false purity may be explicable in terms of painful memories of his own childhood or an overmastering desire to make propaganda, but it involves an artistic betrayal that weakens a good deal of the novel's force. When we consider those contradictions in Oliver's character that I have been discussing, it seems valid to argue that some determinism in Dickens' view of the relationship between the individual and his environment would not have come amiss at this moment in his career.

But the fact that Dickens did not take a determinist view of human personality can be seen in another, opposite way. In his discussion of *Oliver Twist*, Humphry House speaks of Dickens' "desire to demonstrate that the fundamental goodness of human nature can survive almost anything."[23] Dickens' acceptance of the possibility of absolute human *evil* is, however, made clear by the preface to which I have already referred. He is convinced of this possibility with such men as Bill Sikes, who "being closely followed through the same space of time and

[23] *Dickens World*, p. 220.

through the same current of circumstances, would not give, by the action of a moment, the faintest indication of a better nature." The best proof of this certainty is to be found, of course, in the artistic power of these living embodiments of evil. The terror that exists side by side with savage humor in such characters as Dennis the Hangman and Quilp resides in the fact that no adequate external explanation can be found for their malice. Dennis, that "mass of moral filth" as Forster called him,[24] may have been brutalized by his occupation, but this cannot explain the humor with which he enjoys it. The coarseness of this black comedy is at its best in the scene in which he tries to quiet the clamoring of the condemned prisoners in Newgate:

"Will you leave off that 'ere indecent row? I wonder you an't ashamed of yourselves, I do."
He followed up this reproof by rapping every set of knuckles one after the other, and having done so, resumed his seat again with a cheerful countenance. (LXV)

Well conceived as he is, Dennis cannot compare in force with Daniel Quilp, a character who surely answers the charge that Dickens could not depict evil. Whereas Dennis toils laboriously through the mud and filth of the world, Quilp leaps and quivers like a charge of pure energy. There is no suggestion in the story that his stunted, though preternaturally agile, body is the cause of the perversion of his mind. In him, body and mind flow equally from some common source of demoniac vitality. His satanic glee is the expression of the joy of the man who delights in evil for its own sake, as when he appears so unexpectedly before Mrs. Nubbles as she is assisting in the search for Nell:

"Christopher's mother!" he cried. "Such a dear lady, such a worthy woman, so blest in her honest son! How is Christopher's mother? . . . Her little family too, and Christopher? Do they thrive? Do they flourish?" (XLVIII)

The negative qualities of many of Dickens' bad characters are reflected, as they are in Jonas Chuzzlewit, in hints of impotence; but this is far from being true of Quilp, whose wife explains to her friends: "Quilp has such a way with him when he likes, that the best-looking woman here couldn't refuse him if I was dead, and she was free, and he chose to make love to her" (IV).

24 John Forster, *The Life of Charles Dickens* (London: Everyman's Library, 1948), I, 145.

And one of the most disturbing moments in the book comes in the scene in which Quilp makes love to Nell, asking her if she "should like to be my number two, Nelly" (VI).

In the face of such characters, questions of environment seem irrelevant. They represent a principle of total evil which we feel would be unaltered by any circumstances, however softening. That there was, in fact, at this stage in his development a great deal of inconsistency in Dickens' ideas on such matters can be seen from his treatment of, say, the business ability of Mr. Pickwick and the Cheerybles. From this point of view, they resemble Mr. Verver of *The Golden Bowl,* who made his money at what must have been a period of the most intense economic competition, and yet whom we are obviously meant to regard, despite ambiguities in his character, as a man who has a most refined and sophisticated awareness of others. One does not have to subscribe to the caricaturist's view of the capitalist as a top-hatted, cigar-smoking villain to find this a little unconvincing. The fact that Mr. Pickwick made a fortune in business is comparatively unimportant, for it is mentioned merely in passing and is in no sense integral to the story; but this is not so with the Cheerybles. Although Dickens makes no attempt to show the details of their transactions, we are constantly made aware of the fact that they are engaged in a flourishing business. He is presenting us here with an idealized version of a preindustrial, feudal type of business in which the employers consider their duties as well as their rights, in rather obvious contrast to the United Metropolitan Improved Hot Muffin and Crumpet Baking and Punctual Delivery Company of *Nicholas Nickleby.* The degrading employer and employee relationships of the former, however, seem almost as inhuman as the blatant crookery of the latter.

There is no evidence that Dickens had any philosophical position on this question of character and environment, and it would be fruitless to subject his novels to an analysis from this point of view. He placed his faith in living experience rather than abstract speculation, and the events of his childhood and his extensive charitable work led him to a commonsense view of the matter. At each end of the human scale there are natures that, on the one hand, remain adamant in the face of the kindest treatment and, on the other, are capable of rising above the most adverse circumstances. In the middle are the great majority of people who will behave decently if their environment will only give them a chance to do so. Dickens is remarkable for the small extent to which he generalizes from his own experience. The story of his early struggles is well known; they developed in him an iron will to succeed. Forster talks of "the intense individuality by which he effected so much"[25] and the early breeding in him of "a stern and even cold isolation of self-reliance."[26] But Dickens never indulged in the arrogance of the self-made man who claims that anyone else can do what he himself has achieved. He never forgot that "but for the mercy of God, I might easily have been, for any care that was taken of me, a little robber or a little vagabond."[27] It is this intense realization of the power of circumstance that can give to a character like Nancy, despite sentimental evasion and melodramatic exaggeration, a core of reality and truth:

> "Thank Heaven upon your knees, dear lady," cried the girl, "that you had friends to care for and keep you in your childhood, and that you were never in the midst of cold and hunger, and riot and drunkenness, and—and—something worse than all—as I have been from my cradle." (XL)

From an artistic point of view, Dickens' notions on the strength of environment are perhaps more important for the way in which they helped him to form a vision of large social forces rather than in the creation of individual character. In a passage of noble indignation in *Nicholas Nickleby*, Dickens sets his hero's troubles in perspective by drawing a picture of a world in which they are but "an atom in the huge aggregate of distress and sorrow," a world in which "generation upon generation . . . (are) reared from infancy to drive most criminal and dreadful trades . . . by circumstances darkly curtaining their very cradles' heads" (LIII). The dignity of this passage, its complete lack of hysteria, make it all the more impressive a piece of evidence that Dickens was already, in only his third novel, capable of taking a somber view of society. He was trying to create, in a universal way, an effect that he was to render in concrete and particular terms in *Barnaby Rudge*. It might be said that the major character of that novel is the "vast throng . . . whose growth was fostered by bad criminal laws, bad prison regulations, and the worst conceivable police" (XLIX). It certainly provides the most vividly realized and powerful of the novel's scenes. And the horror of its violence is made, if not more excusable, at least more understandable

---

[25] *Ibid.*, I, 418.
[26] *Ibid.*, I, 35.
[27] Autobiographical fragment in Forster's *Life of Charles Dickens*, I, 25.

by the introduction of a conception that was to be one of Dickens' most permanent thoughts about his society. Speaking of the murders committed during the French Revolution, in *Pictures From Italy*, he asks the question: "Was it a portion of the great scheme of Retribution."[28] As Edgar Johnson has pointed out, [29] *Barnaby Rudge* was being written and published at a time of rioting and general social unrest. Although, in his preface to the novel, Dickens claims to have created no more than a work of historical fiction, there can be no doubt that these events were very much in his mind at the time and that he tried, in drawing scenes of ghastly violence, to show that they were the product of unbearable social and economic pressures. Such scenes of macabre power as the attack on Newgate are of value in themselves, but, more important, they point forward to the tragedy of a whole people that was to be created in *A Tale of Two Cities*.

In Dickens' attitude toward poverty and its evil effects, we can see one justification for Edmund Wilson's statement that "of all the great Victorian writers, he was probably the most antagonistic to the Victorian Age itself."[30] For many Victorians, poverty was the result of an almost sinful lack of prudence and industry or a necessity that had to be accepted in humility and resignation. For Dickens, poverty never ceased to be something evil in itself. He says in the chapter on gin shops in *Sketches by Boz*:

Gin-drinking is a great vice in England, but poverty is a greater. . . . If Temperance Societies could suggest an antidote against hunger, distress, or establish dispensaries for the gratuitous distribution of bottles of Lethe-water, gin-palaces would be numbered among the things that were. Until then, their decrease may be despaired of. (Chap. XXII of "Scenes")

The Tragicomedy of Money

For Dickens, in these early novels, money is something both intensely serious and wildly funny. This is clearly brought out by comparing two of the minor characters from *The Pickwick Papers*: The Chancery Prisoner and Wilkins Flasher, Esq. Both

[28] "Lyons, the Rhone, and the Goblin of Avignon."
[29] *Charles Dickens: His Tragedy and Triumph* (London: Gollancz, 1953), I, 312.
[30] "Dickens: The Two Scrooges," in *The Wound and the Bow* (Boston: Houghton Mifflin, 1941), p. 29.

are among the characters who are, in Humphry House's words, "constructed round an attitude to money."[31] In each case money, the absence or presence of it, is the determining factor of existence, and the vividness of these characters stems from what might be called their singlemindedness of function. The descriptive details by which they are sketched-in have none of the seemingly accidental quality of life. They are all geared to the task of producing one simple, but strong, impression.

In the description of The Chancery Prisoner, every detail is designed to make us feel that "the iron teeth of confinement and privation had been slowly filing him down for twenty years" (XLII). And the power of Dickens' indignation at the evil system that has created such suffering is realized in the moving quality of the prisoner's anguished cries: "I am a dead man; dead to society, without the pity they bestow on those whose souls have passed to judgement" (XLII). Dickens is deeply concerned here with the importance of money in his society, but there was another part of him that regarded the "monetary system of the country" (LV) as a farcical game. Wilkins Flasher, Esq., the stockbroker used by Mr. Weller to transfer his funds, is a practitioner of this esoteric but remunerative sport. He can hardly be said to work. He simply waits in his office—"spearing a wafer-box with a pen-knife" (LV)—for whatever may be wafted toward him by the necessary workings of the system of which he is an integral part. The mixture of wary suspicion and respectful astonishment in Mr. Weller and his friends is the response of the simple man in the face of unfathomable, and yet powerful, institutions. The essential lunacy of the whole thing to Dickens is conveyed in Sam's answer to his father's question about the "reduced counsels":

"What are they all a eatin' ham sangwidges for?" inquired his father.

"'Cos it's in their dooty, I suppose," replied Sam, "it's a part o' the system; they're alvays a doin' it here, all day long!" (LV)

A serious concern with the evil effects of poverty on the individual is one of the earliest and most deeply felt of Dickens' subjects. In *Sketches by Boz* we find him, in describing "Shabby-Genteel People," writing of a "timorous air of conscious poverty" that "will make your heart ache—always supposing that you are neither a philosopher nor a political economist,"[32] and of prostitution as "a last dreadful resource, which

31 *Dickens World*, p. 58.
32 "Characters," chap. x.

it would shock the delicate feelings of these *charitable* ladies to hear named."[33] This note is sounded again and again in the early books, but it is significant that it is concerned with the material, external results of poverty or with psychological effects of only the simplest kind. Dickens sums up Mr. Nickleby's ruin in one sentence: "A mania prevailed, a bubble burst, four stockbrokers took villa residences in Florence, four hundred nobodies were ruined, and among them Mr. Nickleby" (I). At this period he is capable of expanding such a hint into a brilliant chronicle of decline. The increasing shabbiness, the recourse to the pawnbroker's, the desperate sense of insecurity in a society that makes only the barest provision for the unfortunate, all this will be presented to us with consummate force. An attempt will be made to show us something of the mental disintegration that may take place, but it will tend to be of the "misery had made her into a devil" variety. The subtle delineation of the breakdown in William Dorrit's character lies far ahead along the path of Dickens' artistic development.

This lack of interest in, or lack of ability to portray, inner complexity is responsible for the static quality of much of Dickens' early characterization. The greed and gambling fever of Nell's grandfather and the miserliness of Ralph Nickleby are part of the unchanging character-equation of each with which we are presented. In neither is there any sense of change or development, nor are we given an adequate psychological explication of their dominant passion. The claim that all Dickens' early villains fall into the category of the traditional miser figure is manifestly unfair. In *Nicholas Nickleby*, for example, this role is taken by Arthur Gride, and compared with him Ralph is a masterpiece of complex characterization (his envious hatred of Nicholas from the very first moment is a good touch). But it remains true that these characters represent "humours" in a fairly simple way.

A concentration on the externals of wealth and a lack of deep interest in character are just as evident in Dickens' treatment of a hero such as Nicholas Nickleby as in the portraits of the villains. In answer to Smike's question "Shall I ever see your sister?" Nicholas replies, "To be sure . . . we shall all be together one of these days—when we are rich, Smike" (XXIX). This seems to be the only necessary condition for happiness for such people as Nicholas, Fanny, and Frank Cheeryble. Born with

[33] "Scenes," chap. iii.

kindness, generosity, and sensibility, they require material prosperity in order that these qualities may flower in the most congenial atmosphere possible. Their lives exist only in terms of
personal relationships; and the worlds of art, politics, or ideas
never rouse their interest. We cannot imagine them putting
their wealth to any fine purpose, for, as Humphry House says,
they "have no style beyond kindness, no taste beyond comfort."[34]

I have already pointed out that Dickens had at this time a
dual attitude toward money. He was only too aware of its importance in his own society, but it also, perhaps for that very
reason, provided him with a wonderfully varied field of comedy.
For the humor of this period is not all of a piece, not just simple
fun, as is so often maintained. There is bitter irony as well as
straightforward comedy in the early novels. But it seems a pity
to dismiss the simple fun as nothing but the easily won effects
of a public entertainer. There is too much of a positive and
joyous comic force in the vision of Mr. Bumble counting the
teaspoons after his proposal of marriage to Mrs. Corney
(XXIII), or of Mr. Mantalini "pouncing with kitten-like playfulness upon a stray sovereign" (XXXIV), to make such a view
easily tenable. And the financial stratagems of Dick Swiveller
are unforgettable:

"I enter in this little book the names of the streets that I can't
go down while the shops are open. This dinner today closes Long
Acre. I bought a pair of boots in Great Queen Street last week, and
made that no thoroughfare too. There's only one avenue to the
Strand left open now, and I shall have to stop that up to-night with
a pair of gloves. The roads are closing so fast in every direction, that
in about a month's time, unless my aunt sends me a remittance, I
shall have to go three or four miles out of town to get over the way."
(VIII)

We feel here a delighted acceptance of life for its own sake, a
glorying in the sheer wonder of ordinary people which prompts
Dickens to say of a character in *The Pickwick Papers* that there
was "a kind of boastful rascality, about the whole man, that was
worth a mine of gold" (XLI). The sanity of the humor that
springs from this delight seems to have a moral force in that it
arouses a response of joyful acceptance in the reader, and this
feeling is reinforced by the fact that Dickens' humor is rarely
cruel or malicious. It can explode nonsense none the less effectively for making us laugh happily at the same time:

[34] *Dickens World*, p. 61.

At length it became high time to remember the first clause of that great discovery made by the ancient philosopher, for securing health, riches, and wisdom; the infallibility of which has been for generations verified by the enormous fortunes constantly amassed by chimney-sweepers and other persons who get up early and go to bed betimes. (*Martin Chuzzlewit*, V)

The comedy of money, however, is capable of producing much more complex effects in these novels. There is irony, for example, informed by passionate indignation. A famous passage is that in which Mr. Bumble describes the buttons on his beadle's coat:

"The die is the same as the parochial sea—the Good Samaritan healing the sick and bruised man. The board presented it to me on New-year's morning, Mr. Sowerberry. I put it on, I remember, for the first time, to attend the inquest on that reduced tradesman, who died in a doorway at midnight." (IV)

Humor of this kind produces a grim smile rather than laughter, and Dickens uses it constantly in order to try to bring home to the complacent the reality of the lives of the poor as they are affected by the institutions that surround them. In the early *Mudfog Papers* he exposes the prejudices of a class for which property is a basic prerequisite of a civilized life by writing of "people not proved poor or otherwise criminal."[35] Perhaps his most brilliant ironic attack on some of the basic early Victorian beliefs is contained in Miss Monflathers' censure of Little Nell:

"Don't you feel how naughty it is of you . . . to be a wax-work child, when you might have the proud consciousness of assisting, to the extent of your infant powers, the manufactures of your country; of improving your mind by the constant contemplation of the steam-engine; and of earning a comfortable and independent subsistence of from two-and-ninepence to three shillings per week? Don't you know that the harder you are at work, the happier you are?" (XXXI)

Child labor, the mechanization of the human spirit, and the gospel of work are all brought under the lash with a Swiftian force; but the most telling feature of the passage is its overall tone of utter coldness and inhumanity, the tone of a voice speaking not to a poor child but to a representative of the class of poor children. Dickens saw very clearly the extent to which we all try to hide behind the abstract in order to escape the

[35] "Report of the Second Meeting of the Mudfog Association."

suffering and unhappiness of others, and he strove always to break down a generalized idea of people into its individual, living components.

The serious use of comedy which I have been discussing occurs only from time to time in the first novels, but in the masterpiece of this early period, *Martin Chuzzlewit*, Dickens succeeds in achieving a fusion of comedy and criticism of society of the highest kind. The prodigal wealth of genius displayed in this novel is allied to an artistic maturity far greater than that of any of its predecessors. The characterization, for example, is more subtle than anything we have encountered as yet. I have already mentioned the comparative simplicity of many of the earlier characters, but in this novel, not content with the creation of a Pecksniff and a Mrs. Gamp, Dickens gives us a hero who experiences some kind of moral development, and he explores with insight the darker regions of the mind of Jonas Chuzzlewit, the chief villain.

A glance at these characters may reveal how some of the scattered themes of the earlier novels are brought into a more significant relationship within the critical framework of *Martin Chuzzlewit*. This world has no place for the genial benevolence of Mr. Pickwick or the more suspect do-goodism of the Cheerybles, while Charity is no more than the name—peculiarly suitable because of her "mild, yet not reproachful gravity" (II)— of one of Pecksniff's daughters. Pecksniff himself is a great "humour" character, and the marvelous subtlety of his presentation lies not so much in the delineation of his inner life as in the exactness of that criticism of hypocritical benevolence that he embodies. After his attempt to force his attentions on Mary Graham, we apprehend his feelings of shame through a purely externalized cataloging of his personal appearance:

Mr. Pecksniff . . . certainly did not appear to any unusual advantage, now that he was left alone. On the contrary, he seemed to be shrunk and reduced; to be trying to hide himself; and to be wretched at not having the power to do it. His shoes looked too large; his sleeve looked too long; his hair looked too limp; his features looked too mean; his exposed throat looked as if a halter would have done it good. For a minute or two, in fact, he was hot, and pale, and mean, and shy, and slinking, and consequently not at all Pecksniffian. (XXX)

Dickens is taking us below the surface of Mr. Pecksniff's personality for a moment, but in an indirect way that does not step outside the formal bounds within which his character is created.

When, however, we find Pecksniff warming his back at a fire "as if it were a widow's back, or an orphan's back, or an enemy's back, or a back that any less excellent man would have suffered to be cold" (II), we realize how tricky a tightrope Dickens is walking. With the sonorous repetitions of his language and such gestures as "keeping his hand in his waistcoat as though he were ready, on the shortest notice, to produce his heart for Martin Chuzzlewit's inspection" (III), Pecksniff is so very close to the outward appearance of a truly benevolent man that benevolence itself seems almost to be called in question. The razor-edge separating moral truth and dishonesty is being presented here with consummate force. We have the nuances of tone and, above all, the evidence of his actions to give us the clue to Mr. Pecksniff's real nature, but despite momentary lapses from his high estimation of his own goodness, he retains the complex hypocrisy of the self-deceived, as his reaction to Mary Graham's dislike of his touch makes clear:

His touch! What? That chaste patriarchal touch which Mrs. Todgers —surely a discreet lady—had endured, not only without complaint, but with apparent satisfaction! This was positively wrong. Mr. Pecksniff was sorry to hear her say it. (XXX)

Martin Chuzzlewit stands out amongst the group of early novels by reason of its significant avoidance of the intrinsically good benefactor. So much is made of this type of character in criticism that we might be forgiven for thinking of Dickens' novels as thronging with simple and openhanded philanthropists. In fact, however, the idea of the dangers inherent in false benevolence is just as important to him. I have already pointed out the serious artistic decline between Mr. Pickwick and the Cheerybles, and some consideration of old Martin Chuzzlewit makes it clear how exercised Dickens was by the problem of presenting charitable actions in a humanly acceptable way. The Cheerybles exist in a social vacuum. They make money with one hand and give it away with the other and there is no convincing continuity between these two sets of actions. With Martin, however, Dickens attempts to set up a meaningful relationship between his character and the possession of wealth. Its evil effects arouse the greed of others and this, in its turn, causes him to retreat into misanthropy:

"I have so corrupted and changed the nature of all those who have ever attended on me, by breeding avaricious plots and hopes within them; I have engendered such domestic strife and discord, by tarrying even with members of my own family . . . that I have . . . fled from all who knew me, and taking refuge in secret places, have lived, of late, the life of one who is hunted." (III)

He plays the benefactor by sending young Martin twenty pounds after he has left Pecksniff, but it was in the hope of bringing "you back, Martin, penitent and humbled. I hoped to distress you into coming back to me" (LII). And some credibility is given to his final distribution of good things by his description of what he suffered as a member of the Pecksniff household.

I am not trying to claim for such attempts at psychological realism the power of, say, George Eliot, but merely to show how, even in the less successful pages of a work of great genius, Dickens constantly explores the possibilities of his art. Even such a total, and odious, failure as Tom Pinch can teach us something, for he reveals to what an extent the possibility of incorruptible goodness retained its fascination for Dickens. The sentimental exaggerations of this character indicate an almost hysterical determination on Dickens' part to stress his purity, a hysteria that may spring from the implicit recognition of how completely at odds the character is with the savagely satirical tone of the novel as a whole. Tom Pinch would be a failure in any novel, but his presence might at least have been more acceptable within the almost unbroken gaiety of *The Pickwick Papers* or the fairy-tale mystery of *The Old Curiosity Shop*. To understand this is to realize something of the true nature of *Martin Chuzzlewit*. Similarly, even a figure as sketchy as young Martin can have some interest for us, because it is possible to follow a development in him from genial selfishness to a finer appreciation of the needs of others. On the other hand, Tom's total divorce from any kind of external influence makes him seem like a character from Enid Blyton rather than an artistic creation: "Who, as thou drivest off, a happy man, and noddest with a grateful lovingness to Pecksniff in his nightcap at his chamber-window, would not cry," etc. (V). Such contempt for the external makes Dickens' treatment of Jonas Chuzzlewit all the more surprising. With the example of Quilp before us, we might expect him to be a figure of total and unexplained evil. But Quilp is elemental, the perfect creature to inhabit a fairy tale. The sober quality of the scenes in which he appears demands that Jonas be cast in a different mold, and it is Dickens' recognition of this necessity that enables him to present the workings of Jonas' mind, in his treatment of Mercy and after the murder, with such understanding. As the preface to *Martin Chuzzlewit* shows, Jonas drew much of his solidity for Dickens from the relationship between his character and his early upbringing:

I conceive that the sordid coarseness and brutality of Jonas would be unnatural, if there had been nothing in his early education, and in the precept and example always before him, to engender and develop the vices that make him odious. But so born and so bred . . . I claim him as the legitimate issue of the father upon whom those vices are seen to recoil.

If the greatness of *Martin Chuzzlewit* is displayed partly in subtler characterization than heretofore, it is even more evident in the sense we experience of a more fully developed unity, despite the novel's multiplicity of characters and abrupt changes of scene. Its pages are crowded—to an extent unknown even in *Nicholas Nickleby*—with scenes of melodrama and pathos, of farce, satire, and comedy of an inspired lunacy, and yet it does seem to possess an overall feeling or tone that the earlier novel lacks. The question of how this was achieved immediately presents itself.

The search for the novel's controlling impulse makes it apparent, in the first place, that it contains a number of limited didactic aims. In the preface, for example, Dickens expresses the hope that he always takes "every available opportunity of showing the want of sanitary improvements in the neglected dwellings of the poor." Again, there is Mr. Bevan's advice to Martin just before he leaves for home:

"If you ever become a rich man, or a powerful one . . . you shall try to make your Government more careful of its subjects when they roam abroad to live. Tell it what you know of emigration in your own case, and impress upon it how much suffering may be prevented with a little pains." (XXXIV)

Forster's view was, of course, that the book's purpose was to show "the number and variety of humours that have their root in selfishness."[36] This is very close to the truth, but there re-

---

[36] *Life of Charles Dickens*, I, 274.

mains a layer of yet deeper meaning. The characters' selfishness
seems to me to arise from a substratum of greed, and so I think
Monroe Engel's comment gets closest to an explanation of the
book's unity: "the ugly, disfiguring effect of money as a social
force is the central or organizing concern of the novel."[37]

This theme of the evil effects of money is suggested by old
Martin in the book's third chapter: "But I have never found one
nature, no, not one, in which, being wealthy and alone, I was
not forced to detect the latent corruption that lay within it,
waiting for such as I to bring it forth" (III). The theme, however, is worked out mainly in terms of comedy and satire. The
comic approach to money constitutes, in fact, the dominant tone
of the novel, the spirit that perhaps above all makes for its unity
of feeling. The Chuzzlewits who surround old Martin like a
group of vultures are not isolated personal phenomena. They
are deeply embedded in a way of life which, from the crookery
of the Eden Land Corporation to the hollowness of the Anglo-
Bengalee Disinterested Loan and Life Assurance Company,
seems entirely given over to greed and deceit. There is a complete integration here between Dickens' public and private concerns. The impertinent chicanery of the Anglo-Bengalee Company is the climax, in this first group of novels, of that sense of
the inherent lunacy of commerce which Dickens first explored
in *The Pickwick Papers*. His treatment there of the "monetary
system of the country" is rather sketchy, but in *Nicholas Nickleby* he devotes a fair amount of space to the promotion of the
United Metropolitan Improved Hot Muffin and Crumpet Baking and Punctual Delivery Company. The objects of the company are of a patriotic and humanitarian nature: "Firstly, by
prohibiting, under heavy penalties, all private muffin trading of
every description; secondly, by themselves supplying the public
generally and the poor at their own homes, with muffins of first
quality at reduced prices" (II). These measures are necessary
to bring to an end such injustices as "the case of an orphan
muffin-boy, who, having been run over by a hackney carriage,
had been removed to the hospital, had undergone the amputa-
tion of his leg below the knee, and was now actually pursuing
his occupation on crutches. Fountain of justice, were these
things to last!" (II). The only object of the directors, of course,
is to sell their own shares as soon as they are at a premium, but
the company is formed amidst scenes of wild enthusiasm and

[37] *The Maturity of Dickens* (Oxford: University Press, 1959), p. 103.

they all go to the office for lunch "as they did every day at half-past one o'clock; and to remunerate themselves for which trouble (as the company was yet in its infancy), they only charged three guineas each man for every such attendance" (II).

Funny as the activities of the Muffin Company are, they are surpassed in humor and seriousness by those of the Anglo-Bengalee. Dickens is now beginning to see more deeply into the evils that afflict an individual and a society given up to the unrestrained pursuit of wealth, and with this greater insight has come an increase in his technical power as a novelist. Because of its place within a novel that is so concerned with the degrading effects of the desire for money, and, even more, because of the imaginative power with which it is presented, we begin to feel that the company stands in some kind of a symbolic relation to the society of which it is a part. By means of devices that are perhaps rather simple—a use of inversion and a concern with surface appearances—but are nevertheless entirely literary, Dickens constructs a comic, an almost mythic, public institution that runs parallel to reality and yet is capable, simultaneously, of forming a criticism of it. Its founder, for example, a sickening confection of glossiness from head to foot, "his fingers, clogged with brilliant rings, . . . as unwieldly as summer flies but newly rescued from a honey-pot" (XXVI), is someone whom we have met before:

And yet, though changed his name, and changed his outward surface, it was Tigg. Though turned and twisted upside down, and inside out, as great men have been sometimes known to be; though no longer Montague Tigg, but Tigg Montague; still it was Tigg; the same Satanic, gallant, military Tigg. The brass was burnished, lacquered, newly stamped; yet it was the true Tigg metal notwithstanding. (XXVII)

By means of that one phrase—"as great men have been sometimes known to be"—Dickens does manage to establish, I think, a significant connection between the mythic Tigg and the real world. Because we know what Tigg was before his transformation, we can see that Dickens is suggesting that there is a fundamental identity between shabby, down-at-heel roguery and expansive financial manipulation.

Just as Tigg himself is newly transformed, so his business is newly created.

The offices were newly plastered, newly painted, newly papered, newly countered, newly floor-clothed, newly tabled, newly chaired, newly fitted up in every way. (XXVII)

But that is no reason for fearing the company's solvency.

Business! Look at the green ledgers with red backs, like strong cricket-balls beaten flat. Solidity! Look at the massive blocks of marble in the chimney-pieces. Publicity! Why, Anglo-Bengalee Disinterested Loan and Life Assurance Company is painted on the very coal-scuttles. (XXVII)

The futility of the company and all its activities is symbolized by the "vast red waistcoat" of its porter.

Whether he was a deep rogue, or a stately simpleton, it was impossible to make out, but he appeared to believe in the Anglo-Bengalee. . . . The whole charm was in his waistcoat. Respectability, competence, property in Bengal or anywhere else, responsibility to any amount on the part of the company that employed him, were all expressed in that one garment. (XXVII)

Under the pressure of a desperate need for money, a red waistcoat seems capable of guaranteeing a release from misery. For it is significant that there is some limit to the inclusiveness of the Anglo-Bengalee as a paradigm of society. Like the Muffin Company, it is run for their own benefit by a group of rogues. At this stage the public is made a victim out of its own economic necessity.

"B is a little tradesman, clerk, parson, artist, author, any common thing you like. . . . B wants a loan. . . . B assures his own life for double the amount, and brings two friends' lives also—just to patronise the office. . . . Do it! . . . B's hard-up, my good fellow, and will do anything." (XXVII)

With the Anglo-Bengalee, Dickens seems to be taking the conspiratorial view of the business world. The company is a vast racket run by a few individuals for their own gain, and the public, caught in the toils of a heartless economic system, are made the victims through no fault of their own. The company thus forms a criticism of certain activities within society, but not of the very nature of society itself. It embodies a critique rather than a vision. If such an attack is to be made wholly inclusive it must work on the assumption either that men are fundamentally evil (especially in their attitudes to money) or that the evils of society are so strong and all-pervasive that they can effect its members almost against their will. With the example of the Eden Land Corporation before us in the same novel, we may be able to foresee a time when there will be an identity of desire between the manipulators and the manipulated, when the manipulated will be made victims of their own greed.

Conclusion

With the exception of *Martin Chuzzlewit*, none of these early novels possesses a fully developed theme, and so any account of them must accept their fragmentary nature. Their great successes lie, of course, in comedy; but as soon as one moves away from this, one discovers various kinds of subject matter, often with important social implications. Dickens seems to be drawn irresistibly toward the depiction of society; we can observe him struggling to execute this with creative power and, frequently, failing. Sometimes the failure is to be found in the lack of formal integration in Dickens' novels at this stage. The satirical indignation of the Dotheboys Hall scenes of *Nicholas Nickleby*, for example, has to coexist with the melodramatic pursuit of Kate by Sir Mulberry and Lord Verisopht and the insanely brilliant comedy of Mrs. Nickleby. The power of Dickens' genius is such that this mixture provides nourishment rather than indigestion, except for an occasional spasm, for most readers; but there is more than narrowminded quibbling involved in claiming that the book's achievement is that of a mélange rather than a novel. The point worth making here is that the book's formal chaos leaves one with no unified imaginative experience. It lives on in one's mind as an increasingly dim memory of bits and pieces; it cannot make itself a part of the texture of one's life in the way that *Middlemarch* or *Anna Karenina* is capable of doing.

At other times, Dickens' failure exists in the isolated scene itself, a failure that often takes the form of a split between the social concern and its artistic embodiment. We perceive the social point, but remain unmoved because of the lifelessness with which it is rendered. It seems clear from this that Dickens has a general interest in social problems and a desire to transform them into art, but that only some of them are capable of inspiring his creative imagination. He exhibits a kind of Pavlovian reaction with regard to social problems, and this accounts for the sense of tiredness that can be found in his treatment of this material from the very beginning: at the merest whiff of a "problem" the old entertainer shuffles into his act and we get his pathos-arousing patter. This effect is most obvious in Dickens' treatment of children throughout his career; it is, I think, what Kafka had in mind when he noted in his diary "Dickens' opulence and great, careless prodigality, but in consequence passages of awful insipidity in which he wearily works over effects he has already achieved. Gives one a barbaric impression."[38] But when the deeper levels of Dickens' creativity are awakened by a subject of social significance, we find that fusion of didacticism and autonomous artistic life which I am suggesting is characteristic of his greatest work.

I think it legitimate to ask if this awakening is caused by some subjects more than others; and when one looks at the range of social problems as they are actually embodied in these early works, it does appear that Dickens is most consistently successful when he is dealing with what I have called the "tragicomedy of money." Even at this stage Dickens can, of course, succeed in other areas of social criticism. The didactic impulse and creative freedom are fused so powerfully in the opening chapters of *Oliver Twist* that they attain the scope of universal ironies, but they eventually fall apart in sentimentality and melodrama. This is the usual fate of Dickens' general social criticism at this period in his career, but when he deals with the effects of money on the individual and society, a theme that can be found throughout his work from the very beginning, we find that it is always embodied with a masterly incisiveness; in fact, he seems incapable of failure whenever he tackles it. And it is relevant here to remember that this theme is a crucial aspect of Dickens' greatest early success, *Martin Chuzzlewit*.

It is possible to understand Dickens' concern with the social as part of the general Victorian attempt to grapple with the problems of the nineteenth century, although this does not account for the peculiar intensity with which he seizes upon the temporal and transmutes it into the material of undying art. Neither does it explain why it is the area of temporal affairs connected with money that so obviously captures Dickens' imagination. When he is dealing with the problems of, say,

[38] *The Diaries of Franz Kafka: 1914–1923* (New York: Schocken, 1949), II, 188–189.

benevolence or progress, Dickens is more than capable of sharing the confusions of his age to the full. His success in dealing with the money theme seems to posit some special degree of understanding that goes hand-in-hand with artistic achievement. If this idea has any substance, it can only be shown by placing Dickens within the context of nineteenth-century life as a whole.

CHAPTER THREE

The Man and His Times

Characteristic of one aspect of the Victorian ethos is a lack of tough, knowledgeable intellect. There are, of course, exceptions. The mental rigor of John Stuart Mill, the moral subtlety of George Eliot, the urbane critical insight of Matthew Arnold, all indicate a high distinction of mind. But when we consider the period as a whole, one of the negative patterns of nineteenth-century life is surely that which gathers around such phenomena as sentimentality, melodrama, and obsessive activity. There is a kind of hysteria of action and feeling in Victorian life. We can see this in the huge literary output of a Trollope, the frantic social activity of a Dickens; in the grief of Lord Jeffrey over the death of Little Nell, and in the absurd fearfulness of the crowds at the New York docks waiting to find out if Dickens had been ruthless enough to kill off his spotless heroine.[1] One widespread social habit that highlights the point I am making here was the public dinner, where the ladies fluttered their handkerchiefs, the gentlemen sobbed their manly tears, and all joined in those endlessly repeated cheers, "three times three and three again," over the fate of the latest subject of social concern, or the retirement of a third-rate actress. As K. J. Fielding remarks in his edition of Dickens' speeches, the "custom of giving vast banquets in aid of a good cause was peculiarly Victorian; and it was typically Victorian that almost everyone realized its absurdity, and yet agreed to keep it going for want of a practical alternative."[2] The genuine flavor of a period is caught in the contemporary account by a young actor, John Coleman, of the banquet in honor of Mac-

---

[1] See Walter E. Houghton, *The Victorian Frame of Mind, 1830–1870* (New Haven and London: Yale Paperbound, 1964), section on "Work," pp. 242–262. Edgar Johnson, *Charles Dickens: His Tragedy and Triumph* (London: Gollancz, 1953), I, 303–304.

[2] (Oxford: Clarendon Press, 1960), pp. xxi–xxii.

ready's retirement: "When all was over Macready left through
an avenue of overwrought men, excited and hysterical as wom-
en. . . . Many who could not get near him, cried 'God bless
you, sir!' or 'God bless you, Mac!' "[3] And one can only wonder
how Dickens could have sat through an occasion such as the
dinner for the General Theatrical Fund of 1851.

Dickens in chair; toasts in rapid succession to "The Queen" (Drunk
three times three, followed by "God save the Queen") and the Prince
of Wales (Cheers were given, three times three, and a glee—"All hail
to the Prince.")[4]

Such manifestations are partly the result of the tensions of
nineteenth-century life. Anxiety and doubt seek their release in
an abandonment to feeling that seems to us excessive. Falsity
of emotion has often been singled out as a weakness of Victorian
literature, and it is a weakness, like melodrama, which we can
see reflected in the life of the times. When we read in the pages
of Mayhew of clergymen's daughters who are violently seduced
into sinful careers, we realize that some alteration is perhaps
required in our attitude toward such seemingly pasteboard
prostitutes as Martha in *David Copperfield*. And although
Victorian sentimentality may be criticized by some ultimate
literary and human standard, this should only follow the attempt to understand its roots in the texture of actual lives
and events.

It is surely one-sided to mention only falsity of emotion in
this context, for such a quality seems to be inextricably bound
up with a sheer lack of responsible intelligence. There does
appear to be a deep-seated imbalance of feeling and intelligence
in the nineteenth century. How else can we account for the
hysteria of Dickens' reaction to Millais' painting of *Christ in
the Carpenter Shop* or Thackeray's maudlin worship of "little
women" in his fiction? In both it may be possible to trace personal, even psychological, reasons for these emotional out-
bursts, but they were also a part of wider public attitudes.
Dickens is sharing a general middle-class view of the Pre-
Raphaelite work, and, much more important, Thackeray's worship of women is an aspect of that idealization of the home
which is such a significant withdrawal from the harshly competitive atmosphere of Victorian society. What strikes one in
the quality of excess in both of these examples is the poverty of

[3] *Ibid.*, p. 118.
[4] *Ibid.*, p. 119.

human response. The wallowing in emotion, the lack of critical intelligence, betray an absence of that awareness which is one of the personal features of a general culture.

This absence of general culture appears continually in Victorian life as a kind of intellectual naïveté. The quality I am attempting to describe can be seen in the work of such an interesting minor figure as Henry Mayhew. A self-made man in his chosen field of serious popular journalism, Mayhew's energy, courage, compassion, and intelligence in human relationships are brilliantly displayed in *London Labour and the London Poor*; and Mayhew is a typical enough figure to make us feel that the work represents some of the best qualities of its age. When we turn to other parts of his large output, however, it is almost impossible to believe that we are listening to the sympathetic voice of *London Labour*. Whereas the latter work contains almost no overt didacticism, his stories for children are weakened by Victorian preaching. The good fairy in his Christmas book *The Good Genius*, for example, turns out to be the "spirit of industry." His travel books on Germany display a chauvinism that moves into realms of fantasy. English superiority is as obvious to Mayhew as it is to Mr. Podsnap, but he found that "it is difficult to make foreigners understand this: as a rule, even our Gallic neighbors are supremely ignorant of English institutions and English habits. . . . Nor is it possible to make continental people comprehend the social and moral enormities that offend English families directly they set foot on foreign soil. . . . Englishmen can say with justice that there is no nation, either past or present, which will, for a moment, admit of comparison with their own." And the "philosophising" of Mayhew's educational works maintains a level of total banality.[5] The qualities we see in *London Labour* would lead us to expect a sympathetic understanding of the lives and thought of other men and other periods, but instead we find unawareness of the most blatant kind. The same kind of unawareness is ruthlessly exposed by George Eliot in *Middlemarch*, where Mr. Casaubon's labors of a lifetime are destroyed by his lack of knowledge of what German scholars have achieved in his own field of study. This provincial ignorance can be seen also in the pathetic Victorian insistence on the

[5] For the information contained in this section and its general viewpoint I am indebted to an unpublished M. A. thesis of the University of Birmingham, *The Literary Career of Henry Mayhew, 1812–1887*, by Angela M. Hookham.

evils of the French novel and its corrupting effect on English
morals. Typical here are the remarks of James Miller, Professor
of Surgery at Edinburgh University, in a pamphlet entitled
"Prostitution Considered in Relation to its Cause and Cure,"
published in 1859:

We blame modern works of fiction also. Not a few of these are
tainted with impurity; borrowing largely, in this, from the French
school; and yet they are read by old and young with a growing
avidity. The mind thus becomes familiarized with things and
thoughts which, if not absolute strangers to it, ought at least to be
banished and shut out as often as they appear.[6]

That the road to morality should be cleared by simply averting
one's gaze from what is unpleasant, and that this advice should
be given by a medical scientist, is powerful testimony to the
Victorian sense of the anarchic implications of sexual freedom.
Even Matthew Arnold himself, the great critic of cultural
provincialism, can fall a victim to it when, for example, he
attacks "the worship of the great goddess Lubricity":

That goddess has always been a sufficient power amongst mankind,
and her worship was generally supposed to need restraining rather
than encouraging. But here is now a whole popular literature, nay,
and art too, in France at her service![7]

The reasons for the lack of general culture that I have been
discussing are obviously very complex. It would be absurd to
accuse Matthew Arnold, say, of provincial ignorance. His reaction to French fiction is representative of that strain of Victorian earnestness that looked so fearfully upon any breakdown in accepted standards of moral behavior. That such a
sensitive mind could subscribe to the general view on this
point reveals both the strength of the popular feeling and the
large area of common interest that could exist among all sections of the middle class at this period. One of the most
difficult problems with Dickens is to separate the deeply
revolutionary creative artist from the man who enjoyed and
sympathized with so many aspects of his own culture. Henry
Mayhew is again relevant to the argument. Despite his background of classics at Westminster School, Mayhew had a self-
conscious awareness of himself as a new man well suited to

---

[6] This quotation and other relevant material can be found in William
Logan, *The Great Social Evil* (London, 1871), p. 232.
[7] Quoted in W. E. Houghton, *Victorian Frame of Mind*, p. 360.

the demands of a new age. His belief in the complete suprem-
acy of England and things English was such that, even as a boy,
he resented the time he felt was wasted on the study of "dead"
languages. This cultural chauvinism is revealed with devasting
effect in his educational works, with their patronizing disregard
of such figures as Plato and their advancing of the merest
platitudes as world-shattering discoveries. The roots of this
attitude of mind lie ultimately in the massive sense of England's
mercantile and industrial power felt by so many of her inhabitants. Carlyle himself, one of the earliest and most bitter
critics of Victorian complacency, can share it to the full in
talking of the modern Englishman:

Thy very stupidity is wiser than their wisdom. A grand *vis inertiae*
is in thee; how many grand qualities unknown to small men! Nature
alone knows thee, acknowledges the bulk and strength of thee; thy
Epic, unsung in words, is written in huge characters on the face of
this Planet,—sea-moles, cotton-trades, railways, fleets and cities,
Indian Empires, Americas, New-Hollands; legible throughout the
Solar System![8]

As so often in examples of Victorian self-adulation, one can
detect the note of hysteria, expressed here in the wild apos-
trophizing of the blindly magnificent Englishman in pseudo-
biblical rhetoric. Once again, there is that excess of feeling,
in this instance surely related to a guilty awareness of the
foundation of human misery on which England's greatness is
based.

It strikes one as peculiarly appropriate that Mayhew should
have been able to make his self-made way in the new field of
serious popular journalism. It is one of the strengths of this
journalism that in it Mayhew could find full expression for his
commitment to a radical approach to human suffering (it is
important to remember that *London Labour* began as a series
of articles in the *Morning Chronicle*), but in the last analysis
its demands gave a sanction to the cultural ignorance that men
such as Mayhew were ready to embrace almost, it seems, with
eagerness. The writing from which Mayhew earned his living
over a lifetime (some representative titles are *"But, However—,"* a farce in one act; *What to Teach and How to Teach
It: So That the Child May Become a Wise and Good Man; The
Great Exhibition Described; The Wonders of Science, or Young*

[8] *Past and Present,* ed. A. D. M. Hughes (Oxford: Clarendon Press,
1918), p. 145.

Humphry Davy; The Rhine and its Picturesque Scenery) was
part of a process that, in Richard D. Altick's words, led "to a
far-reaching revolution in English culture. No longer were
books and periodicals written chiefly for the comfortable few;
more and more, as the century progressed, it was the ill-
educated mass audience with pennies in its pocket which
called the tune to which writers and editors danced."[9] A glance
at these works of Mayhew will clearly show that the middle-
class audience that gave him his success was not likely to
demand much in the way of fierce intelligence from its writers.
A process of democratization was at work here which, whatever
its achievements, did lead undoubtedly to a lowering of intellectual standards.

Some idea of the level to which mid-Victorian intellectual
standards could sink can be gained from Arthur A. Adrian's
biography of Mark Lemon, friend of Dickens and first editor
of *Punch*. Professor Adrian devotes a chapter to *"Punch* Table
Talk," and after recounting some grisly moments of *Punch*
humor, makes the following comment:

Only occasionally was the current of serious Table talk checked
by such frothy eddies. More often the stream flowed steadily in its
deep channel, carrying its cargo of thoughtful comment. For here
were some of the best-informed men of their time, conscious of
their cultural heritage.

After this buildup, one might be forgiven for expecting sallies
of Johnsonian wit and profundity, but what we are given is
perhaps something less than that.

But what is poetry? Its aim, the Table decided, is the truthful representation of the beautiful. Since suggestiveness is its chief charm,
horrors should not be described but hinted at, as in Scott's "here an
arm, there a leg." This is more terrible in its directness, all admitted,
than the cut-and-dried terrors of superior writers. Poetry suggests
pictures to the mind; it is something more than music—the sound
pleases and the thought remains. Finally, the poet must always be
above art.[10]

The serious point is that this is the talk of men who *were*
"some of the best-informed . . . of their time," the intimates of

    [9] *The English Common Reader* (Chicago and London: Phoenix Books,
1963), p. 5.
    [10] *Mark Lemon: First Editor of Punch* (London: Oxford University
Press, 1966), pp. 68, 69.

Thackeray and Dickens, molders of opinion who helped to set the tone of their age. Mayhew himself was one of the original members of this circle, and with the exception of the really distinguished creative writers, achieved more with his *London Labour* than most of the rest of them put together. And yet Mayhew was guilty of the monumental ignorance and bad taste that I have already pointed out.

It would be comforting to believe that these were qualities unshared by the greatest Victorian writer, but the facts of Dickens' biography make it abundantly clear that this was not so. One factor, however irrelevant, that delayed the recognition of Dickens' true greatness was surely his blatant lack of intellectuality. The cultural emptiness of his characters' lives, his avoidance of any theoretical discussion of the novel, and the banality of the very small number of remarks on art in general in those thousands of letters, all point firmly to a mind sublimely indifferent to the interest of ideas. And the thought of the dummy books in the library at Gad's Hill with titles such as *Forty Winks at the Pyramids, Socrates on Wedlock, Malthus's Nursery Songs* is enough to bring a blush to the conscientiously intellectual modern cheek.[11] Despite this, I claim that one of the most important strands of Dickens' genius is a profound understanding of the period through which he lived. With all great art one seeks to experience as deeply as possible the total meaning made up of the union of form and content. Dickens does, of course, possess this twofold greatness of embodiment and insight; but to the insights into character and human nature which we expect from literature he adds a knowledge of the essential nature of the nineteenth century, both in its general implications and in its specific influence on the lives of individuals. And so my task in this chapter is to show that Dickens did, in fact, understand the nineteenth century, and to explain how he came to this understanding. I try to do so by tracing a significant relationship between Dickens and his age.

The question of whether Dickens understood what was going on in his society immediately raises a problem of method. I think I should make it clear that my method is not that of the historian as such. Too many literary studies attempt to ac-

[11] Edgar Johnson, *Charles Dickens: His Tragedy and Triumph* (London: Gollancz, 1953), II, 749–750.

quire scholarly respectability by means of an easy marshaling of historical facts that are often found to be available to all in well-known secondary sources. Many of the most interesting problems of the nineteenth century—changes in the standard of living of the working classes, for example—are of such a highly technical nature that they remain subjects of controversy to professional historians, as the following passage from the brilliant introduction to a new edition of Chadwick's *Sanitary Report* makes clear.

Recent years have seen much difference of opinion between historians over the questions of the changing fortunes of the working class in the late eighteenth century and the first half of the nineteenth century. There is no doubt, however, that there were substantial increases in both aggregate real income and average real incomes during the first half of the nineteenth century. Average incomes, however, tell nothing of the distribution of income, and very few of the participants in this important debate have been able to throw much light on the trends in real income of, say, the bottom fifty per cent, or the bottom twenty per cent of the income scales. . . . not enough is known about *changes* in income distribution to determine with any certainty whether the growth of average real income during the early nineteenth century offset an increasingly unequal distribution sufficiently to raise the real income of the lowest income groups, or the reverse.[12]

In any event, I do not think it either necessary or desirable that I should deal exhaustively with the minutiae of the age. This is legitimate because my aim is not to illuminate the historical features of the nineteenth century, but to throw light on a body of works of literature. It follows that I am more concerned with what the creative minds *thought* of their period than whether they were factually correct in what they thought. Nevertheless, there is such an amazing unanimity of view concerning what I consider to be the most crucial aspects of the inner life of the time that one seems justified in accepting that these phenomena were, objectively, a part of Victorian England. My method in justifying this opinion is to document the social insights of as representative a selection of writers as I can muster.

One aspect of this unanimity of view is the widespread nature of Victorian social criticism. Almost all the best minds of the nineteenth century—Carlyle, Arnold, Ruskin, Mill, Newman, Tennyson, Browning, Dickens, Thackeray, George Eliot—

[12] *The Sanitary Condition of the Labouring Population of Gt. Britain,* ed. M. W. Flinn (Edinburgh: University Press, 1965), pp. 3–4.

and a host of lesser figures such as Mayhew, Clough, Hood, Kingsley, are more or less dissatisfied with their age. We are involved here with the same paradox I mentioned earlier with regard to Dickens: the dichotomy between the creator's criticism of, and the man's attachment to, his society. Most of these writers succumb to the lure of their own age or feel a commitment to its institutions in some area or other, but running counter to this is the critically conscious rejection or the anguish of an alienation not fully understood. This is no doubt true of the great figures of many historical periods, but the peculiarly Victorian feature is the intensity of both the criticism and the commitment and the tension of ambiguities that spring from it. Tennyson, for example, the laureate of the age in so many ways, can range from the triumphant cry of

. . . Forward, forward let us range
Let the great world spin for ever down the ringing grooves
   of change

to the "two nations" mood of

And the vitriol madness flushes up in the ruffian's head,
Till the filthy by-lane rings to the yell of the trampled wife,
And chalk and alum and plaster are sold to the poor for bread,
And the spirit of murder works in the very means of life.[13]

Tennyson's intellectual difficulties with the nineteenth century are revealed in In Memoriam, which attempts to assimilate the discoveries of science into the framework of Victorian thought. As the culmination of this attempt, Hallam becomes the forerunner of a new evolutionary vision:

Whereof the man, that with me trod
   This planet, was a noble type
   Appearing ere the times were ripe,
That friend of mine who lives in God.

But Tennyson is only prepared to listen to science when it tells him, or when he makes it tell him, what he wants to hear:

I trust I have not wasted breath:
   I think we are not wholly brain,
   Magnetic mockeries; not in vain,
Like Paul with beasts, I fought with
   Death;

[13] Locksley Hall and Maud, Pt. I, sec. i, stanza x.

Not only cunning casts in clay:
Let Science prove we are, and then
What matters Science unto men,
At least to me? I would not stay.[14]

And from an emotional point of view, Tennyson's inability to identify himself completely with his age is surely one reason for that poignancy of loss which is such a pervasive note in his poetry.

However paradoxical the relations between the great Victorians and their society, one is faced, in looking at the period as a whole, with a social criticism that is formidable in its dimensions. This mass of discontent can easily provoke the rage for order, but it may still be valid to wonder if it possesses any common factors. At the risk of appearing partial, I maintain, nevertheless, that the feature of their own times that consistently struck nineteenth-century writers with a shocked surprise was the emergence of money as a social fact with the widest possible implications for themselves and their society. One can see this dominance of money being expressed in a huge wealth of documentary evidence from widely different minds all through the nineteenth century. The keynote to this recognition of the power of money is struck by Southey in 1808:

The commercial system has long been undermining the distinctions of rank in society. . . . Mushrooms are every day starting up from the dunghill of trade, nobody knows how. . . . They who are in the lucky scale rise as others sink; and merchants and bankers and contractors make their way by wealth even into the ranks of nobility. . . . The power of the old nobles [is] gradually transferred to a set of new men, to an aristocracy of wealth.[15]

We can find this recognition not only in direct statements concerning an increase in materialism, but also in the way in which criteria of wealth are seen to operate in all forms of human activity. As early as 1829, Carlyle's scornful opinion of the majority of his contemporaries is that with them

[Religion is] a matter, as all others now are, of Expediency and Utility; whereby some smaller quantam of earthly enjoyment may be exchanged for a far larger quantum of celestial enjoyment. Thus Religion too is Profit, a working for wages.[16]

14 *In Memoriam*, closing section and sec. cxx.
15 *Letters from England*, 2d ed., Vol. III, letter lx, pp. 83, 90, 92.
16 "Signs of the Times," in *Critical and Miscellaneous Essays* (London, 1857), p. 113.

Only a few years later, we find Bulwer Lytton in agreement:

As the first impression the foreigner receives on entering England is that of the evidence of wealth, so the first thing that strikes the moral enquirer into our social system is the respect in which wealth is held . . . with us, Money is the mightiest of all deities.[17]

Again, Emerson was amazed by the English attitude to money on his visit of 1856:

There is no country in which so absolute a homage is paid to wealth. In America, there is a touch of shame when a man exhibits the evidence of a large property, as if, after all, it needed apology. But the Englishman has pure pride in his wealth, and esteems it a final certificate.[18]

In 1865, Ruskin spoke scathingly of the financial system to an audience at the Camberwell Working Men's Institute:

The first of all English games is making money. That is an all-absorbing game; and we knock each other down oftener in playing at that, than at football, or any other roughest sport.[19]

And looking back to her mid-Victorian childhood, it seemed to Beatrice Webb that her mother, who was the wife of a capitalist and a deeply religious woman, believed that "it was the bounden duty of every citizen to better his social status; to ignore those beneath him, and to aim steadily at the top rung of the social ladder. . . . No one of the present generation realises with what sincerity and fervour these doctrines were held by the representative men and women of the mid-Victorian middle class."[20] The possession of money was the sign that they had arrived; yet this has more significance than is apparent. Ruskin and Beatrice Webb complement each other here, for his theory is enforced by her experience. In his bitter attack on the popular doctrine of Political Economy, Ruskin says that "what is really desired, under the name of riches, is, essentially, power over men."[21] Beatrice Webb found that "the shifting mass of wealthy persons" whom she met in London society in the 1880's formed a kind of club of "professional profit-makers; the old-established families of bankers and brewers, often of Quak-

---

[17] *England and the English* (London, 1833), Bk. II, chap. 1.
[18] *English Traits* (1856), chap. x.
[19] *The Crown of Wild Olive* (London, 1866), lecture 1, "Work," sec. 24.
[20] *My Apprenticeship* (London, n.d.), chap. 1.
[21] *Unto this Last* (London: Longmans, n.d.), Essay II, "The Veins of Wealth."

er descent, coming easily first in social precedence." And that "Deep down in the unconscious herd instinct of the British governing class there *was* a test of fitness for membership of this most gigantic of all social clubs . . . the possession of some form of power over other people."[22] Finally, to give only one example from the many that could be taken from poetry, there is surely a significant weight of implication in Clough's revision of the Decalogue:

> Thou shalt not steal; an empty feat,
> When it's so lucrative to cheat.[23]

This can serve as a reminder of Blake's parody of a new version of the Lord's Prayer:

Our Father Augustus Caesar, who art in these thy Substantial Astronomical Telescopic Heavens, Holiness to Thy Name or Title, & reverence to thy Shadow. . . . Give us day by day our Real Taxed Substantial Money bought bread; deliver from the Holy Ghost whatever cannot be taxed.[24]

This reminder is salutary, not merely because Blake's savage brilliance defines Clough's rather cut-and-dried simplicity, but because it serves to illustrate how often Blake's prophetic insights continually anticipate the nineteenth century's judgment of itself (and, in aphorisms such as "Newton's philosophy has ruined England," some of those of the twentieth also).

The question that seems to pose itself here is whether there is anything in the facts of the historical process that will confirm the sense of a response to something new in all these varied statements. Greed for money in itself and desire for the material possessions that it can buy are of such ancient standing that they have achieved the status of constants in human behavior. Social criticism concerned with the desire for wealth can be found in all literary periods, in Chaucer's *The Pardoner's Tale*, for example, the plays of Ben Jonson, the satires of Pope. But in such examples this vice is seen as one amongst many, and the satirical attack is leveled against the individual who is evil in general terms, as in Chaucer, or against the traditional figure of the miser. What is new in the nineteenth century is

[22] *My Apprenticeship*, chap. 1.
[23] *Poems*, ed. H. F. Lowry, A. L. P. Norrington, and F. L. Mulhauser (Oxford: Clarendon Press, 1951), pp. 60–61.
[24] *Poetry and Prose*, ed. Geoffrey Keynes (London: Nonesuch Library, 1961), p. 827.

the notion that greed for money lies at the very heart of almost all personal and social evil, that other forms of wrongdoing are superstructures erected upon this one essential foundation, and that it is diffused throughout the whole of society. As I have tried to show, it is the key to most of the direct attacks made upon the period by its critics, but it is also present as the fundamental ground upon which the most sophisticated critiques are based. For both Matthew Arnold and John Stuart Mill, it is taken for granted as a basic given of their society.

Wealth, again, that end to which our prodigious works for material advantage are directed,— the commonest of commonplaces tells us how men are always apt to regard wealth as a precious end in itself; and certainly they have never been so apt thus to regard it as they are in England at the present time. Never did people believe anything more firmly, than nine Englishmen out of ten at the present day believe that our greatness and welfare are proved by our being so very rich.[25]

Mill takes a remarkably similar line in explaining why he "thought the predominance of the aristocratic classes, the noble and the rich, in the English constitution, an evil worth any struggle to get rid of":

Secondly . . . because the respect of the multitude always attaching itself principally to that which, in the existing state of society, is the chief passport to power; and under English institutions, riches, hereditary or acquired, being the almost exclusive source of political importance; riches, and the signs of riches, were almost the only things really respected, and the life of the people was mainly devoted to the pursuit of them.[26]

One is not surely falling into any kind of Marxist trap in seeing in all of this a response to the commercial and financial developments of the industrial revolution. In purely practical terms, money acquired greater importance than it had ever had before. Statements of this kind, especially in a context of literary criticism, must take into account L. C. Knights's classic study *Drama and Society in the Age of Jonson,* for Knights makes the point that whichever "of the larger industries we select in this period we find developments that until quite recently were regarded as peculiar to the late eighteenth and

[25] Matthew Arnold, *Culture and Anarchy,* ed. J. Dover Wilson (Cambridge Paperback, 1963), p. 51.
[26] *Autobiography* (London: The World's Classics, 1924), p. 145.

early nineteenth centuries."[27] Professor Knights is very much
concerned, in his "background" chapters, to establish a new
significance for money in the age of Jonson as a result of the
increase in commercial, industrial, and mercantile activity in
the period. Many of his observations on Jonson and his society
are very similar to those I wish to make about Dickens and his.
And so, with this question of money, it might seem as though
one were engaged on a task similar to the description of that
rise of the elusive middle classes, who are sent conveniently
on the move as an explanation of many diverse literary phenomena. But there are, I think, important discriminations to be
made between these two periods and the relationship with
their literatures. Professor Knights himself says that "the
strongest tendency of the age was towards the free investment
of capital; and the medieval ordering of commercial relationships was finally to give way before the increase in competition.
At the period that we are considering, however, the old and
the new were still blended, even in those forms of commercial
enterprise which, in the long run, were the most powerful
solvents of the traditional organization."[28] But that "long run"
did take several centuries to reach its climax, and indeed, the
image suggested by the phrase is not a happy one. The industrial revolution is marked, especially in the minds of those
who lived through it, not by a sense of gradualness, a blending
of old and new, but by an explosiveness of change that seemed
to destroy the old and replace it by the new almost overnight.
The Victorians appeared to themselves to be living "without leisure and without pause—a life of *haste*—above all a life of excitement, such as haste inevitably involves—a life filled so full . . .
that we have no time to reflect where we have been and whither
we intend to go . . . still less what is the value, and the purpose,
and *the price* of what we have seen, and visited."[29] As Walter E.
Houghton remarks, such a statement "seems far more modern
than Victorian. But if the speed of life has increased in the
twentieth century, the sense of speed has declined, for what has
become commonplace today was then a startling novelty. Our
greatgrandfathers may have had more leisure than we do but
it seemed less."[30] This point can be substantiated by another
reference to Professor Knights: "Even in the capitalist indus-

[27] (Penguin Books, 1962), p. 63.
[28] *Ibid.*, p. 57.
[29] Quoted in *Victorian Frame of Mind*, p. 7.
[30] *Ibid.*, p. 7

tries the small working masters did not completely disappear until the Industrial Revolution."[31] Once again, it is in the nineteenth century that the decisive break with tradition takes place.

It is possible, however, to fix on crucial differences between these periods with still more accuracy. In comparing the Middle Ages and the late-Renaissance with respect to money, Professor Knights has a passage that, at first sight, would seem to be equally applicable to the nineteenth century:

There had been medieval satires on Lady Meed; medieval preachers had denounced those who had money for their god, and that *"Pecuniae obediunt omnia"* had been a complaint of Erasmus; but, in England at least, it was in the early seventeenth century that the Lady Pecunia became, in a special sense, "the Venus of the time and state." Money and competition were becoming the prime movers of economic life.[32]

One of the aims of this study is to show that in the nineteenth century, in the view taken of it by its most critical minds, money and competition *had* become the prime movers of human life as such. The quotations from Arnold and Mill cited above show clearly enough that they shared this view, and the briefest reference to Dickens will reveal how central this is to his vision. Both Pip and Wemmick, in their different ways, and the society of which they are a part, are essentially motivated by money and the seeming magic it can work. And this reference to literature brings me to my most important point. The following passage is Professor Knights's explanation of why the "only economic 'diagnosis' that we find on the Jacobean stage should take the form of satire on particular individuals or classes of individuals":

A character in one of Dos Passos's novels remarks: "Don't blame people for things; it's the system." This could not have been said in the reign of James I. The capitalist "system" was taking shape, and "impersonal" causes were already responsible for a good deal; but the individuals who were helping to form that system were, I think, more prominent, more obviously capable of exerting economic pressure, than their successors in the nineteenth century.[33]

Relevant here is one of the key errors in Dickens criticism, the temptation to see his work solely in terms of a thronging gallery

[31] *Drama and Society* (Penguin Books, 1962), p. 66.
[32] *Ibid.*, p. 105.
[33] *Ibid.*, pp. 148–149.

of characters, even of Jonsonian "humour" figures. Dickens at his greatest, if not his most Dickensian, displays a genius very different from this. It is to be found in his ability to represent, in the elaborate structure of his later novels, a complex vision of society in which individuals are subordinated to the pressures of a web of relationships that symbolizes the intimate, yet inhuman, contacts of modern capitalism. As I later try to show in detail, he is able to create, in works such as *Little Dorrit*, mythical worlds that are not, in T. S. Eliot's words, "fancy, because they have a logic of their own; and this logic illuminates the actual world, because it gives us a new point of view from which to inspect it."[34] In doing so he was reflecting one of the major facts of the nineteenth century, its enormous increase in commerce and industry, and the processes by which the hardly new human desire for money achieved significantly new institutionalized forms in the life of the nation. A social economist sees one of these processes at work in the railway boom of the mid-forties which created "a national market for the investment of money . . . drew from the hoards of the small tradesman and 'the frugal operative' the pent-up savings of years. . . . It accumulated idle capital, while it innoculated even the poorest with the itch for aquisition."[35]

But it is not purely in practical terms that we should see the results of what Carlyle called "the supreme triumph of Cash."[36] Side by side with this has been an increase in the power of money—"the father of ultimate illusion and lies," as Lionel Trilling calls it[37]—as an almost abstract or metaphysical force in the life of society. Man is constantly threatened by the domination of the very machinery that he has himself created to make his life easier. Nowhere is this process more sinister in its operation than in the workings of money: money should have value only because it represents objects, but it seems more and more in capitalist society as though objects come to have value only because they represent money. To use the words of Marx, it is an *"alien intermediary* . . . whereas man himself should be the intermediary between men—man sees his will, his activity and

[34] "Ben Jonson," in *Elizabethan Dramatists* (London: Faber Paperback, 1963), p. 78.
[35] Edith Batho and Bonamy Dobrée, *The Victorians and After* (London: Cresset Press, 1938), p. 137.
[36] In *Chartism*, first published, 1839.
[37] *The Liberal Imagination* (New York: Doubleday Anchor Books, 1953), p. 110.

his relation to others as a power which is independent of him and them."[38] The great increase in share manipulation and company promotion in the nineteenth century was the register of a process of money begetting money in a way that seems to short-circuit the "natural" method of producing articles because they are needed. And out of the power of money in its realm of abstract economic manipulation comes one of the major causes of what seems to me the second great spiritual fact of the period which was clearly seen by the critics of Victorian society, that of isolation, loneliness, alienation. Carlyle's vision of a time when even the serf "had the inexpressible satisfaction of feeling himself related indissolubly, though in a rude brass-collar way, to his fellow mortals in this Earth" and when "*Cash Payment* had not then grown to be the universal sole nexus of man to man"[39] may have been idealized. But it formed a solid enough moral basis from which to criticize the treatment of human beings which reduced them, in the words of Marx in describing the use of the terms "full-timers" and "half-timers," to "nothing more than personified labor time. All individual distinctions are merged."[40] They were merged equally by that process of mechanization which destroyed the idiosyncrasy of traditional trades and crafts—"nothing is now done directly, or by hand. . . . The shuttle drops from the fingers of the weaver, and falls into iron fingers that ply it faster"[41]—and the herding together of people in huge towns demanded by the processes of mass production.

I think it true that along with the development of the railways, this enormous increase in the size of towns was the most noticeable change in the physical environment of the Victorian period. At any rate, it appeared so to its contemporaries, as Asa Briggs points out: "Most Victorian writers on society thought of their age as 'an age of great cities.' . . . About the facts themselves there could, of course, be no dispute. The population of England, in Ruskin's words, was being 'thrown back in continually closer crowds upon the city gates.' "[42] And that this was part of a European process is clear when we remember that the nineteenth century saw the beginning of

[38] T. B. Bottomore and M. Rubel, eds., *Karl Marx* (London: Watts and Co., 1956), p. 172.
[39] *Past and Present*, Bk. III, chap. xiii, p. 191; and *Chartism*.
[40] *Das Kapital* (London: Allen and Unwin, 1928), p. 244.
[41] Carlyle, "Signs of the Times," p. 100.
[42] *Victorian Cities* (London: Odhams Press, 1963), p. 57.

that movement whereby the city has come to play a peculiar
role in our consciousness, what Richard Wollheim has called
"the sense of disruption, of potential violence, of despair and
alienation that are held to be endemic to the condition of the
modern metropolis."[43] The sense that we are dealing with a
phenomenon that is, once more, new is reinforced both by
contemporary documentation and by contrast with the concept
of the "town" that is of great importance in literary forms such
as Restoration Comedy and the satire of Pope. The judgment
of the town is used sometimes as an object of satirical attack
and at others as the basis for moral condemnation, but it always
contains the idea of a coherent, homogeneous, and civilized
group. For Congreve, the town represents the hypocritical
consensus of a licentious upper class:

"Why do we daily commit disagreeable and dangerous actions? To
save that idol reputation. If the familiarities of our loves had produced that consequence, of which you were apprehensive, where
could you have fixed a father's name with credit, but on a husband?
I knew Fainall to be a man lavish of his morals, an interested and
professing friend, a false and a designing lover; yet one whose wit
and outward fair behaviour have gained a reputation with the town,
enough to make that woman stand excused, who has suffered herself
to be won by his addresses."[44]

But even this suggests the intimacy of a society where a man
can be as jealous of a woman as a "Cheapside husband of a
Covent Garden wife."[45] In Congreve we find almost a parody
of an "organic" community, but Pope's implicit use of the idea
of the town is deeply serious. At the beginning of *An Essay
on Man* he states what it will be necessary for him to do in
order to "expatiate free o'er all this scene of Man":

> Together let us beat this ample field,
> Try what the open, what the covert yield;
> The latent tracts, the giddy heights explore
> Of all who blindly creep, or sightless soar;
> Eye Nature's walks, shoot Folly as it flies,
> And catch the Manners living as they rise.[46]

[43] *Encounter*, May, 1962, p. 26.
[44] *The Way of the World*, Act II, scene iv.
[45] William Wycherley, *The Country Wife*, Act I, scene i.
[46] In *Poems*, ed. John Butt (London: University Paperbacks, 1965),
p. 504, ll. 9–14.

The wit of this metaphor from the life of the natural scene is made even more pointed by our awareness of the contemporary meaning of "manners," the moral as well as the social behavior of a homogeneous group. In other words, the complex of sanctions, habits, and ideals of men attempting to live in civilized contact with one another. Pope's satire arises from the fact that this attempt is never wholly successful, but he does not seek a solution in isolation or a flight to nature. In practical terms, his allegiance may shift to the country house as the center of an ideal life, but that ideal remains essentially social, for the country house may be regarded as a perfect town in miniature. In attempting to sum up the spirit of the eighteenth century, A. R. Humphreys remarks that the "task which the age made particularly its own, was to live in widespread harmony, abjuring the hazards of war and fanaticism which had convulsed the seventeenth century. By instinct and intention men strove for a congenial society."[47] And they were aided in this task by even some of the physical realities of their London, which was "nowhere more than a mile away" from the country.[48]

Pope is committed to a vision of man's life that forms part of a tradition that was broken only by the double assault of the Romantic sensibility and the pressures of the industrial revolution. Although the banished Duke in Shakespeare's *As You Like It* assures us, in speaking of his existence in the forest, that he "Finds tongues in trees, books in the running brooks, / Sermons in stones, and good in everything. / I would not change it,"[49] it is remarkable how willingly everyone does accept the change back to the court. The point seems to be that man needs a balanced relationship between nature and civilization for his spiritual and moral health, but that the court and the town are the places where man's finest qualities must find expression after being purified by contact with natural beauty. And even in the forest the Duke and his lords are far from being natural men. When Orlando, made desperate by hunger, breaks in upon their banquet he is rebuked in terms that show that a civilized mode of life is being kept up even there:

> Art thou thus bolden'd, man, by thy distress,
> Or else a rude despiser of good manners,
> That in civility thou seem'st so empty?[50]

[47] *Augustan World* (New York: Harper Torchbooks, 1963), p. 1.
[48] *Ibid.*, p. 13.
[49] Act II, scene i, ll. 16–18.
[50] Act II, scene vii, ll. 90–93.

It is true, of course, that one of the minor traditions of English
poetry, to which both Pope and Dr. Johnson contributed, consists of satirical abuse of the town and praise of rural con-
tentment, but this does not radically weaken my argument. One
can point out, in passing, that works in this genre often possess
a witty artificiality that expresses itself in a conscious indebted-
ness to classical imitation. Again, one might be permitted the
somewhat stale reminder that for Dr. Johnson, whose poem
"London" is a vigorous part of this tradition, "the man who
is tired of London is tired of life." Serious writers deserve to
be met on more serious ground, however, and I would cite
Pope's "A Farewell to London. In the Year 1715" as a work
that makes clear how different are his and later reactions to
the same subject.

> Dear, damn'd, distracting Town, farewell!
>   Thy Fools nor more I'll teize:
> This Year in Peace, ye Critics, dwell,
>   Ye Harlots, sleep at Ease!
>
> *Lintot*, farewell! thy Bard must go;
>   Farewell, unhappy *Tonson*!
> Heaven gives thee for thy Loss of *Rowe*,
>   Lean *Phillips*, and fat *Johnson*.
>
> Why make I Friendships with the Great,
>   When I no Favour seek?
> Or follow Girls Seven Hours in Eight?—
>   I need but once a Week.[51]

The tone here is surely of great importance. Pope is keenly
aware of the evils of London, but he sees them revealed in
purely personal terms. We are still in the intimate world of the
Town, and so a witty particularity is Pope's mode of attack:
the glancing malice reflects a known and manageable world in
which the general vices of humanity are seen instinctively as
a drama of individuals. It is, once more, the prophetic voice of
Blake that marks the transition to the modern view of the city.
A comparison of only the first line of his "London" with Pope's
poem will indicate some significant changes in attitude.

> I wander thro' each charter'd street,
>   Near where the charter'd Thames does flow,

[51] *Poems*, p. 245.

And mark in every face I meet
Marks of weakness, marks of woe.

But most thro' midnight streets I hear
How the youthful Harlot's curse
Blasts the new born Infant's tear,
And blights with plagues the Marriage hearse.[52]

The unpunctuated weightiness of that opening line immediately communicates a sense of monotony and uniformity which is strongly reinforced by the repetition of "mark." We are in an utterly different place from Pope's "dear, damn'd, distracting Town." Blake's tragic vision is of an inhumanly ordered nightmare in which the streets, the purely external, are recognizable, while the inhabitants of those streets are unknown except for the suffering and evil of which they are all a part. This is not the town of Lintot, Rowe, and Johnson, but the city of abstractions such as the Chimney-sweeper, the Soldier, and the Harlot whose facelessness is an epitome of the blank misery that Blake sees as an essential feature of London.

We can move from Blake into the nineteenth century, for his city has all the horror of Carlyle's:

How men are hurried here; how they are hunted and terrifically chased into double-quick speed; so that in self-defence they *must not* stay to look at one another! . . . There in their little cells, divided by partitions of brick or board, they sit strangers. . . . It is a huge aggregate of little systems, each of which is again a small anarchy, the members of which do not *work* together, but *scramble* against each other.[53]

It has also the total lack of communication that Engels found:

It occurs to no man to honour another with so much as a glance. The brutal indifference, the unfeeling isolation of each in his private interest becomes the more repellent and offensive, the more these individuals are crowded together, within a limited space. And, however much one may be aware that this isolation of the individual, this narrow self-seeking is the fundamental principle of our society everywhere, it is nowhere so shamelessly barefaced, so self-conscious as just here in the crowding of the great city. The dissolution of

---

[52] *Poetry and Prose*, p. 75.
[53] Carlyle's 1831 Journal, quoted in James Anthony Froude, *Carlyle: First Forty Years* (London: Longmans, 1882), Vol. II, chap. ix.

mankind into monads, of which each one has a separate principle, the world of atoms, is here carried to its utmost extreme.[54]

It is interesting to notice that this passage refers to London, which Engels found even more frightening than the big industrial towns of the Midlands and North. And with the exception of some of the social-problem novels of the 1840's such as Mrs. Gaskell's *Mary Barton* and Disraeli's *Sybil*, and Dickens in *Hard Times*, it was London that represented the type of the modern city to the creative minds of Victorian England, rather than what one might think of as the more typical Manchester, Birmingham, or Leeds. This was not simply because it was the city they knew most about; the crucial factor was that its substitution of abstract financial manipulation for direct manufacture and its quality of complete isolation made it, for them, the most direct symbol of the characteristic features of their age.

In the foregoing pages I have tried to outline and justify what I see as the most important phenomena of nineteenth-century life, important both in their broad social movement and in their effect upon the lives of individuals. Now it is necessary to justify the claim that the understanding of these phenomena is a basic part of Dickens' artistic genius; that is, that his understanding was not cerebral, but expressed in the concrete embodiment of specific works of art. I shall try eventually to show that his profound grasp of social forces is mirrored in the very form of the novels themselves, but the first question that presents itself concerns the nature of this understanding which, in my view, he displays so clearly. As I have already pointed out, and it is not a point that needs to be labored, Dickens is firmly of his age in his lack of intellectuality. And so it is impossible to find any general statement of his quarrel with Victorian society. The letters to Forster on the "condition of England" are powerful and moving, but they do not in any sense amount to a theoretical critique. It is, however, only our modern conception of the writer that makes this surprising to us. Dickens is a novelist in the fullest sense, in that he keeps his deepest use of intelligence and feeling for his fiction. It is there, expressed in all the subtlety of the concrete moment, that we find those situations, events, and characters that possess

[54] *The Condition of the Working Class in England in 1844* (London: Sorrenscheim and Co., 1892), chap. ii.

both the vitality of life and the weight of a generalizing, but, never abstract, insight.

But how was this insight gained, if not by the exercise of mind? Partly, of course, by observation and experience. From his early work in the law office of Ellis and Blackmore, through the sometimes desperate whirl of his life as a parliamentary reporter, to the excitement and travel of his years of fame, Dickens had ample opportunity to gain firsthand knowledge of many aspects of English life amongst every social class. Something of what his reporting days meant to him is conveyed by a speech Dickens made to a Newspaper Press Fund banquet in May, 1865:

I have been, in my time, belated on miry by-roads, towards the small hours, in a wheelless carriage, with exhausted horses and drunken postboys, and have got back in time for publication. . . . I have never forgotten the fascination of that old pursuit.[55]

The implications of all this for a future novelist are illuminated by a comment on coach travel which George Eliot makes in her introduction to *Felix Holt*. Speaking of the early thirties, she says that "the happy outside passenger . . . gathered enough stories of English life . . . to make episodes for a modern Odyssey." Combined with this experience was Dickens' immense curiosity about the world he lived in, a curiosity governed by a brilliant intelligence. For although G. H. Lewes may have been shocked by the meagerness of Dickens' library when he visited him at Doughty Street in 1838,[56] there is ample evidence, in the life as well as the work, of that keenness of intelligence to which Forster testifies in words that stress the lack of any abstract quality in Dickens' mental equipment. For him, Dickens' face as a young man had an aspect "which no time could change, and which remained implanted on it unalterably to the last. This was the quickness, keenness, and practical power, the eager, restless, energetic outlook on each several feature that seemed to tell so little of the student or writer of books, and so much of the man of action and business in the world. Light and motion flashed from every part of it."[57] But do these qualities account for, if anything can finally account for, the highest kinds of genius; the embodied under-

<hr>

[55] In *The Speeches of Charles Dickens*, K. J. Fielding, ed. (Oxford: Clarendon Press, 1960), p. 347.
[56] Edgar Johnson, *Charles Dickens: His Tragedy and Triumph*, I, 269.
[57] *Ibid.*, I, 187–188.

standing of the nature of nineteenth-century society which
we find in, say, *Little Dorrit*? We may perhaps come somewhere close to understanding how Dickens achieved this degree of insight by attempting to see if there is any relationship
between the facts of Dickens' life and the facts of the nineteenth century. Therefore, I now examine Dickens' life in the
light of those social pressures which I have argued are of the
greatest importance in understanding Victorian England: the
role of money in society and the nature of alienation. A related
aspect of this task is to look at London as the setting in which
these pressures attain their most extreme manifestation.

Dickens' knowledge of London, to begin with the city, was
immense, a fact of which every Dickensian is only too well
aware. It continued to fascinate him, although the quality of
that fascination changed throughout his life and his exploration of it began at an early age. One of his recreations as a
young clerk was to investigate "the life of London. No aspect
of its teeming activity and its gigantic proliferation of streets
and squares escaped his extraordinary observation.[58] And to
reinforce this point, Edgar Johnson quotes the reminiscences of
George Lear, one of Dickens' colleagues at Ellis and Blackmore's.

"I thought I knew something of the town . . . but after a little talk
with Dickens I found that I knew nothing. He knew it all from
Bow to Brentford. . . . He could imitate, in a manner that I never
heard equalled . . . the low population of the streets of London in
all their varieties, whether mere loafers or sellers of fruit, vegetables,
or anything else."[59]

But I am not concerned here with the kind of information that
is to be found in works of the "wandering down London by-
ways with Dickens" type. It is the meaning of London, not
its topography, which is of overwhelming importance in Dickens. And this meaning is to be found in the dark richness of
his symbolic use of the city that recurs again and again in his
fiction after *Martin Chuzzlewit*. In a sense Dickens' imagination is haunted by images of mystery, terror, and complexity
that arise from his contemplation of the city, and his involvement with it is deeper than that of any other Victorian novelist.

In novels such as *Great Expectations*, London is never merely
a lifeless background or a crudely painted, melodramatic back

[58] *Ibid.*, I, 55.
[59] *Ibid.*, I, 55.

cloth. It has always a meaningful role to play within the story and it is brought alive by a subtlety as well as a range of detail. Indeed, its ultimate importance is to be seen in its indissoluble conjunction of insight with the living detail that gives that insight embodiment. We can find this mastery even in a novel such as *David Copperfield*, which lacks the artistic unity of the later works.

The neighborhood was a dreary one at that time; as oppressive, sad, and solitary by night, as any about London. There were neither wharves nor houses on the melancholy waste of road near the great blank prison. A sluggish ditch deposited its mud at the prison walls. Coarse grass and rank weeds straggled over all the marshy land in the vicinity. In one part, carcases of houses, inauspiciously begun and never finished, rotted away. In another, the ground was cumbered with rusty iron monsters of steam-boilers, wheels, cranks, pipes, furnaces, paddles, anchors, diving-bells, wind-mill sails, and I know not what strange objects, accumulated by some speculator, and grovelling in the dust, underneath which—having sunk into the soil of their own weight in wet weather—they had the appearance of vainly trying to hide themselves. The clash and glare of sundry fiery Works upon the river-side, arose by night to disturb everything except the heavy and unbroken smoke that poured out of their chimneys. Slimy gaps and causeways, winding among old wooden piles, with a sickly substance clinging to the latter, like green hair, and the rags of last year's handbills offering rewards for drowned men fluttering above high-water-mark, led down through the ooze and slush to the ebb-tide. There was a story that one of the pits dug for the dead in the time of the Great Plague was hereabout; and a blighting influence seemed to have proceeded from it over the whole place. Or else it looked as if it had gradually decomposed into that nightmare condition, out of the overflowings of the polluted stream. (XLVII)

The heavy weight of descriptive adjectives—"dreary," "blank," "sluggish," "rank"—and the meaningfully bizarre images—"carcases of houses," "rusty iron monsters of steam-boilers"—do more than create an externalized "atmosphere." They give the passage the force of a metaphor that is capable of imbuing Martha, the otherwise rather sketchy figure of the prostitute, with a range of human misery and evil that is representative, even universal.

As if she were a part of the refuse it [the polluted stream] had cast out, and left to corruption and decay, the girl we had followed strayed down to the river's brink, and stood in the midst of this night-picture, lonely and still, looking at the water.

The final greatness of this writing stems from the fact that there is a unifying vision at work in the selection and arrangement of the detail. It is rooted in an imagined treatment of one tiny facet of the industrial revolution: "the clash and glare of sundry fiery Works." The relationship between the elements of the passage is significant. Those fearfully alive "rusty iron monsters of steam-boilers," for example—their quality of life stems from the active thrust of language itself, *grovelling in the dust*"—had been "accumulated by some speculator." The power of the writing is so great that, for a moment, we are drawn into a world of complete rottenness, even the "carcases of houses" seem to have "rotted away," and this is the rottenness of the modern capitalist city as Dickens increasingly came to view it. We shall see, in his later work, that the city becomes the complete symbol of the greed and alienation of nineteenth-century society.

THE CITY

Dickens is, in part, the chronicler of the rootless city-dweller who lives on his wits: street Arabs like Jo and Young Bailey; lawyers such as the disreputable Dodson and Fogg, the respectable Kenge and Carboy, both essentially similar beneath their differing exteriors; clerks such as Guppy and Dick Swiveller; Bucket the official detective, Nadgett the secret searcher-out of information; and, perhaps above all, the Smallweeds, sterile in body, dead to all claims of affection or human relationship, unproductive even in their labor, the hideous epitome of a society constantly in search of money. These are, in the words of Peter Quennell, the new townspeople:

Thrown up by the struggle for existence conducted on principles of economic *laissez-faire* . . . they constitute the all-important background of any Dickens' story—the creepers and the climbers, the grovellers and the schemers, scrambling over one another in the dark confusion of their pestiferous ant's nest.[60]

The inhabitants of the Dickens' city are not the productive members of his society, but the bill collectors and discounters, the middle men, the fixers. Similarly, the city in which they exist is not usually a place of mills and foundries, but the seat of bureaucracy, of financial speculation, of legal chicanery. The London that Dickens came to think of as "a vile place"[61] was a great exchange, a huge unproductive sink that swallowed the country's lifeblood and gave nothing in return. Beneath its

[60] *Mayhew's London* (London: Pilot Press, 1949), Introduction, p. 16.
[61] Letter to Bulwer Lytton, Feb. 10, 1851, in *Letters*, ed. Walter Dexter (Nonesuch ed.; London, 1938), II, 272.

facade of order, strength, and beauty lay the loathsome sanitation, foul slums, and swarming underworld that seemed to him
so much more real. For Dickens, that duality represented the
fatal dichotomy of a system that valued materialism rather than
human worth.

I have been trying to show that Dickens possessed much
more than an observer's eye for vivid detail in his fictional use
of London. His imagination is saturated by the symbolic meaning of the city, and his knowledge of this meaning comes from
two things: the incomparable richness of his everyday experience of the city and his insight into the nature of his own age.
It is now time to attempt to account for this insight. We have
seen that Dickens' intelligence is not of the kind that could find
sustenance in the play of abstract ideas. But it did involve itself
with great vigor in the social, political, and economic affairs
of the time. What gave him the power to understand these
affairs so profoundly? I want to suggest that his native intelligence in these matters was reinforced, and crucially reinforced,
by certain episodes in his own life.

One vitally important way in which Dickens' personal experience coincided with a significant fact of his society was the
part played in his life by what he called "those little screws of
existence—pounds, shillings, and pence."[62] In discussing Dickens' boyhood, Una Pope-Hennessy remarks: "There was never
a time in young Charles's life when he did not hear of money
difficulties."[63] This is something of an exaggeration, for it is
unlikely that Dickens, with all his childish acuteness, was much
aware of such problems until the year immediately preceding
his incarceration in the blacking factory. But from then on,
certainly, he was brought into close contact with them. With
the beginning of the Bayham Street period, at the end of 1822,
Dickens' schooling ceased until after he left the factory, and
so he was well placed, staying at home all day, to observe the
decline in his family's fortunes. Such shifts as his mother's
farcically ineffective attempt to start a school and his own visits
to the drunken pawnbroker gave him experience of one of the
characteristic phenomena of Victorian life, what Margaret Dal-
ziel calls the "extraordinary omnipresence of debt." Her analysis shows that in the popular fiction of the day the "financial
position of individuals was often alarmingly insecure" and that

[62] See p. 23 n. 11.
[63] *Charles Dickens* (London: Chatto and Windus, 1945), p. 4.

debt "was like a congenital physical or mental infirmity."[64] There is no doubt that this reflected a widespread social reality, and we can see that Dickens' own life contrived to give him the opportunity to study it at firsthand.

His father's eventual imprisonment for debt and the task of husbanding his own tiny resources once he went to work made Dickens even more aware of the importance of money both in social and in personal terms. It is clear that this period saw the growth of Dickens' determination never to live a life like his father's and the forging of the iron will that was to make that determination a reality. Money continued to play a large part in Dickens' adult life, for his father's frequent improvidence, his sense of responsibility toward his brothers and sisters, and then the claims of his own large family all combined to make it an ever-present necessity to him. This was reinforced by the strain of extravagance and dandyism in Dickens' own character which made him adopt a style of life beyond what he could comfortably support. The fact of his way of life seeming sometimes dangerously close to that of the Veneerings is evidence of certain ambiguities in Dickens' attitude toward money. It is certain that he was genuine in his hatred of materialism, both as expressed in his novels and in the note of real horror we find in a letter to Clarkson Stanfield concerning payment for Christmas book illustrations: "Heaven forbid that there should be any of that same dirty metal in the leaven of our friendship, ever!"[65] And Forster reports a statement Dickens made after a discussion between Jerrold and Thackeray "about money and its uses": "No man . . . attaches less importance to the possession of money, or less disparagement to the want of it, than I do," a statement that receives the Forsterian imprimatur, "to which I may add the confirmation of all our years of intercourse."[66] Yet he was capable of pursuing that "dirty metal" with a hardheaded determination very different from the timidity and self-abnegation that form the moral touchstone of so much of his work. Dickens' relations with his publishers make this particularly clear, but he was more than ready to fight for what he considered his rights in any situation in which he found himself. It is remarkable that a man so concerned with his own

[64] *Popular Fiction A Hundred Years Ago* (London: Cohen and West, 1957), pp. 156–157.

[65] Oct. 4, 1845, in *Letters*, I, 707.

[66] *The Life of Charles Dickens* (London: Everyman's Library, 1948), II, 94.

individuality should have created a fictional universe in which humility is one of the principal virtues and that he should have done it with such triumphant success. The self-sacrifice of his heroines may be irritating on occasion, but the moral beauty of a character such as Joe Gargery is beyond question. The explanation lies, no doubt, in the scar left on Dickens' personality by those early experiences of poverty. He hated a society in which the possession of the good things of life, which he enjoyed so much, was made dependent on the ability to amass money. And he loved those who, without any sense of their own worth or what was due them from their exploiters, were totally unfitted for that harsh struggle. Dickens would obviously have preferred to live in a Pickwickian world of benevolence and goodwill, but he found himself in a world of bitter realities, and as he was neither ascetic nor humble, he worked ceaselessly to keep intact the wall he had managed to erect between himself and poverty of even the most genteel kind.

Nevertheless, these ambiguities in Dickens' attitude toward money are of interest in adding to our knowledge of the complexity of his character rather than in affecting our estimate of the novels. In them, his hatred of materialism—made personal in the moral blindness of a Mr. Dombey, mythologized in life-destroying institutions such as the Court of Chancery—is entirely self-consistent and draws the strength of its inner unity from deeply felt personal experience.

It is not difficult to discover other biographical facts that were decisive both in forming Dickens' view of his world and in the evolution of some of his most important fictional material. In an essay published in *Household Words* in May, 1856, Dickens recorded a touching scene he had observed in a French public driveway:

In the same place, I saw, nearly every day, a curious spectacle. One pretty little child at a window, always waving his hand at, and cheering, an array of open carriages escorted by out-riders in green and gold; and no one echoing the child's acclamation . . . four great streams of determined indifference I always saw flowing up and down; and I never, in six months, know a hand or heard a voice to come in real aid of the child.[67]

When it has been noticed at all, this passage has usually been connected with another sentence from the essay as making some kind of allusion to Dickens' own childhood: "I am not a

[67] *Household Words* (Collected ed.; London, 1856), XIII, 386.

lonely man, though I was once a lonely boy; but that was long ago." This is certainly true, but I think the passage has also a more general force. The picture of the lonely child continually striving to enter into some relationship, however transitory, with those around him and being met with nothing but "four great streams of determined indifference" can be seen as a paradigm of that loneliness and alienation which its contemporaries felt to be so characteristic of the nineteenth century. It is, in fact, a minor example of one of Dickens' great themes, the alienation of the individual from his own true self or from the human reality of the society of which he forms a part. This reveals, yet again, the amazing unanimity of view among nineteenth-century critics of Victorian civilization. We have seen how deeply felt was Carlyle's concern for the human suffering involved in this situation; and another passage from this essay, describing a Parisian pavement café, makes it amply clear that Dickens was equally aware of this problem, particularly as it affected the inhabitants of what he called "that awful machine, a great working town":[68]

It is surely better for me, and for the family group, and for the two old ladies, and for the workman, to have thus much of community with the city life of all degrees, than to be getting bilious in hideous black-holes, and turning cross and suspicious in solitary places!

For Carlyle, the isolation of classes and individuals in Victorian England was indissolubly connected with the "Cash Nexus" that made up the operative heart of English society. The similarity of his statement with the more rigorously technical analysis of Marx is surely significant. Marx was attempting generalizations that would apply to the whole universe of modern industrial capitalism, but his conception of that universe was formed, of course, from his detailed examination of the English industrial revolution and its aftermath in the rest of the nineteenth century. Whatever may be one's opinion as to the final value of Marx's concept of alienation as a general theory, one is forced to the conclusion that it is fruitfully applicable to the social conditions from which it itself arose. In any event, the important point for this study is that Dickens is in essential agreement with these other writers in seeing a link between personal isolation and the greed of a materialistic society. The merest glance at the character of Wemmick in

[68] Letter to Miss Coutts, Sept. 2, 1852, in *Letters*, II, 414.

Great Expectations will prove the point and illustrate, at the same time, the power and economy of his artistic embodiment of this theme. I want now to try to account for the force and insight with which Dickens treats this aspect of his work.

I believe their origins are to be found in what I take to be the single most important experience in Dickens' life, his incarceration in the blacking factory, for in this episode Dickens himself went through a process of personal alienation of a powerfully disturbing kind. Some attempts have been made to minimize the horrors of this experience. Dickens was only twelve years old and worked from eight in the morning until eight at night, but, it has been objected, thousands of other children began to work much earlier and labored much harder than Dickens ever did. Signs of self-pity and social snobbery have been detected in Dickens' agonized description of the sufferings he endured at that time. It is surely imperative, however, to remember the differences in the backgrounds involved before making a final assessment of Dickens' own statements. Many of those thousands of unfortunate children were inured to hunger, cold, foul sanitation, evils of all kinds, from their earliest years, and the necessity of their getting out to work as soon as possible was an ever-present certainty. Even if Dickens' consciousness of his own abilities and worth is left out of account, it remains true that the affection and admiration he received at home, his education, the whole tenor and direction of his life, made such an abrupt change in his circumstances seem quite unthinkable. Our imaginative picture of the experience is of a sensitive boy being plucked from a warm, friendly, well-lit family circle and thrust into a dark world of loneliness, deprivation and monotonous labor.

Dickens' ordeal had more than a personal significance. He endured the acting-out of a public as well as a private drama. What he went through was a microcosm of the social fate of thousands in the industrial revolution. People moved from a way of life that had remained the same for hundreds of years to sudden immolation in a dark factory and the performance of mechanical tasks for an unvarying number of hours every day with, at night, the return to a crowded, stinking slum. It is easy to sentimentalize over this change. The rural way of life was undoubtedly a hard one and the move to the city did, in the long run, produce the benefits of a higher standard of living. Again, it is possible to exaggerate the benignant effects of the beauties of nature: as Coleridge pointed out, to a low peasantry, "the ancient mountains, with all their terrors and all their glories, are pictures to the blind, and music to the deaf."[69] Nevertheless, when every allowance has been made for the idealistic fancies of the townsman, it is still possible to agree with Trevelyan that agriculture represented "a way of life, unique and irreplaceable in its human and spiritual values."[70] The sense of fulfilling one of the most fundamental human needs, the variety of necessary tasks, and the chance to pursue each one through to its conclusion, the contact with animals and the processes of growth and decay, all surely made for a more dignified personal existence than the monotonous scramble of the factory. And the village community allowed for both a greater recognition of personal individuality and a social organization that, because of its roots in human contact, placed some emphasis on obligation as well as right. Even those whose only change was from one form of industry, the rural, to another, experienced new and harsh external pressures, as the Hammonds point out in describing the "irregular and undisciplined atmosphere of the old industry"[71] as compared with the new. It is not unreasonable to think that many who experienced these upheavals were left with feelings of despair and disorientation, feelings that would not be lightly overcome.

It is certainly true that Dickens' memories of his blacking-factory period stayed with him until the end of his life. Because it was impossible for him to conceive that they could ever come to an end, the sufferings of this time were burned ineradicably into the depths of his personality. (Dickens himself wrote, "I have no idea how long it lasted; whether for a year, or much more, or less."[72] But Edgar Johnson states that it could not have been more than five months at the most.[73]) The frequent recurrence of the theme of the lost and unloved child is enough to show this. And the sense of loss and abandonment produced in him by those sufferings never left him, as a letter, written when he was forty, clearly reveals: "This is one of what I call my wanderings days before I fall to work. I seem to be always

---

[69] *Biographia Literaria* (London: Everyman's Library, 1952), p. 167.

[70] *English Social History* (London: Longman's, 1948), p. 554.

[71] J. L. Hammond and B. Hammond, *The Age of the Chartists* (London: Longman's, 1930), p. 28.

[72] Autobiographical fragment quoted in Forster's *Life of Charles Dickens*, I, 32.

[73] *Charles Dickens: His Tragedy and Triumph*, I, 45.

looking at such times for something I have not found in life."[74]
It is the intensity of this felt experience which distinguishes
Dickens so absolutely from the "social-problem" novelists and
which contains the source of his ability to combine social criticism and didactic purpose with myth-making and a poetic apprehension of the world. Because he had felt what his society
could do to the human being before he tried, or indeed before
he was able, to understand it, Dickens was incapable of con-
structing a tract for his age in purely didactic terms; for in
attacking the alienation of Victorian society, he was tapping one
of the truest currents of his emotional life.

The variety of interpretation to which great works of art are
susceptible is evidence not of the perversity of critics, but of
the richness of their created universes. Dickens is no exception
to this, and the sources of his enduring strength have been seen
to exist in many different aspects of his art. But the significance
of his profound understanding of nineteenth-century, and so of
modern, life, does seem to form one general area of agreement.
I have been attempting to show that this understanding stems
from the peculiar intensity of the relationship that existed between Dickens and his age. I hope now to establish a further
relationship between Dickens' social insight and the artistic
power of his later fiction.

[74] To Mary Boyle, July 22, 1852, in *Letters*, II, 403.

CHAPTER FOUR

The Mob And Society: America and *Martin Chuzzlewit*

The subtlety of novels such as *Little Dorrit* and *Great Expectations* is so great that the critic is liable, fearfully, to seek an escape in easy abstractions of his own making. Firmly blinkered by a single idea, that of the role of money in society perhaps, one can gallop wildly through Dickens' fictional landscape and see nothing of the terrain's real features. A continual return to the works themselves is the only way of avoiding a total one-sidedness. I have tried to show that money was a factor of crucial significance in the texture of nineteenth-century civilization, but it would be foolish to pretend that all of the normal human activities we hold in common with the Victorian age were determined by only one pressure. And even when money does have an effect on the personal lives of men and women, it obviously often works in ways other than a simple-minded greed. I hope to prove that the complexity of structure in these later novels is intimately connected with Dickens' understanding of the economic complexity of his society; however, if a crude distinction may be drawn between form and content, my discussion of their subject matter will be concerned with more than the raising of shrill cries (or, worse, the drawing of graphs) at every mention of the word "money." In these works money has the function, as a substratum of external pressure, which it has in life. Destructive personal emotions such as Mr. Dombey's pride, Pip's snobbery, Arthur Clennam's sense of alienation, and Bradley Headsone's self-destructiveness are connected with the partially determining force of money which flows as a kind of ground swell below them; but they must also be examined in and for themselves. The elucidation of what I take to be Dickens' unifying ideas, combined with the appreciation of their personal manifestations, is clearly a very difficult task, and so I wish to clarify my approach by looking briefly at what I think is an obvious example of the successful fusion of didacticism and creative autonomy organized around the theme of money.

Many earlier discussions of Dickens seem to assume that he was interested only in the creation of characters, comic and melodramatic. Again and again the lists are set down—Mr. Micawber, Sam Weller, Mrs. Gamp, Squeers, Fagin—as though the novels were nothing but fortuitous collections of individuals. The personal and idiosyncratic remained of great interest to Dickens, but he was also fascinated by the spectacle of people in the mass: in his early work, by the anarchic gang that made up the mob; in the later, by the organized group that made up the society.

At one stage in his literary career, Dickens seems to have been drawn to the violence, the energy, the sheer *size* of the mob when a large number of people are gathered together. In *Barnaby Rudge*, for example, when Lord George is reviewing his men, we find this stress on size for its own sake.

So they went on and on, up this line, down that, round the exterior of this circle, and on every side of that hollow square; and still there were lines, and squares, and circles out of number to review. (XLVIII)

Even in its moments of repose, the vastness of such a crowd is guarantee enough of its potential vitality. Dickens usually sees this vitality as something evil and destructive, but it does occasionally work for positive ends. After the murder of Nancy, Bill Sikes loses himself, physically and psychologically, in the task of fighting a fire.

There were half-dressed figures tearing to and fro. . . . Women and children shrieked, and men encouraged each other with noisy shouts and cheers. . . . He shouted, too, till he was hoarse; and flying from memory and himself, plunged into the thickest of the throng. (XLVIII)

But the fact that a fire is being put out seems almost incidental to the frenzy that is engendered by collective action. In its spirit, the scene is not so very different from the terrible one of the burning of the Haredale mansion.

On the skull of one drunken lad—not twenty, by his looks—who lay upon the ground with a bottle to his mouth, the lead from the roof came streaming down in a shower of liquid fire, white hot; melting his head like wax. (LV)

In the same scene, Dickens catches the violence of those who feel themselves released from personal responsibility in the general fury of the mob:

There were men there, who danced and trampled on the beds of flowers as though they trod down human enemies, and wrenched them from the stalks, like savages who twisted human necks. (LV)

For Dickens, the mob is not only almost always violent, it is also an entity that has a kind of mind of its own. In a last attempt to escape from his pursuers, Sikes climbs out onto the roof of a house.

The crowd had been hushed during these few moments, watching his motions and doubtful of his purpose, but the instant they perceived it and knew it was defeated, they raised a cry of triumphant execration to which all their previous shouting had been whispers. (L)

Like a herd of fierce animals, it runs here and there as though at the behest of some blind instinct.

On pressed the people from the front—on, on, on, in a strong struggling current of angry faces. . . . There were tiers and tiers of faces in every window; cluster upon cluster of people clinging to every house-top. Each little bridge (and there were three in sight) bent beneath the weight of the crowd upon it. Still the current poured on to find some nook or hole from which to vent their shouts, and only for an instant to see the wretch. (L)

Although, as I have said, the anarchic violence of such crowds obviously exerts a hateful fascination over Dickens, he is prepared to search for extenuating circumstances even here. The mob of *Barnaby Rudge* was "composed for the most part of the very scum and refuse of London"; nevertheless, its growth was fostered "by bad criminal laws, bad prison regulations, and the worst conceivable police" (XLIX). This would seem to contradict Humphry House's view that "Dickens ultimately accepted the distinction between the deserving and the undeserving poor, and in that he was a man of his time";[1] for even at the level of the mob, there are distinctions to be drawn between a Dennis and a Hugh, between personal evil and the evil produced largely by society. Dickens did, of course, differentiate between the mob and the poor. In writing to Forster of his hatred of Malthusian doctrines, he remarks: "There is a sense and hu-

[1] *The Dickens World* (London: Oxford Paperbacks, 1960), p. 85.

manity in the mass, in the long run, that will not bear them";[2]
and, again, in another letter, "I have great faith in the Poor."[3]
It is obvious, given one's general knowledge of his work, that
by "the Poor" Dickens means the Plornishes of his world: the
humble, decent working classes who strove so desperately to
stay on the right side of respectability. Plornish is blind to the
forces that control his life in its externals, but there is a core of
simple humanity in him that prevents his going very far wrong
in the realm of personal relations. Yet even a Jo is permitted to
emerge fleetingly from the dark, submerged mass of those who
have given up the struggle for a life approximating the human,
or who were never in a position to make it in the first place,
and to show that he also belongs to the world of men. And although he felt that if the mob rose up, it had to be crushed for
the sake of organized society, Dickens never ceased his efforts,
both in his life and work, to destroy the conditions that had
given it birth.

The obvious imaginative power of Dickens' scenes of mob
violence has caused many writers to interpret them as expressions of a dissatisfaction with society at a deep level. Edmund
Wilson sees in them a hidden identification with the criminal,[4]
while for Humphry House they are the rationalization of a
sense of political impotence.[5] It seems impossible to mediate
such views, based as they are on nothing more than intelligent
guesses as to the state of the Dickensian unconscious. Personal
introspection may make it easier to accept another of House's
statements, that Dickens' fear of the mob stemmed from a
"knowledge of the hidden depths of bestiality in every man."[6]
Connected with this sense of our universal original sin is the
powerful link made by the Victorians between it and their lower
classes. The possibility of revolution, and the chaos that would
follow it, was an ever-present fear in the Hungry Forties, and
that this was more than a surface emotion is shown by Bertrand
Russell's story of his grandfather, who on his deathbed in 1869,
"heard a loud noise in the street and thought it was the revolution breaking out."[7] The exact part played by the darker

(margin annotations: THE MOB / FEAR OF REVOLUTION)

---

[2] Aug. 24, 1846, in *Letters*, ed. Walter Dexter (London: Nonesuch
Press, 1938), I, 781–782.

[3] To James Verry Staples, April 3, 1844, *Letters*, I, 589.

[4] "Dickens: The Two Scrooges," in *The Wound and the Bow* (Boston:
Houghton Mifflin, 1941), p. 20.

[5] *Dickens World*, p. 214.

[6] *Ibid.*, p. 180.

[7] Quoted in Walter E. Houghton, *The Victorian Frame of Mind, 1830–
1870* (Yale Paperbound, 1964), p. 54.

aspects of Dickens' personality in the genesis of these crowd scenes is problematic, but it is certainly possible to see in them an important fusion of personal and public feeling. In yet another way, Dickens appears as the perfect interpreter of his age. It has been pointed out,[8] for example, that the period of the publication of *Barnaby Rudge* was one of widespread industrial violence, and this must have given it a much greater contemporary relevance than we can easily appreciate today. Again Dickens is issuing his warning of the dire consequences that may follow that neglect of ignorance and want which he sees as so much a part of his society. Coupled with this is his delight in setting himself a difficult technical problem. This true novelist's joy in "the fascination of what's difficult" is seen in a letter to Charles Ollier, in which he is talking of Lord George and the riots: "as to the riots, I am going to try if I can't make a better one than he did."[9]

Despite some recent attempts to rehabilitate it,[10] it seems to me that if there is a failure amongst Dickens' novels, *Barnaby Rudge* is the closest approach to one. There is a stale quality about it; it has the feeling of a job being performed mechanically because it simply must be done (it bears, in fact, all the signs of being what Edgar Johnson calls it, "that often postponed task," although it should in fairness be pointed out that Johnson thinks that Dickens "had at last found a potent motivating force" for it in the agitation of the Chartists[11]). The facetiously treated dullness of John Willet and Barnaby's tiresome wise-fool quality seem fair representatives of the domestic side of the novel, while the historical events have not the range and significance to escape the limitations of their contemporary topicality. For the character of Barnaby, for example, Steven Marcus suggests some interesting literary progenitors, including such figures as the Holy Fool, Tom o'Bedlam, and Wordsworth's Idiot Boy, and remarks that "the influence of *King Lear* on this novel is . . . of considerable interest."[12] The influence of this play can be seen at work in *Barnaby Rudge*, as it can in

[8] Edgar Johnson, *Charles Dickens: His Tragedy and Triumph* (London: Gollancz, 1953), I, 312.

[9] June 3, 1841, in *Letters*, I, 324.

[10] See for example Steven Marcus, *Dickens: From Pickwick to Dombey* (London: Chatto and Windus, 1965).

[11] *Charles Dickens: His Tragedy and Triumph*, I, 305.

[12] *Dickens: From Pickwick to Dombey*, p. 191.

Melville's *Moby Dick*, but the question for literary criticism is what use is made of this influence, and there can be little doubt that the comparison serves only to reveal Dickens' limitations in a devasting manner.

Nevertheless as I have indicated, the book contains several powerful scenes whose sudden flashing into creative life makes the rest appear even paler in comparison. This vitality is, perhaps, suspect, since so much of its force seems to stem from a morbid, even hysterical, interest in the mob's activity. This morbidity can also be found in other parts of the novel, in the unpleasantly erotic passages dealing with the threat of rape to Dolly Varden and Emma Haredale, for example:

Poor Dolly! Do what she would, she only looked the better . . . and tempted them the more. When her eyes flashed angrily, and her ripe lips slightly parted, to give her rapid breathing vent, who could resist it? When she wept and sobbed as though her heart would break . . . who could be insensible to the little winning pettishness which now and then displayed itself. . . . When, forgetful for a moment of herself . . . what mortal eyes could have avoided wandering to the delicate boddice . . . the neglected dress . . . of the blooming little beauty? . . . Not Hugh. Not Dennis. (LIX)

Not Dickens either, one might add. Those slightly parted ripe lips belong more to the world of G. W. M. Reynolds' *Mysteries of London*[13] than to a great novelist, and the general air of prurience is increased by the incredible unreality of the way in which Hugh and Dennis put the matter off until their chance is eventually lost. The erotic element is not common in Dickens, but the hint, and sometimes more than the hint, of sadistic outrage can often be felt in his work. A famous example is when Pancks cuts off Mr. Casby's hair in *Little Dorrit*, although that extraordinary and, for once, genuinely Freudian shearing of a false Samson has a thematic relevance to the novel as a whole. Gratuitous and so deeply unpleasant are scenes such as the flogging of Wackford Squeers, for which Dickens can find a sanction, though he fortunately eschews their barbarity of detail, in his beloved eighteenth-century novel; in this instance, the attack on the schoolmaster in *Roderick Random*. But even if one does think that the vitality of the scenes of mob violence in *Barnaby Rudge* is exaggerated, their power remains undeni-

13 Published 1846–1848. Reynolds was a prolific writer of sensational and prurient literature for the working-class audience. See Louis James, *Fiction for the Working Man* (London: Oxford University Press, 1963).

able, and from it we can learn something of great importance
to our understanding of Dickens.

In a sense the mob is the most important character in *Barnaby
Rudge*—it is certainly the center of interest—and Dickens' concern with the group and his ability to create it in a fully realized
way is to be crucial to his whole future development as a novelist. The mob had ceased to be a living social reality by Dickens'
day, although its presence made a suitable background to the
brutal underworld of *Oliver Twist*, and the sense of its former
terror found an echo in the apparently dangerous Chartist
movement (a danger that was found to have been illusory upon
its collapse in 1848). From the very beginning of his career,
in *The Pickwick Papers*, Dickens displayed what one might
call a "panoramic" ambition, and his method of achieving this
in his early work can be understood by reference to three related points. There is, first, the question of literary inheritance.
Dickens, like any other artist, had to begin his career by borrowing from somewhere, and his borrowings were, of course,
from the eighteenth-century novel. The form, if one can use
the word, of his early works is that of the English picaresque,
whose one point of structural reference lies in the wanderings
of the hero. A writer such as Fielding is often said to have a
mastery in his presentation of English society, but the world
of *Tom Jones* does not surely stay in our imagination as an interrelated whole. The characters, incidents, and setting are brought
into juxtaposition by nothing more significant than the presence
of Tom himself, and so the novel's overall impression is essentially fragmentary, as F. R. Leavis suggests: "He [Fielding] is
credited with range and variety and it is true that some episodes take place in the country and some in Town, some in the
churchyard and some in the inn, some on the high-road and
some in the bed-chamber, and so on."[14] Dickens takes over this
method and in some of his works leavens it with the activities
of the mob in order, I would suggest, to escape the aimless
wanderings of a Nicholas Nickleby, and because he is groping
toward some sense of a wider social unit.

Dickens was, in fact, able to renew the picaresque form with
a validity that is surprising, as it had seemed beyond even the
point of collapse. (I mean in terms of literary tradition; the
popularity of Surtees may have something to do with the habits
of the reading public, but it has nothing to do with the tradi-

---

[14] *The Great Tradition* (Penguin Books, 1962), p. 12.

tion of the novel.) His success in this was due to the power of his genius working on an imagination stored with childhood reading of the eighteenth-century novel—Dickens himself pictured his childhood as "a summer evening, the boys at play in the churchyard, and I sitting on my bed, reading as if for life"[15] —and because in his early twenties Dickens was able to taste something of the life for the depiction of which the picaresque novel had been an adequate vehicle. This latter fact brings me to my second major point concerning Dickens' panoramic ambition. I have already suggested that Dickens' work as a reporter brought him into touch with the last phases of the life of the road and what this life could mean to the future novelist.[16] The methods and slowness of travel before the complete dominance of the railways meant that although the highest social classes traveled in their own coaches and the lowest on foot, a very wide cross section of the community traveled and lived together, often for fairly long periods. It is not, surely, a misuse of autobiography to imagine that Dickens' contact with this world could have made him feel that his childhood impersonating of his favorite characters had become a reality: "I have been Tom Jones . . . for a week together. I have sustained my own idea of Roderick Random for a month at a stretch."[17] But, as has often been described, the speed of the railways and the class divisions they imposed on the public brought this social reality to an abrupt end in the late 1830's and early 40's. The leisurely opportunity of varied social types to get to know each other by anecdote and shared experience was over and with it the novel of the road as a valid literary form. But Dickens' panoramic ambition remained, and so he was faced with the task of finding another form that would fulfill its demands.

Yet even if the advent of the railways had not destroyed the possibility of the English picaresque's continuation, the limitations of the form would have become more and more obvious, and this is the third point I want to make on this topic. The fact is that however appropriate Fielding's kind of novel was for the representation of life in eighteenth-century England, it was no longer adequate for the task of mirroring a society that had undergone a radical transformation, the extent of which is indicated by the words of David Thomson.

[15] *Charles Dickens: His Tragedy and Triumph*, I, 21.
[16] See p. 75.
[17] *Charles Dickens: His Tragedy and Triumph*, I, 21.

The generation of Englishmen between 1815 and 1850 suffered from the combined aftermath of two great social and political revolutions, the American and the French; of two great social and economic upheavals, the agrarian and the industrial revolutions; of two great foreign wars, the French Revolutionary and the Napoleonic Wars.[18]

And it is certainly true that if we compare *Tom Jones*, say, and *Little Dorrit*, the sense of society they present to us is entirely different. The only feeling of unity we gain in Fielding is from the presence of Tom himself and the novel exists basically on a "horizontal" plane, the series of events from A to Z which encompasses Tom's adventures. The world of *Little Dorrit* can be imagined as a sphere from the unifying center of which runs a set of connecting lines to the surface of character, action, and setting. And this unifying center of the work of art is, at the same time, an insight into the nature of the nineteenth century which sees it as a structure dominated by the desire for money and permeated by personal loneliness. But this insight was not something that Dickens won easily. It came only as the result of the most intense personal and social experience and with a constant development of artistic form which was agonizing in its creative demands. Nothing could more clearly reveal the utter unity of form and content than the story of Dickens' fictional career. At the beginning, one aspect of his genius, genial social comedy of a Shakespearian amplitude, found perfect expression in the structure of *The Pickwick Papers*. That book does not reflect the general social reality of England in 1836, but rather the fusion of Dickens' profound imaginative involvement in the eighteenth-century novel with a paradisal embodiment of the myth of an Old England. Thereafter, there is a dichotomy between Dickens' subject matter, especially his increasing social awareness, and a structure that simply cannot contain it. But Dickens constantly experiments in an attempt to balance his social insight with the artistic form that will most perfectly embody it. After he had brought his treatment of the anarchy of the mob to its highest point of expression in *Barnaby Rudge*, it was to be the complex groupings of social interconnection which were to seize Dickens' imagination more and more powerfully. And it is in the American scenes of his next novel, *Martin Chuzzlewit*, that we find

[18] *England in the Nineteenth Century (1815–1914)* (Penguin Books, 1950), p. 33.

him attempting the vastly difficult technical and creative problem of delineating a whole society for the first time.

The characteristic tone of these scenes is brilliantly crude exaggeration, and in keeping with this, the relationship between money and society is savagely simplified: Dickens presents the worship of money as the sole organizing principle of the society he is depicting. The effects of this money worship are more than ugly and disfiguring;[19] it causes a complete inversion of *all* values. Although the English business world may not have been taken over entirely by Tigg Montagues, American commerce is a fraud from beginning to end.

> In commercial affairs he was a bold speculator. In plainer words he had a most distinguished genius for swindling, and could start a bank, or negotiate a loan, or form a land-jobbing company (entailing ruin, pestilence, and death, on hundreds of families), with any gifted creature in the Union. This made him an admirable man of business. (XVI)

And such men are universally admired as shining examples of freedom and smartness. Moral values are equally determined by the one criterion of material success, as when Colonel Diver tells Martin that America does possess an aristocracy: "Of intelligence, sir, . . . of intelligence and virtue. And of their necessary consequence in this republic, Dollars, sir" (XVI).

Some idea of how Dickens attempted to deal with the problem of drawing a whole society may be gathered from comparing *Martin Chuzzlewit* with *American Notes*, which appeared the year before, in 1842. The latter is a sober, straightforward, fairly interesting account of what Dickens did and saw in America. He criticizes many aspects of the life and institutions he encountered, but the tone throughout is that of the unsensational travel book. He comments, for example, in his best propaganda style on the lack of social graces to be found in America, the haste with which food is despatched, and the lack of conversation during the course of the meal.

> But I may venture to say, after conversing with many members of the medical profession in America, that I am not singular in the opinion that much of the disease which does prevail, might be avoided, if a few common precautions were observed. Greater means of personal cleanliness, are indispensable to this end; the custom of hastily swallowing large quantities of animal food, three times a-day,

[19] See p. 47.

and rushing back to sedentary pursuits after each meal, must be changed. (XVIII)

One or two isolated quotations from the novel will show, I think, what happens to this simple observation when it is infused with imagination. As Martin is walking back to his New York hotel with three gentlemen, they hear the loud ringing of a bell.

The instant this sound struck upon their ears, the colonel and the major darted off, dashed up the steps and in at the street-door (which stood ajar) like lunatics; while Mr. Jefferson Brick, detaching his arm from Martin's, made a precipitate dive in the same direction, and vanished also.

Martin imagines that he has heard an alarm-bell, warning of a fire, and then follows a scene that foreshadows a favorite gag of the silent film.

As Martin faltered on the pavement, three more gentlemen, with horror and agitation depicted in their faces, came plunging wildly round the street corner; jostled each other on the steps; struggled for an instant; and rushed into the house, a confused heap of arms and legs. (XVI)

Martin follows them anxiously and discovers that the bell was announcing dinner and that the rush was made necessary by the speed with which food disappears from the table.

Again, when Martin gives his levee, he is visited by two reporters.

Two gentlemen connected with the Watertoast Gazette had come express to get the matter for an article on Martin. They had agreed to divide the labour. One of them took him below the waistcoat; one above. Each stood directly in front of his subject with his head a little on one side, intent on his department. If Martin put one boot before the other, the lower gentleman was down upon him, he rubbed a pimple on his nose, and the upper gentleman booked it. He opened his mouth to speak, and the same gentleman was on one knee before him, looking in at his teeth, with the nice scrutiny of a dentist. (XXII)

In both instances Dickens is attacking things he dislikes about America by exaggerating them to a fantastic degree, but a connection with reality is still maintained. The national failings he is satirizing are none the less real for being transposed into a farcical key. For Gissing, Dickins in America was

"Dickens the satirist without the counterpoise of his native tenderness."[20] Nevertheless, although Dickens is unremitting in his fierceness, there is compensation for this lack of tenderness in the growth of new powers of organization, which become yet more evident if we go on to consider the characters who inhabit these American scenes and the language that they speak.

In his preface, Dickens remarks that with the exception of Mr. Bevan "the American portion of this story is in no other respect a caricature, than as it is an exhibition, for the most part, . . . of a ludicrous side, *only* of the American character." But such characters as Mr. Jefferson Brick and Dr. Ginery Dunkle move beyond caricature into the realm of true imagination. When Martin first sees Mr. Brick he is sitting behind a desk, "a figure with a stump of a pen in its mouth and a great pair of scissors in its right hand, clipping and slicing at a file of Rowdy Journals." Martin thinks that he is Colonel Diver's son:

Upon the upper lip of this young gentleman were tokens of a sandy down: so very, very smooth and scant, that, though encouraged to the utmost, it looked more like a recent trace of gingerbread than the fair promise of a moustache.

Because of this belief Martin comes very near to destroying Anglo-American relations.

He had begun to say that he presumed this was the colonel's little boy, and that it was very pleasant to see him playing at Editor in all the guilelessness of childhood, when the colonel proudly interposed and said: "My War Correspondent, sir." (XVI)

The first appearance of Dr. Ginery Dunkle is equally disconcerting. He is one of a party who wish to give the Honourable Elijah Pogram a levee.

The deputation entered to announce this honour: consisting of six gentleman boarders and a very shrill boy.
"Sir!" said the spokesman.
"Mr. Pogram!" cried the shrill boy.
The spokesman thus reminded of the shrill boy's presence, introduced him. "Doctor Ginery Dunkle, sir. A gentleman of great poetical elements."

[20] *Critical Studies of the Works of Dickens* (New York: Greenberg, 1924), p. 75.

Other introductions are made and the spokesman attempts to continue:

"Sir!"

"Mr. Pogram!" cried the shrill boy.

"Perhaps," said the spokesman, with a hopeless look, "you will be so good, Dr. Ginery Dunkle, as to charge yourself with the execution of our little office, sir?"

As there was nothing the shrill boy desired more, he immediately stepped forward. (XXXIV)

These almost surrealist transpositions stem from Dickens' observation, recorded soberly enough in *American Notes*, of the youthful-looking quality of many American men. In the process of being transmuted into art, this piece of observed social reality becomes the means of turning America into a land of myth. It forces upon us a vision of that country thronging with tiny figures—closely resembling the midget-headmaster of the film "Zero de Conduite," complete with frock coat and top hat—between whose appearance and social role there is a complete lack of continuity.

Like all the inhabitants of this insane country, Dr. Dunkle is more than glad to have an opportunity to demonstrate his powers in the Columbian Rhetoric department. We meet the Rhetoric in, perhaps, its purest form in the great attack on the British Lion from "a pallid lad of the Jefferson Brick school."

"Lion! . . . where is he? Who is he? What is he? Show him to me. Let me have him here. Here!" said the young Columbian, in a wrestling attitude, "upon this sacred altar. . . . Bring forth that Lion! Alone I dare him! I taunt that Lion. I tell that Lion, that Freedom's hand once twisted in his mane, he rolls a corse before me, and the Eagles of the Great Republic laugh ha, ha!" (XXI)

The accuracy of Dickens' observation here is shown by F. O. Matthiessen's discussion of "Eloquence" in his *American Renaissance*: "Oratory, moving with the Revolution from the pulpit to the political forum, was . . . the one branch of literature in which America then had a formed tradition"; and by the ripe example of the style that Matthiessen quotes: "Standing beneath this serene sky, overlooking these broad fields now reposing from the labors of the waning year, the mighty Alleghenies dimly towering before us, the graves of our brethren beneath our feet, it is with hesitation that I raise my poor voice to break the eloquent silence of God and Nature."[21] But

[21] (New York: Oxford University Press, 1941), pp. 18, 20 n. 8.

the Columbian Rhetoric is even more powerful, if in a more
homespun form, from the lips of Mr. La Fayette Kettle, who
describes Queen Victoria as "that young critter, in her luxurious
location in the Tower of London" (XXI), and in the stirring
words of the Honourable Elijah Pogram:

> "Our fellow-countryman is a model of a man, quite fresh from
> Natur's mould! . . . Verdant as the mountains of our country; bright
> and flowing as our mineral Licks; unspiled by withering conven-
> tionalities as air our broad and boundless Perearers! . . . and his
> boastful answer to the Despot and the Tyrant is, that his bright
> home is in the Settin Sun." (XXXIV)

This last passage is comic poetry of a high order. Its very
rhythm follows the outline of saloon-bar ranting, and the dying
fall of the last sentence, with its pause at "is," exposes merci-
lessly the chauvinist's sentimentality. It forms a criticism of
something debased, and yet, with the paradox of art, it is infused with a soaring vitality. The language of *Martin Chuzzlewit* is the most striking feature of the genius that is scattered
so prodigally throughout the book. The gentlemen at Todgers',
Young Bailey, Mr. Mould the undertaker, Pecksniff, and, supremely, Mrs. Gamp—all display their comic idiosyncrasy in
the particularity of speech. And speech forms the artistic cement
of the American scenes, for it is by the consistent use of a comic
language that Dickens binds together the disparate elements of
that world of the imagination based on social reality.

The relationship between *Barnaby Rudge* and *Martin Chuzzlewit* is, then, a significant one. There is a distance in time
of only two years between them, but the distance in terms of
the development of Dickens' art is enormous. And I think it
is possible to argue that *Martin Chuzzlewit* is the crucial novel
in Dickens' literary career taken as a whole; it contains both
his last extended use of the picaresque framework in the wanderings of Martin and Mark Tapley, and it adumbrates the form
that he was to perfect in his later fiction. This Janus-like quality of looking to the past and the future may help to account
for the work's chaotic structure. The clumsiness of the transitions from England to America and back again is blatant, but
forgivable if one is aware just how much Dickens is attempting
new things with other aspects of the work's form. In *Barnaby
Rudge* we saw Dickens' last use of the mob as some kind of
symbolic representation of society at large, and it is this method,
as well as the work's actual setting, which condemns the novel

irredeemably to a sense of belonging to a worn-out past.
The necessary fusion of didacticism and creative autonomy in
Dickens' greatest work, and its essentially complementary quality, is revealed here, negatively, by its total absence. There is
no organizing principle at work in the novel, and this is mirrored in the lack of any organizing insight into the nature of
the society that is being depicted. The interest of the American
scenes of *Martin Chuzzlewit* is that they contain both sides of
the Dickensian equation of genius.

The lives of men of supreme greatness seem often to possess
a meaning in even the smallest details, and Dickens is no exception to this. Indeed, the points of contact between his personal life and that of the nineteenth century are more varied
and significant than is true with any other Victorian literary
figure. Dickens' journey to America falls within this same pattern of significance, and although the story is too well known
to need retelling here,[22] the meaning of this journey for Dickens'
artistic development will perhaps emerge from a brief discussion of it. Dickens was wildly excited at the thought of visiting
a country that appeared to him, at a safe distance, to be genuinely free, and free above all of class privilege and its accom-
panying social stratification. His subsequent disillusion with
America has the peculiar bitterness of high hopes disappointed,
as a letter to W. C. Macready makes clear: "I infinitely prefer
a liberal monarchy—even with its sickening accompaniments
of court circulars—to such a government as this. . . . I see a
press more mean, and paltry, and silly, and disgraceful than
any country I ever knew."[23] To liberals of Dickens' stamp,
America seemed a unique example of a workable democracy,
and there can be little doubt that Dickens' disappointment with
it was a very real factor in the increasingly gloomy view that
he took of social affairs. If democracy could not be a success
in America, there seemed little reason to hope that it could
be a success anywhere else, and with the end of this hope a
note of desperation began to enter into Dickens' thoughts about
society and so, necessarily, into his artistic realization of them.

Another important fruit of this experience was the insight
Dickens gained into the machinery of a whole society. A general sense of social dissatisfaction is evident in all of Dickens'
early work after *The Pickwick Papers*, but it is equally evident

22 See *Charles Dickens: His Tragedy and Triumph*, I, 357–446.
23 March 22, 1842, in *Letters*, I, 413–414.

that he had not yet grasped the motivating forces of his society at that stage. Scattered references to money were to be
found in the early novels, but they were not organized into
any artistic or, which is to say the same thing, social unity.
Even Dickens' young genius was baffled by the pressures of
early nineteenth-century life; thus a major result of his trip
to America was the escape it afforded him from the complexities and confusions of his own direct environment to the
apparent simplicities of a fresh scene—an escape that enabled
him to enlarge his vision to a hitherto unthought-of extent. Glib
generalizations are a common result of foreign travel, and there
is, certainly, some crudity in Dickens' reduction of America
to a society founded on nothing but the principle of money
worship, but the compensation for this singleness of view is to
be found in the brutally direct brilliance of Dickens' rendering
of America. At his greatest, Dickens never repeats his effects,
and the note that is struck here is one that he did not return to
again. These scenes are comedy as fantastic as anything in
which Mrs. Gamp is involved, but such is the novel's variety,
fantasy is the only quality they have in common. The humor
of Mrs. Gamp stems from a lunatic discontinuity of speech,
the absurd juxtapositions of which form a poetry of comic
inflation. Like Falstaff, she seems distended to gigantic size
by language of such rich comedy that she appears to our
imagination purified by the laughter she causes; a figure of
huge, amoral beneficence. And she exists almost entirely in
terms of what she says; she is concerned with action and
event of an interior kind only.

The comedy of the American scenes works in a reverse way,
in terms of a savage reductiveness. Speech is just one factor
among many here, and despite its poetic exuberance, it assists
in the process of comic depreciation by highlighting the ridiculous hypocrisy of figures who are truly evil. And the fantasy
of the humor is controlled and directed by a didactic purpose
far beyond that of narrow reformism into an internally consistent world of the comic spirit. With the exception of Mr.
Bevan, who functions as both a plot device to enable Martin
to escape from America and as a necessary counterpoise to a
picture of otherwise totally unrelieved depravity, Dickens'
America contains no artistic inconsistencies. Its boylike rhet-
oricians, swindling businessmen, crooked politicians, and their
fantastic language that rolls and reverberates from one side of
the vast land to the other are all of a piece with the wild farce

of the incidents in which they are involved. Dickens does seem to have created in this novel, to risk a much-abused critical term, a mythological world that is, nevertheless, rooted in an observed reality.

In his ruthless presentation of American lust for money, we might feel that Dickens is in the grip of an *idée fixe*, but as I have tried to show in the preceding chapter, this is an insight of profound significance to the nineteenth century as a whole. His journey to America seems to have given Dickens the ability to realize the implications of the "Cash nexus" and to understand that it was built into the very structure of capitalist society at a deep level. And with this understanding came the awareness that it could be a principle of artistic organization, as well as a tool for the analysis of society. No longer did the panoramic ambition have to remain content with the wanderings of a, hopefully, unifying central figure, the shapeless aggregation of disparate individuals. From now on a principle would be at work, a shaped and shaping response to both the external and the fictional world. And it is for this reason that the artistic universes Dickens was to bring into being are, at one and the same time, self-sufficient entities and critiques of the civilization of which they form a mythological counterpart. In *Martin Chuzzlewit*, Dickens intuitively balances didacticism and creativity with perfect assurance: the relative simplicity of his social insight is embodied, in the American scenes, in a style limited to caricature. But this experience, social as well as artistic, liberated powers in him that were to find expression in the mythic structures of English society of the later novels.

CHAPTER FIVE

The Middle Years

Dombey and Son

With *Dombey and Son*, published between 1846 and 1848, we come to the first fully realized achievement of Dickens' maturity. Dickens is able to use much of what he had learned in the writing of *Martin Chuzzlewit* in this novel, but he is also struggling to create those elements of form that will best satisfy the peculiar demands of his new subject matter, for "each venture is a new beginning, a raid on the inarticulate." However devastingly successful are the American scenes of *Martin Chuzzlewit*, some necessary qualifications may help to bring out how much more Dickens is attempting in *Dombey*. The American scenes form, of course, only a fairly small part of a very long novel, and, more important, in them Dickens abjures his love of narrative complication. And with Dickens, narrative complication is more than just plot manipulation for its own sake, as I hope to show. The wanderings of Martin and Mark form a picaresque tale of the simplest type, for it is as though the problems Dickens set himself were so great that they could be solved only by a close concentration on the matters directly in hand and so left him no imaginative energy with which to indulge in complications of plot. We find that in *Dombey* Dickens is able to combine his new-found ability to deal with society on the large scale with a complex formal structure, and to this is added exploration of character of a new subtlety.

It is well known that *Dombey and Son* was very carefully planned. Forster tells us that "the design affecting Paul and his father had been planned from the opening, and was carried without real alteration to the close," and that "it was to do with Pride what its predecessor had done with Selfishness."[1] But Dickens himself was notoriously disinclined to theorize about his work, and just as it is possible to argue that selfishness is not

[1] *The Life of Charles Dickens* (London: Everyman's Library, 1948), II, 19–20.

the deepest organizing principle of *Martin Chuzzlewit,* so it may be valid to seek a more fundamental determining reality behind the simple fact of Mr. Dombey's pride. It may, in fact, be possible to discover the reason for that pride.

Three elements combine to form the substance of Mr. Dombey's master passion: class, the notion of people as possessions, and money. Humphry House remarks of Mr. Dombey that "a good deal of his pride is class-pride,"[2] and we get an early clue to this complex of feeling when Miss Tox speaks of the wet nurse engaged for Paul: "She must consider it a privilege to see a little cherub closely connected with the superior classes, gradually unfolding itself from day to day at one common fountain" (II). Again, toward the end of the book, when Edith suggests a separation, her husband's reaction is determined entirely by social considerations:

"Did you ever hear of Dombey and Son? People to say that Mr. Dombey—Mr. Dombey!—was separated from his wife! Common people to talk of Mr. Dombey and his domestic affairs! Do you seriously think, Mrs. Dombey, that I would permit my name to be handed about in such connexion?" (XLVII)

Walled in his impenetrable fortress of class superiority, Mr. Dombey is insulated from the possibility of entering into any kind of human relationship with those whom he regards as almost of another race. His ruthless self-alienation from the springs of human feeling is seen at its most destructive in the scene with Toodle at the railway station, when Toodle tries to offer his sympathy for the death of Mr. Dombey's son. With masterly compression, Dickens indicates that Toodle is in mourning for Paul: his offer of money having been refused, Mr. Dombey tries to brush past him.

His attention was arrested by something in connexion with the cap still going slowly round and round in the man's hand.

"We lost one babby," observed Toodle, "there's no denyin'."

"Lately," added Mr. Dombey, looking at the cap.

"No, Sir, up'ard of three years ago, but all the rest is hearty."

Toodle changes the subject; but Mr. Dombey has seen enough to know that he is in mourning for Paul.

So from high to low, at home or abroad, from Florence in his great house to the coarse churl who was feeding the fire then smoking before them, every one set up some claim or other to a share in his

---

[2] *The Dickens World* (London: Oxford Paperbacks, 1960), p. 153.

dead boy, and was a bidder against him! . . . To think that this lost
child, who was to have divided with him his riches, and his projects,
and his power . . . should have let in such a herd to insult him with
their knowledge of his defeated hopes, and their boasts of claiming
community of feeling with himself. (XX)

It is impossible for Mr. Dombey to conceive of a communal
grief that is genuine. His vision of the world is competitive at
even the most personal levels, and those who share his sorrow
can only be regarded as "bidders" seeking to buy some knowledge of him in what he considers the degradation of his grief.
Mr. Dombey is a private man in the very worst sense of the
word, for his contacts with the outside world are limited to the
pursuit of purely external ends. Any relationship between
such personal life as he does possess and humanity in general
is, by definition, a besmirching of his sense of unique selfhood.
And by means of a wonderful irony, Dickens hints that Mr.
Dombey feels a kind of hatred for his son because of his act
of dying; not merely has this meant the end of his plans, it
has also left him open to the insulting grief of a "herd" of
mourners.

In his total sense of isolation, Mr. Dombey cannot even admit to a community of feeling with those who are more or less
his social equals. And at this point we move beyond the level
of class-consciousness into the realm of an even greater moral
evil that contains, perhaps, the seeds of the first: that of regarding human beings as things to be owned and used. The necessity of hiring a wet nurse is a terrible blow to Mr. Dombey,
for it stresses his son's, and by extension his own, inescapable
involvement with a common humanity at the most basic level.

That the life and progress on which he built such hopes, should be
endangered in the outset by so mean a want . . . was a sore humiliation. . . . He viewed with so much bitterness the thought of being
dependent for the very first step towards the accomplishment of his
soul's desire, on a hired serving-woman . . . that in every new rejection of a candidate he felt a secret pleasure. (II)

But the thing must be done, and when, finally, Polly Toodle
is engaged, Mr. Dombey seeks to convert her into a possession
in an act that Dickens symbolizes by his forcing her to change
her name when she enters his house: "It is not at all in this
bargain that you need become attached to my child, or that
my child need become attached to you" (II). Mr. Dombey
desires to "make it a question of wages, altogether" (II), and

so Polly ceases to be a human creature and becomes nothing
but a milk-producer.

A passage at the very beginning of the book shows us that
it is not just people that Mr. Dombey wishes to own:

The earth was made for Dombey and Son to trade in, and the sun
and moon were made to give them light. Rivers and seas were
formed to float their ships; rainbows gave them promise of fair
weather; winds blew for or against their enterprises; stars and
planets circled in their orbits, to preserve inviolate a system of
which they were the centre. (I)

The whole universe has been turned into a machine to serve the
ends of a monstrous egotism. Frightening as such an attitude is
when applied to the inanimate, its denial of individuality to
the human being becomes terrifying. Mr. Dombey deplores
the thought of his first wife's dying in giving birth to his son.

He would find a something gone from among his plate and furniture, and other household possessions, which was well worth the
having, and could not be lost without sincere regret. Though it
would be a cool, business-like, gentlemanly, self-possessed regret, no
doubt. (I)

And in marrying his second wife he purchases a valuable
object on the open market, as she herself makes clear:

"He sees me at the auction, and he thinks it well to buy me. . . .
When he came to view me—perhaps to bid—he required to see the
roll of my accomplishments. . . . When he would have me show one
of them, to justify his purchase to his men, I require of him to say
which he demands, and I exhibit it. I will do no more." (XXVII)

Neither she nor Dickens shirks the knowledge of the true nature
of her relationship with her husband:

"What are you, pray? What are you?"
"I have put the question to myself," said Edith, ashy pale, and
pointing to the window, "more than once when I have been sitting
there, and something in the faded likeness of my sex has wandered
past outside; and God knows I have met with my reply." (XXX)

A living relationship with another person is impossible for
Mr. Dombey because he cannot value, cannot even grasp, the
notion of distinctive personality, of "otherness," in the people
around him. Other people only exist in so far as they have a
subordinate relation to himself. This is true even of his beloved
Paul. Dickens convinces us that Mr. Dombey loves his son in

his own way, but he, too, must have a function, and is used as a pawn in Mr. Dombey's personal game. His child's value stems from nothing personal or idiosyncratic, but simply from the fact that he "was to have divided with him his riches, and his projects, and his power and . . . shut out all the world as with a double door of gold" (XX).

The nature of Mr. Dombey's contact with people is summed up by Cousin Feenix's ghastly joke at the wedding feast:

" 'Well, Jack, how are the ill-matched couple?' 'Ill-matched,' says Jack. 'Not at all. It's a perfectly square and equal transaction. *She* is regularly bought, and you make take your oath *he* is as regularly sold!' " (XXXVI)

Those words "bought" and "sold" take us to the heart of Mr. Dombey's view of the world and of the society of which he is an important and respected member. His own pride and his conviction that other people, indeed the whole universe, exist only for his benefit arise ultimately from his sense of the importance of money. This is reflected even in his personal appearance:

Mr. Dombey, who was one of those close-shaved close-cut moneyed gentlemen who are glossy and crisp like new bank-notes, and who seem to be artificially braced and tightened as by the stimulating action of golden shower-baths. (II)

Many scattered references throughout the book help to complete the portrait of a man for whom money is the only final criterion of value. For example, when Major Bagstock protests that it is an honor to know him, "Mr. Dombey, in his estimation of himself and his money, felt that this was very true, and therefore did not dispute the point" (XX). And again, when Mrs. Skewton praises the changes he has made in his house in order to receive Edith, he reacts in a similar way.

"It is handsome," said Mr. Dombey, looking round. "I directed that no expense should be spared; and all that money could do, has been done, I believe."
"And what can it not do, dear Dombey," observed Cleopatra.
"It is powerful, madam," said Mr. Dombey. (XXXV)

The final clue to our understanding of Mr. Dombey's character and of the meaning of the book is contained in the famous scene where father and son sit, side by side, gazing into the fire: "Mr. Dombey stiff with starch and arrogance; the little image by inheritance, and in unconscious imitation. The

two so very much alike, and yet so monstrously contrasted."
Paul asks the question, "Papa! what's money?" His father,
doubtful of his being able to understand its full wonder,
murmurs something about guineas, shillings, half-pence; but
Paul remains unsatisfied: "I mean what's money after all . . .
what can it do?" To which his father answers: "Money, Paul,
can do anything." On being asked why it could not save his
mother from death, Mr. Dombey is provoked into giving a
general defense of his god:

> Mr. Dombey . . . expounded to him that money, though a very
> potent spirit, never to be disparaged on any account whatever,
> could not keep people alive whose time was come to die; and how
> that we must all die, unfortunately, even in the City, though we
> were never so rich. But how that money caused us to be honoured,
> feared, respected, courted, and admired, and made us powerful and
> glorious in the eyes of all men; and how that it could, very often,
> even keep off death, for a long time together.

But Paul is unconverted by his father's attempt at indoctrina-
tion:

> This, with more to the same purpose, Mr. Dombey instilled into the
> mind of his son, who listened attentively, and seemed to understand
> the greater part of what was said to him.
> "It can't make me strong and quite well, either, papa; can it?"

Dombey is so disconcerted by Paul's dispassionate discussion
of his own symptoms of physical weakness that his pathetic
attempt at personal communication quite breaks down: "Mr.
Dombey was so astonished, and so uncomfortable, and so perfectly at a loss how to pursue the conversation, that he could
only sit looking at his son by the light of the fire" (VIII).
   In the short but beautiful scene that follows, Dickens displays, with perfect tact, the self-destructiveness of Mr. Dombey's creed of the material. Dombey stands passively looking
on at a moment of human contact as Florence carries Paul off
to bed: "She was toiling up the great, wide, vacant staircase,
with him in her arms . . . they went, toiling up; she singing all
the way, and Paul sometimes crooning out a feeble accompani-
ment." And for an instant he is humanized as he seems to sense
faintly the existence of an area of experience from which he has
shut himself off completely.

> Mr. Dombey looked after them until they . . . passed out of his
> sight; and then he still stood gazing upwards, until the dull rays

of the moon, glimmering in a melancholy manner through the dim skylight, sent him back to his own room. (VIII)

One final example will serve to complete this picture of the alienating effects of money worship. Having failed in his attempt to indoctrinate Paul, Mr. Dombey seizes a practical opportunity for demonstrating the power of money to his son. When Walter Gay comes to ask him to help his uncle in his financial troubles (contracted in giving aid to Walter's father), Mr. Dombey asks Paul if he "would like to begin to be Dombey and Son, now, and lend this money to young Gay's uncle?" Paul, moved principally by his sister's unhappiness, is eager to do so.

"Then you shall do it," returned his father. "And you see, Paul . . . how powerful money is, and how anxious people are to get it. Young Gay comes all this way to beg for money, and you, who are so grand and great, having got it, are going to let him have it, as a great favour and obligation." (X)

There is no mention of human feeling or responsibility, only the old reduction of people to units that can be manipulated by the exchange of cash. And on this occasion we feel that Mr. Dombey's doctrine has made some headway:

Paul turned up the old face for a moment, in which there was a sharp understanding of the reference conveyed in these words: but it was a young and childish face immediately afterwards: when he slipped down from his father's knee, and ran to tell Florence not to cry any more, for he was going to let young Gay have the money. (X)

At the level of authentic human contact, then, money is a divisive force. It turns society from a community into a series of individual personal units linked only in a web of external, material relationships. Shut fast within the constricting boundaries of their own egos, men deny their common humanity.

Look round upon the world of odious sights—millions of human creatures have no other world on earth—at the lightest mention of which humanity revolts, and dainty delicacy living in the next street, stops her ears, and lisps "I don't believe it!" (XLVII)

But community of a kind does exist in this world where the possession of money is the criterion not only of success but almost, it seems, of personal goodness. If moral evil could be made palpable it would be seen "rolling slowly on to cor-

rupt the better portions of a town . . . overhanging the devoted
spots, and creeping on, to blight the innocent and spread
contagion among the pure . . . and from the thick and sullen
air where Vice and Fever propagate together, raining the
tremendous social retributions which are ever pouring down,
and ever coming thicker!" (XLVII). If men could break
through to a realization of this fact they would see that they
are all united with each other.

Men . . . like creatures of one common origin, owing one duty to
the Father of one family, and tending to one common end, to make
the world a better place!
    Not the less bright and blest would that day be for rousing some
who never have looked out upon the world of human life around
them, to a knowledge of their own relation to it. (XLVII)

These passages are expressions of the organizing principle
around which the concrete details of *Dombey and Son* cohere:
the opposition between the alienating effect of money and the
force of human love. In order to grasp the special flavor of the
novel, it is necessary to observe how it differs from what immediately preceded it and what was to follow. The theme of
Dombey is obviously closely related to that of both *Martin
Chuzzlewit* and *Bleak House*, but its embodiment is worked
out in deeply "personal" terms. By this I mean that on the one
hand, the characters of *Dombey* are much more rounded and
psychologically realistic than the strutting caricatures of the
American scenes of *Martin Chuzzlewit*, and on the other, *Dombey and Son* is not dominated by any large-scale, mythic institution like the Court of Chancery that dominates *Bleak House*.
The closest we come to this is in Walter's description of his
first day in Mr. Dombey's office. Walter's uncle is eager to "hear
something about the firm."

"Oh! there's not much to be told about the firm, uncle. . . . It's a
precious dark set of offices, and in the room where I sit, there's a
high fender, and an iron safe, and some cards about ships that are
going to sail, and some boxes, and a lot of cobwebs, and in one of
'em, just over my head, a shrivelled-up blue bottle that looks as if
it had hung there ever so long."

Old Solomon is disappointed at this lack of evidence of the
excitements of high finance.

"No bankers' books, or cheque books, or bills, or such tokens of
wealth rolling in from day to day?" said old Sol, looking wistfully at

his nephew out of the fog that always seemed to hang about him, and laying an unctuous emphasis upon the words. (IV)

Walter can only report that these tokens are hidden away in the private offices of the firm's principals. What we get here is akin to that "tragicomedy of money" which I have already discussed,[3] the sense of money begetting money in ways that are totally beyond the ordinary man's comprehension. The murky office, with its shriveled bluebottle—symbol of Mr. Dombey's emotional sterility, the fate of the firm's financial victims, the society that honors Dombey and all his activities—is at once ludicrous and sinister. We seem to be at the center of a vast spider web whose threads stretch out in a limitless menace, and this connects the business, in its disruptive effect on the lives of individuals, with the huge upheaval of the railways.

The first shock of a great earthquake had . . . rent the whole neighbourhood to its centre. . . . Houses were knocked down; streets broken through and stopped; deep pits and trenches dug in the ground; enormous heaps of earth and clay thrown up; buildings that were undermined and shaking, propped by great beams of wood. . . . There were a hundred thousand shapes and substances of incompleteness, wildly mingled out of their places, upside down, burrowing in the earth, aspiring in the air, mouldering in the water, and unintelligible as any dream. Hot springs and fiery eruptions, the usual attendants upon earthquakes, lent their contributions of confusion to the scene. Boiling water hissed and heaved within dilapidated walls; whence, also, the glare and roar of flames came issuing forth; and mounds of ashes blocked up rights of way, and wholly changed the law and custom of the neighbourhood. (VI)

Dickens' attitude to all this activity is ambiguous, for despite his evident fascination with the railways' trailing "smoothly away, upon its mighty course of civilization and improvement" from "the very core of all this dire disorder" (VI), it remains a cause of terror and pain. And both it and the world of business make the strongest possible contrast with Solomon Gills' inability to come to terms with the new age.

"You see, Walter . . . in truth this business is merely a habit with me. I am so accustomed to the habit that I could hardly live if I relinquished it: but there's nothing doing, nothing doing. When that uniform was worn," pointing out towards the little midshipman, "then indeed, fortunes were to be made, and were made. But com-

[3] See pp. 38–50.

petition, competition—new invention, new invention—alteration, alteration—the world's gone past me. I hardly know where I am
myself; much less where my customers are." (IV)

Despite the importance of the firm of Dombey and Son to the
novel as a whole, it is surely a mistake to talk, as one critic
does, of the "World of Dombeyism."[4] To do so is to impute to
the novel a greater richness of imaginative realization than
can easily be justified. We must be careful not to confuse
seriousness of purpose and a degree of thematic unity with
total artistic success. Mr. Dombey's business is felt as a representative force in the society depicted by the novel, but it is
simply not made to work, creatively, with the universality of
institutions such as Chancery and the Circumlocution Office.
For one thing, we never learn as much of the mechanics of its
operations as we do with the other two institutions. These are
anatomized with such detailed power that they permanently
enlarge our awareness of this key area of modern life, the
chaotic strength of financial and bureaucratic institutions. A
question of language is vitally involved here. In *Dombey*, Dickens lacks the resources of symbol and image pattern that force
a complete imaginative acceptance of the structures of his
later works. *Dombey and Son* has its recurrent images—the sea,
for example—but they are limited to the novel's private world,
to Paul and Florence. Dickens is unable, at this stage, to
make use of images such as the fog and, especially, the prison
which will unite the novel's private and public worlds and so
create a continuously unified vision. We understand the importance of the firm of Dombey and Son, but we are not made
to feel it enveloping the whole texture of society and con-
taminating thousands who never appear directly within the
pages of the novel.

It might be argued that this limitation stems from Dickens
having attempted to give a general social significance to a
merely private business, but the character of Merdle will help
to prove that this is not so, and will also throw some more
light on the "personal" nature of *Dombey and Son*. There can
be little doubt that the work's evil characters represent the
social linkings of nineteenth-century society. Joey Bagstock,
the retired army officer; James Carker, the smoothly efficient
"new man" of business; the Hon. Mrs. Skewton, decayed member of a decaying aristocracy—all are held together by nothing

[4] Edgar Johnson, *Charles Dickens: His Tragedy and Triumph* (London:
Gollancz, 1953), II, 626.

but their relation to the economic center of their society, Mr. Dombey. It is he alone who gives them a reason for living, just as, Dickens suggests, money represents the only reason for living to a society divorced from all claims of love and responsibility. But Dickens' method here is perhaps too much limited to the direct personal relationship to gain all the effect he desires. We perceive Merdle's impact on a small circle of developed characters, but we are more impressed by his tenuous and shadowy influence on thousands who exist outside this circle.

He was in everything good, from banking to building. He was in Parliament, of course. He was in the City, necessarily. He was Chairman of this, Trustee of that, President of the other. The weightiest of men had said to projectors, "Now, what name have you got? Have you got Merdle?" And the reply being in the negative, had said, "Then I won't look at you." (Bk. 1, XXI)

In *Little Dorrit*, structure, symbol, and language combine to reveal Merdle's involvement with his society at every level. The various worlds of *Dombey and Son* are, by contrast, not sufficiently integrated for us to feel the full force of what Mr. Dombey stands for.

When we turn to the novel's good characters, however, we find that their involvement with each other is personal in a positive sense. Indeed, this must be so, for in Dickens' later fiction the good are always more or less isolated figures whose lives are carried on outside, or on the very boundaries of, a society whose organizing principle is the selfish pursuit of individual interest. From some points of view, these good characters are not a very distinguished group. Walter is conventionally brave and bright, and completely uninteresting, but the others are unassuming, humble, and not particularly intelligent. Toots, in fact, is downright half-witted. Yet they have an undeniably successful power, for they are all characterized by an unselfish response to the joy and suffering of others. They enter, gladly and quite intuitively, into relation with the lives of those around them. They are all, in their different ways, fools in the eyes of the world, but wise fools in the love they feel for each other. And we respond to their positive qualities partly because of the laughter they release in us, as in the scene where Captain Cuttle gives Walter a farewell present.

The captain immediately drew Walter into a corner, and with a great effort, that made his face very red, pulled up the silver watch, which was so big, and so tight in his pocket, that it came out like a bung. "Wal'r," said the captain, handing it over, and shaking him heartily by the hand, "a parting gift, my lad. Put it back half an hour every morning, and about another quarter towards the arternoon, and it's a watch that'll do you credit." (XIX)

One seems to detect here memories of Mr. Shandy dragging the handkerchief out of his pocket, and the effect gained is akin to, although in a diluted form, the mixture of pathos and humor in Uncle Toby. And Toots is surely immortalized by his lunatic, yet completely apt, addressing of Walter Gay as Lieutenant Walters.

The novel's most important affirmation lies, of course, in Florence's frustrated love for her father. Once again, it is possible to discern Dickens' Shakespearian ambition at work, this time in the relationship between Florence and Mr. Dombey. We may doubt the success of Dickens' attempt to suggest a sense of Lear-like isolation in Dombey, the Victorian business-man; but there is more than a superficial resemblance to Cordelia in the unwavering persistence and total unselfishness of Florence's love. Her love has an absolute value because it asks for nothing in return, and in this it is at the furthest possible remove from her father's attitude to personal relation-ships. Dickens depicts with fine psychological insight the hu-man desire for love and the feeling of unreality that envelopes the personality when it is withheld.

And now the void in Florence's own heart began again, indeed, to make a solitude around her. . . . Thus living, in a dream wherein the overflowing love of her young heart expended itself on airy forms, and in a real world where she had experienced little but the rolling back of that strong tide upon itself, Florence grew to be seventeen. (XLVII)

Despite all the rebuffs she receives, Florence holds to her love because in it she discovers the strongest sense of her own individuality. She knows herself by the love she feels for some-one else. There is nothing selfish in this, for like George Eliot's Dorothea, "no life would have been possible" to Florence "which was not filled with emotion."[5] In seeking to express her love, she is only giving vent to a necessity of life as primi-tive as the need for breath. And so she will go to any lengths to hide from herself the fact that her father regards her love as quite without value, for this would be to destroy the basis of her own existence.

[5] *Middlemarch*, "Finale."

Her father did not know—she held to it from that time—how much she loved him. She was very young, and had no mother, and had never learned, by some fault or misfortune, how to express to him that she loved him. She would be patient, and would try to gain that art in time, and win him to a better knowledge of his only child. (XXIII)

These passages show an interesting variation from Dickens' usual fictional method. He generally works to a sense of inner life by means of a vividly realized externality, but his picture of Florence is supplemented by direct analysis and creates an emotional realism new in his work. That, even in his earlier work, Dickens is not limited to a view of human character based on nothing but the "ruling passion"[6] is shown by the famous example of Jonas Chuzzlewit's mental state after the murder of Montague Tigg.

And he was not sorry for what he had done. He was frightened when he thought of it—when did he not think of it?—but he was not sorry. He had had a terror and dread of the wood when he was in it; but being out of it, and having committed the crime, his fears were now diverted, strangely, to the dark room he had left shut up at home. He had a greater horror, infinitely greater, of that room than of the wood. Now that he was on the return to it, it seemed beyond comparison more dismal and more dreadful than the wood. His hideous secret was shut up in the room, and all its terrors were there; to his thinking it was not in the wood at all. (XLVII)

This is brilliant, but it is not developed into anything like a full-scale portrait, and Jonas remains an essentially melodramatic villain. In his depiction of Florence, however, Dickens is obviously attempting something much more subtle, and the degree of success he achieves is evidence of his constant development. Even in his presentation of external detail, there is a greater richness, stemming from its organic relationship to a unifying theme. Scenes such as the following haunt the imagination, not merely because of their spontaneous freedom, but also because of the depth of understanding they give us into Florence's predicament.

Florence lived alone in the great dreary house, and day succeeded day and still she lived alone; and the blank walls looked down upon her with a vacant stare, as if they had a Gorgon-like mind to stare her youth and beauty into stone.

[6] Dickens uses this phrase in chap. li of *Martin Chuzzlewit*, in describing Nadgett's reluctance to make known his secret information.

No magic dwelling-place in magic story, shut up in the heart of a thick wood, was ever more solitary and deserted to the fancy, than was her father's mansion in its grim reality, as it stood lowering on the street: always by night, when lights were shining from the neighbouring windows, a blot upon its scanty brightness; always by day, a frown upon its never-smiling face . . . there was a monstrous fantasy of rusty iron, curling and twisting like a petrifaction of an arbour over the threshold, budding in spikes and corkscrew points, and bearing, one on either side, two ominous extinguishers, that seemed to say, "Who enter here, leave light behind!" . . . Noise ceased to be, within the shadow of the roof. The brass band that came into the street once a week, in the morning, never brayed a note in at those windows; but all such company, down to a poor little piping organ of weak intellect, with an imbecile party of automaton dancers, waltzing in and out at folding-doors, fell off from it with one accord, and shunned it as a hopeless place. (XXIII)

This brief discussion of Dickens' method of character creation in *Dombey and Son* suggests two more aspects of what I have called the personal nature of the book. The unusually high proportion of analysis is obviously one. Dickens seems prepared in this novel to risk sacrificing a certain amount of dramatic color in the purely objective presentation of character, in the attempt to produce a more rounded, subtler, *quieter* sense of human personality. It seems clear that Mr. Dombey and Florence are meant to possess a range of interest, a complexity of spiritual life, far beyond anything Dickens had yet aspired to. And in thematic terms, they are the poles of opposition around which the novel's meaning revolves. The greed and selfishness of nineteenth-century society are embodied in the private motives and actions of Mr. Dombey; the unchanging reality of unselfish love is the prime motivating force of Florence's character. Whether this weight of thematic relevance is, artistically, too heavy a burden for such characters to bear is a point I return to later.

The implied richness of meaning is especially important in Florence, and this brings me to the second personal aspect of *Dombey*, one that I think is entirely successful. The constantly recurring image of Florence as the lonely princess in the evil castle, gazing out sadly at the wealth of life around her in which she seems forever unable to take part, is surely related to the picture of the child "at a window, always waving his hand at, and cheering, an array of open carriages" and being greeted with "four great streams of determined indifference."[7]

7 See p. 81.

The profound autobiographical significance to Dickens of the lost child theme is amply evidenced by its frequent occurrence, but the real question to be considered is, as always, to what use personal experience is put. The story of the deprived child is transposed here into a delicately imagined study of the alienating loss of identity that, as we have seen, was felt to be one of the crucial facts of their age by Victorian critics of society. But, in keeping with the essential nature of this novel, the loss of selfhood is not connected directly with the effects of the industrial and financial process as in such characters as Wemmick and Pancks. Dickens connects the attack on Florence's personality with the most private of losses, that of love and respect for her individuality, but one does not have to falsify her story in order to see its intimate connection with the public world. The depreciation of human worth and dignity was one of the more intangible, but none the less real, accompaniments of the industrial revolution and permeated a great deal of Victorian charity, as some well-known words of W. R. Greg in the *Westminster Review* of June, 1845, make clear.

The prevailing idea evidently is . . . *to give benefits to an inferior,* not to *do justice to a fellow man.* There is something essentially pauperising in all their conceptions. It pervades alike the factory and mining legislation of Lord Ashley; the "cricketing" condescension of Lord John Manners, and the insulting rewards and prizes offered by ostentatious landlords to the hampered farmers and the starving peasantry. We are weary of this cuckoo-cry—*always charity, never justice;*—always the *open purse,* never the *equal* measure.

In a speech a year before this, Dickens had made a very similar appeal for benefits rather than charity: "a just right which honest pride may claim without a blush."[8] Both writers were reacting bitterly against what Carlyle called "the feeling of *injustice* that is insupportable to all men. . . . The real smart is the soul's pain and stigma, the hurt to the moral self."[9] The background of all this can be understood, perhaps, from the harsh, unfeeling tone of a passage from the Report of the Poor Law Commission of 1834.

We deplore the misconception of the labourers in thinking that wages are not a matter of contract, but of right; that any diminution of their comforts occasioned by an increase in their numbers, with-

---

[8] June 4, 1844, to the Sanitorium, in *The Speeches of Charles Dickens,* K. J. Fielding, ed. (Oxford: Clarendon Press, 1960), p. 69.
[9] *Chartism,* first published, 1839.

out an equal increase of the fund for their subsistence, is an evil to be remedied, not by themselves, but by the magistrates; not an error, or even a misfortune, but an injustice.[10]

Dickens does not labor the point of the relation of Florence's deprivation to the social realities of nineteenth-century England; he does not need to. We understand enough of Mr. Dombey's representative function to realize that what he does to his daughter is a deeply spiritual reflection of what the power of Dombeyism was capable of inflicting on others in Victorian society. And this realization is conveyed by means of a personal relationship whose symbolic significance is allowed to flow from the perfectly chosen richness of its incidental detail and never from any schematically imposed, external meaning.

When Florence is finally made to accept the fact of her father's unmistakable hatred of her, after Edith has deserted him, the shock is so great that she seeks refuge in the attempt to deny the reality of his existence. Her sense of her own value, indeed of her very reality, depends absolutely on the love she feels for her father and the hope that she might win his in return. It is impossible for her to live with the knowledge that her father actively and constantly hates her. And so, with the gradual growth of that knowledge, comes the end of her father's reality for her.

Florence loved him still, but, by degrees, had come to love him rather as some dear one who had been, or who might have been, than as the hard reality before her eyes. Something of the softened sadness with which she loved the memory of little Paul, or of her mother, seemed to enter now into her thoughts of him, and to make them, as it were, a dear remembrance. Whether it was that he was dead to her, and that partly for this reason, partly for his share in those old objects of her affection, and partly for the long association of him with hopes that were withered and tenderness he had frozen, she could not have told; but the father whom she had loved began to be a vague and dreamy idea to her: hardly more substantially connected with her real life, than the image she would sometimes conjure up, of her dear brother yet alive, and growing to be a man, who would protect and cherish her. (XLVII)

But Florence cannot be allowed to remain in these fantasies that have been such an important part of her existence.

Shadowy company attended Florence up and down the echoing house, and sat with her in the dismantled rooms. As if her life were

[10] Report of the Poor Law Commission (London, 1834), p. 280.

an enchanted vision, there arose out of her solitude ministering thoughts, that made it fanciful and unreal. (XXIII)

Dickens is never farthest from his sentimental strain than in his ruthless attack on fantasy, which for him is always evil at its heart no matter how essential its indulgence may be for the preservation of some kind of spiritual balance. Illusion must be shattered and it is shattered for Florence in the most violent manner imaginable, when her father strikes her.

She looked at him, and a cry of desolation issued from her heart. For as she looked, she saw him murdering that fond idea to which she had held in spite of him. She saw his cruelty, neglect, and hatred dominant above it, and stamping it down. She saw she had no father upon earth, and ran out, orphaned, from his house. (XLVII)

But this is no mere manipulation for an external effect: Florence's subsequent behavior is entirely within the bounds of an inherent and beautifully observed probability. She does not lose her profound capacity for forgiveness, but the depth of her former love for her father means that he must be denied, as in the scene where she sees the bruise from Mr. Dombey's blow.

Her tears burst forth afresh at the sight; she was ashamed and afraid of it; but it moved her to no anger against him. Homeless and fatherless, she forgave him everything; hardly thought that she had need to forgive him, or that she did; but she fled from the idea of him as she had fled from the reality, and he was utterly gone and lost. There was no such Being in the world. (XLIX)

And the capacity for love that has been the cornerstone of her life is too important to be jettisoned with her idea of her father. It is perfectly fitting that when she is alone and in despair in the streets of the city she should turn to old Sol whose shop is a haven of all the qualities she had failed to find at home. At this point, as her love begins to flow with a self-healing power toward Walter Gay, a distinction has to be drawn between thematic and psychological plausibility and artistic success. The relationship between Florence and Walter is devoid of any potential for imaginative involvement on our part, mainly because of the almost total emptiness of Walter Gay's character. Here one does feel the pressure of a purely mechanical arrangement of events. There is nothing in Walter, of whom we know so little (because there is so little to be known), which can make us believe he was capable of arousing the love of Florence, of whom we know so much.

A similar weakness mars the novel's ending, for the eventual reconciliation of Florence and Mr. Dombey, the possibility of which is made credible by the overwhelming importance of Florence's love for her father, is brought about in a totally melodramatic way. A single chapter of "spectral, haggard" figures in the "wasted likeness" of Mr. Dombey who brood and brood over empty fireplaces, "wild, loud, piercing, loving, rapturous" cries and trickling pools of blood are thrown together to bring to a conclusion a relationship the earlier tracing of which had marked a new peak in Dickens' achievement. The dialogue is redolent of melodramatic circumlocution: "Papa, love, I am a mother. I have a child who will soon call Walter by the name by which I call you" (LIX). This is like an unconscious echo of Augustus Moddle's immortal letter of rejection to Charity Pecksniff in *Martin Chuzzlewit*: "I love another. She is Another's. Everything appears to be somebody else's" (LIV). But the artistic insight with which Florence's love has been depicted convinces us that it has the strength to perform the function assigned it: to bring Mr. Dombey into communion with the world of feeling. Victorian sentimentality may dictate that, unlike Lear, Mr. Dombey must live, but the change finally wrought in him by suffering and love is satisfying both psychologically and as a symbol of the change that society must undergo if it is to return to spiritual health. His expiation, in the love he feels for Florence's daughter, is domestic rather than tragic, but it has its own kind of beauty and power.

He hoards her in his heart. He cannot bear to see a cloud upon her face. . . . He fancies that she feels a slight, when there is none. He steals away to look at her, in her sleep. It pleases him to have her come, and wake him in the morning. He is fondest of her and most loving to her, when there is no creature by. (LXII)

Interregnum

The achievement of *Dombey and Son*, considered in relation to Dickens' literary career as a whole, is that with it he found a form capable of imposing some kind of unity on his seemingly boundless imagination, with its linking of didacticism and creativity, its desire for a wide canvas, its need to depict man in society, and its mixture of comedy and melodrama. Despite its variety of incident and character, the novel has an underlying thread of consistent meaning around which much of the action is organized, and so it can leave a generalized impression on the mind—a flavor of its own—in a way that a book such as *Nicholas*

Nickleby can never do. Certain key scenes, that in which Mr. Dombey instructs Paul in the power of money, for example, or when Florence in her loneliness looks out the windows of the great empty house at a happy family across the street, contain within themselves the essence of the novel in a way that constitutes a fresh departure for Dickens. His thematic control of the novel is so great that it can contract from its unifying task to find embodiment in a dramatic scene or inhere in the very texture of a mood of solitary introspection. Even the comedy of Captain Cuttle and Toots, unlike that of a Mantalini, does not exist only in and for itself. It is an integral part of the character of those who in their simplicity form an unspoken criticism of Mr. Dombey and his whole way of life.

It is, however, still possible to doubt whether Dickens had yet found the form that would exactly embody his unique vision, his utterly personal fusion of didacticism and creative autonomy. A poetic expansion of the social novel would appear to be the form that Dickens was struggling toward; thus, some discussion of what this form might be seems appropriate at this point. To succeed within its own terms of reference the social novel must be carried effectively into the public sphere. The way in which this is done differentiates crucially between the pamphleteer, whose didactic aim, however sincere, operates on a purely cerebral level, and the real artist. Disraeli is an example of the propagandist pure and simple who uses the novel for purposes totally unconnected with those of art. His imagination is as tawdry as that of the shoddiest Hollywood scriptwriter; documentary realism and a lack of priggishness, the usual vice of the propagandist, are his only saving graces. Mrs. Gaskell is a fine novelist, but too often her social indignation and her fine artistry do not cohere. The novelist in whom these qualities are merged, whose artistic imagination is fired by external, public issues—or, rather, who understands the inner meaning of such issues in their effect on individuals and groups—is a very rare figure. He alone, if we care at all for the novel as a form, is worthy of being called a social novelist, and he alone will rise above such devices as forcing political discussions into the mouths of his characters or indulging in narrative description of public institutions. His passionate apprehension of social or political reality will be embedded in organizations such as Kafka's Castle or the Circumlocution Office whose inhumanity is made personal and whose mythic force, stemming from the concretely realized detail of an abstract conception, enables them to bear the weight of an indictment not merely of specific abuses, but of the whole of modern society. Within the books that contain them, such institutions take on the role of characters and are an integral part of the creative web of the novels' artistic lives.

If *Dombey and Son* is measured against this exacting scale it will be seen to fall short, and it falls short for a reason that at first sight seems a curious one to apply to any novelist and to Dickens above all: it is too much a novel of character. We will be told, in the first place, that it is the major business of *every* novelist to concern himself with human character, and, second, that as everyone knows Dickens is preeminently the novelist of character, or at least of characters. It is easy enough to assent to the proposition that whatever their philosophical or social preoccupations, concentration on the personal should be the major business of *most* novelists. The theme of *Crime and Punishment*, for example, is of the widest possible human interest, but its universal moral application grows out of the inner struggle of Raskolnikov himself. It is self-evident that Dickens is concerned with the personal effects of poverty, bureaucracy, and greed for money, but the mention of a novel such as *Crime and Punishment* makes it clear that he deals with them, at this stage, in some way other than by the depiction of the human reality of a mighty central character. No Dickens novel is built around and within a Myshkin, a Madame Bovary, or an Anna Karenina. Steerforth may have been the inspiration for Stavrogin;[11] yet we feel that this is an instance where the pupil has clearly outstripped the master.

The reason is to be sought partly in that Victorian domesticity which forbade the rigorous examination of character in its fullest depths and screened off the wild and unpleasant aspects of humanity in a way that effectively prevented the creation of character on the deepest level. No major Victorian writer, other than the Brontës, ventured into that realm in which animal impulse rather than social awareness is of primary interest. Only perhaps in *The Last Chronicle of Barset*, with Mr. Crawley, do we meet a fully realized character whose passionate, even pathological, moral intensity refuses to be kept tidily in place by considerations of respectability. We find in this lack a reinforcement of the social interest that is so much a part of the

[11] George Katkov, "Steerforth and Stavrogin," *Slavonic and East European Review*, XXVII (1949), 469–488.

tradition of the English novel and yet, at the same time, a kind
of debasing of that tradition; for we feel that the Victorian
interest in the social world is often used as an escape from the
wildness of idiosyncratic human behavior. This escape was
particularly dangerous to a writer like Thackeray whose genius
should have come to fruition in that area of human experience
forbidden him by public timidity. But, in yet another way, we
find Dickens to be a man of and for his time in that this timidity
was much less damaging to him as a writer.

The Dickens world, with its farce and comedy, its melodrama
and tragedy, its greed, hypocrisy, cruelty, and benevolence,
its frenetic gaiety and glowering menace, both touched by
hints of instability, is not yet a place for the triumphant nor-
mality of such characters as Dorothea and Lydgate. Wildness
or eccentricity are its true inhabitants. We may find later characters closer to the spirit of George Eliot, but for the moment
Dickens chooses to people his world with eccentrics rather
than with fully adult, if anguished, beings. He is seen here
to be following particularly closely in the footsteps of his
teachers, the eighteenth-century novelists, in whom the robust
externalization of comic figures contrasts with the sentiment
of the often palely realized heroes and heroines. Dickens, however, is not simply reacting to public pressures (as even
he may have been forced to do to a certain extent) or mechanically following in a tradition. In concentrating on the
eccentric he shows an awareness of where his best powers
of characterization then lay. As I have suggested, eccentricity
and wildness are both suited to a melodramatic setting, and
they form a contrast with a more obviously realistic method of
characterization. But wildness and realism are closer to each
other than either is to eccentricity in that they demand a certain
degree of psychological insight for their successful embodiment.
By the standards of everyday life the actions of a Raskolnikov
may seem improbable; yet the understanding of the springs of
motive in his character is such that we are convinced of their
authenticity and of the self-consistent reality of his existence.
The essence of eccentricity is not merely its impenetrability,
but that we feel no desire to understand the actions that arise
from it. The disconnectedness of eccentric behavior—the cause
of its comic or, sometimes, sinister impact—has no moral or
spiritual significance. To attempt to understand it would be
an exercise of the same kind as solving a crossword puzzle: it
is more profitable to continue to enjoy it for its own sake. For

the writer this means that the obsessional tic can take the place of psychologically convincing behavior. External detail, if observed with sufficient accuracy and realized with sufficient vividness, can take the place of a deeply felt inner life.

The meaning of my earlier statement that *Dombey and Son* is less than a total success because it is too much a novel of character may now be clearer. It is not fully a social novel in the sense in which I earlier tried to describe the form, and this means that Mr. Dombey and Florence have to carry the entire weight of the book's implied and embodied social, as well as personal, criticism. Neither is a "big" enough character to be able to do this. In my discussion, I compared their roles to those of Lear and Cordelia, and such a comparison is not entirely unfair; for Dickens shared with Keats the Shakespearean ambition. It cannot be denied, however, that on such a mighty scale they appear as rather small figures. Mr. Dombey is at best a domesticated Lear. His moral failings are real and convincing enough, but he lacks all grandeur and presence. It is asking too much for such a character to contain within himself the whole "World of Dombeyism."

Dombey and Son falls, in fact, between two styles. It is not entirely a novel of the social group, nor is Dickens' genius yet of the kind to make it completely successful as what might be called a fully personal novel. Such a verdict may raise the question of just what sort of novel it is whose primary interest does not lie in the presentation of the inner life of its one or two major characters. An examination of *Bleak House* may help provide an answer.

Bleak House

An approach to *Bleak House* based on the expectation of finding its meaning purely within the characters who inhabit it seems doomed to failure. The book *has* a central character, of course, but with a function very different from that of a Raskolnikov. Esther may have her amiable qualities, but the depth of her personality and the complexity of her problems are rather less than those of Anna Karenina or Madame Bovary. If we look elsewhere, we see a host of sharply etched and vividly realized people, but they are not delineated in such a way as to convince us that what we are dealing with is primarily a study of character. Consider, for example, Mr. Tulkinghorn and Lady Dedlock. Both are masterly exercises in that unification of details of dress, physical appearance, manner, and gesture which can give the strongest impression of external reality. But this feeling of physical presence is not complemented by any profound sense of their inner reality. Why, for instance, does the one pursue the other so remorselessly?

It may be that he pursues her doggedly and steadily, with no touch of compunction, remorse, or pity. It may be that her beauty, and all the state and brilliancy surrounding her, only gives him the greater zest for what he is set upon, and makes him the more inflexible in it. . . . Whether he be any of this, or all of this . . . (XXIX)

That, Dickens seems to be saying, is impossible to tell. Mr. Tulkinghorn is a figure of motiveless evil, but so, we may be told, is Iago. The latter, however, is a poetic presentation of *absolute* evil, and as such is imbued with a more than personal force, while the lawyer is a realistic figure whose delineation is impaired by his lack of adequate motivation. Again, with Lady Dedlock at the great crisis of her life there is a similar lack of psychological insight.

Thus, a terrible impression steals upon and overshadows her, that from this pursuer . . . there is no escape but in death. Hunted, she flies. The complication of her shame, her dread, remorse, and misery, overwhelms her at its height; and, even her strength of self-reliance is overturned and whirled away, like a leaf before a mighty wind. (LV)

This has a certain nervous power of its own, but of a generalized, theatrical kind that forms no satisfactory substitute for the personal analysis that could have added subtlety to Lady Dedlock's character at that moment.

If, then, our first interest is not to be given to the novel's characters, on which aspect of the book should we fix our attention, from which center can we trace the growth of its meaning? Setting, atmosphere, language, tone, organization— all play their part within the structure of the work. Each of the first four may constitute the unifying force of a particular kind of novel. It is possible to argue, for example, that the setting of *The Return of the Native* forms one of its chief interests to both reader and author; and the manipulation of language certainly seems to be a major focus of a work such as *The Red Badge of Courage*. It is significant, however, that both these books are considerably shorter than *Bleak House*, and it would appear that only organization is capable of sustaining a work of its length and complexity. At any rate, I think it may prove fruitful to begin a study of *Bleak House* from that point of view.

The organization of a novel can operate on two levels: that of plot and that of significance. By plot I mean the complications of the detective story, introduced merely to mystify or thrill the reader, or, on a slightly higher plane, the bringing of characters into relationship in a purely external way, through the workings of chance or accident. By significance I mean something very different: that ordering of people or events which stems inevitably from the inner meaning of character or circumstance. The art that conceals art in an attempt to catch the shifting, transient, aimless surface of life—as in *The Catcher in the Rye*—is one method of doing this, the method of the novel rather than the romance, to use Hawthorne's brilliant distinction. But it is the romance, which presents its truths "under circumstances . . . of the writer's own choosing or creation,"[12] which is relevant to the artistry of Dickens. In its formal aspects his work is akin to a novel such as *The Great Gatsby* in which we are constantly reminded, because of Nick's function as narrator and because he tells us that he himself wrote the book we are reading, that we are involved with art as a means of getting to grips with life and not with life itself. In such works, the writer is self-consciously unafraid of making us aware of his artistry in the novel's shaping because he wishes us to judge as he judges, rather than lose ourselves in the flux of purely spontaneous experience. Imbued with a unifying vision of man or society, these novels try to avoid the fortuitous in the hope of creating a world in which this vision can operate most consistently. They are, however, radically unlike purely didactic works that are pieced together mechanically in order to illustrate some doctrine or point of view. In them, the novelist's view of reality is so strongly felt, so much a part of his being, that he cannot help but write in accordance with it. His degree of success will depend on how far he refuses to inhibit it through, say, fear of public opinion, or the extent to which it has been thought out as well as deeply felt; but if he gives it any play at all, it will so order the novel's characters and events that they will acquire symbolic and social meanings.

In *Bleak House* there are three main organizing strands: the mystery of Esther's birth, the murder of Tulkinghorn, and the

[12] Preface to *The House of the Seven Gables*.

events and characters that surround the Court of Chancery. In order to understand the novel fully it is necessary to examine all three. The least important strand, that concerning Esther, does not require a great deal of attention, for its main interest lies in illuminating the distinctions about organization which I tried to make earlier. It is a device of plot rather than significance, because the relationship it discloses between Esther and Lady Dedlock is not important at the book's deepest levels of meaning. It might possibly be argued that Oliver Twist's relationship with the Maylies is significant, since through it Dickens is attempting to show that Oliver's appalling misadventures could happen just as much to middle-class little boys as to members of the lower orders; however, no hidden purpose is at work in the relationship of Esther and her mother. Their consanguinity enables Dickens to bring about Lady Dedlock's downfall (for him, an important feature of the novel) in an economical way. At the same time, this particularizes the general comment he made about two seemingly very different worlds at the beginning of his second chapter: "It is but a glimpse of the world of fashion that we want on this same miry afternoon. It is not so unlike the Court of Chancery, but that we may pass from the one scene to the other, as the crow flies." Through them a host of disparate characters— Nemo, Jo, Guppy, Tony Weevle, Krook, George, the Smallweeds, Mr. Snagsby, Guster, Bucket, Tulkinghorn—and the worlds they inhabit are brought into connection, but their function begins and ends there.

The fabric of events that surround Tulkinghorn's murder presents us with rather more problems. When we first survey that complicated series of incidents, the question that seems to suggest itself is not, I think, "what is the meaning of Tulkinghorn's murder?" but rather "what is its purpose?" There seems to be too much of the externalized mystery-making of the detective story here, too much suspense for its own sake. In particular, Tulkinghorn's holding of the threat of exposure over Lady Dedlock seems the very cheapest of melodramatic devices. It reflects that abominable delight Dickens took in the creation of gratuitous mysteries (of which the worst example in the book is the marriage theme of Esther, Woodcourt, and Mr. Jarndyce where the delaying tactics of Mr. Jarndyce take on a positively indecent air). Also, there is something distasteful in the hounding of Lady Dedlock to death for an action that most people would think expiated by years of anguished self-reproach.

There seems to be a determination to extract the moral pound
of flesh here which can only stem from a real terror of any departure from conventional sexual mores.

Perhaps we are mistaken, however, in accepting these events
too much at their face value. *Bleak House* is a highly objectified
novel, and as has been well pointed out, the "character" of the
third-person narrator is as consistently maintained as that of
Esther herself. His mood of "detached and playful irony"[13]
should perhaps suggest to us that Lady Dedlock's persuit by
Tulkinghorn is something more than a piece of melodrama.
And when we remember that she is, like Dickens himself, a
social upstart, a parvenu who has won her way solely through
her beauty and intelligence, then some possible levels of meaning do begin to appear. Are we to see the lawyer as the soulless
representative of a class into which one can buy one's way with
money, but which forbids entry to more personal and human
qualities? Or is he even the moral spokesman of a puritanical
society for whom Lady Dedlock's love affair is a sin to be
punished with ruthless severity? Such a view reminds us of
Edmund Wilson's conception of Captain Hawdon as the embodiment of an older, happier England, brave and gay, adored
by women, worshipped by his men.[14] The trouble is that this
does seem to be more a creation of Wilson than of Dickens.
The interpretation might possibly be valid, but it goes quite
beyond the evidence contained within the texture of the novel
itself. Captain Hawdon is mentioned so rarely that only Dickens' genius, in Jo's description of how the captain "wos wery
good to me, he wos," could invest such a shadowy figure with
any sense of character. But, for anything we know to the contrary, Hawdon could as well have been a dissolute Regency
rake as the man Wilson suggests to us. We simply do not know
enough about him. And, similarly, the opacity of motive which
I observed earlier in Lady Dedlock and Tulkinghorn prevents
their attaining a complexity sufficient to enable them to bear
the burden of a symbolic or social meaning in the way that the
characters of *Great Expectations* will eventually be seen to do.

The climax of the difficulties concerned with this aspect of
the book comes with Lady Dedlock's death at Hawdon's grave-
yard. Are these loathsome surroundings the fitting scene for the

[13] M. E. Grenander, "The Mystery and the Moral: Point of View in
Dickens' *Bleak House*," *Nineteenth Century Fiction*, X (1956), 305.

[14] "Dickens: The Two Scrooges," in *The Wound and the Bow* (Boston:
Houghton Mifflin, 1941), pp. 40–41.

punishment of two sinners, or is their meeting in death meant
to arouse compassion for the memory of a truer, more deeply
human life that they both once shared? Or, take a third alternative, is this simply the most suitable ending for a series of
essentially theatrical adventures? As in Eliot's *The Waste Land,*
we are faced with several conflicting conclusions and there
seems to be no valid reason for choosing one rather than another. But the confusion of Eliot's poem is, in a sense, fruitful,
since it may be held to mirror the very confusions of the world
that it depicts. No such saving explanation is possible for *Bleak
House.* If Dickens intended the story of Lady Dedlock and Mr.
Tulkinghorn to carry any subterranean meaning he failed in his
task. When we remember some of the story's other episodes,
however, it seems unlikely that this is true. The use of Hortense
to dispose of Mr. Tulkinghorn, for example, is very unsatisfactory: we may be convinced that she is capable of murder, but
the only person she could have killed with any psychological
consistency would have been her mistress (her supposed
wrongs at the hands of Mr. Tulkinghorn are trifling compared
with the causes of grievance she feels she has against Lady
Dedlock). And her actual unmasking through the fact of being
Mrs. Bucket's lodger is nonsense that would make any self-
respecting detective-story writer blush to his ears. Finally, the
desperate chase through the night, whatever its literary superiority to other attempts of the kind, is all of a piece with the
theatricality that mars the Dedlock-Tulkinghorn story. The
charge against Dickens here is more serious than that of failing
to realize a significance he had intended. It is, rather, that he
is still dealing in the tired conventions of popular melodrama
without imbuing them, despite the skill he shows in their use,
with a meaning sufficient to raise them above the level of entertainment.

I have dealt so far with some of those flaws that do undeniably mar the total greatness of *Bleak House,* but it is time now
to turn to that feature, the Court of Chancery, which works
with triumphant success. We find in it the real organizing crux
of the book, a structure that embodies both plot and significance. And through it the unity of didacticism and creative
autonomy is displayed on a new level, for it forms at one and
the same time a criticism of a society—perhaps, indeed, of
modern society as a whole—and a brilliant technical contribution to the novel. It is the means to the creation of a new kind
of novel that will enable Dickens to realize fully themes that

are damagingly limited to the personal in *Dombey and Son.*

I have tried to show how important to Dickens is the theme of money in its public and private effects. We have followed it from the scattered references in the earlier books through the farcical satire of the American scenes of *Martin Chuzzlewit* to the attempt to embody it in the novel of character in *Dombey*. Now, in a leap forward that is crucial in his development, Dickens bodies it forth in the workings of a public institution. In doing so he displays not only complete awareness of what will best suit his artistic purposes, but also a profound insight into the nature of his own society. Once again we can detect the vibration of that instinctive understanding by the man of his time. For, however ancient the Court of Chancery itself may have been, the large-scale organization and institution were characteristic features of the new era ushered in by the industrial revolution. The worlds of industry, finance, and government were all involved in this process. As David Thomson points out, the "age of machinery was also the age of organization: and industrial relations became more impersonal, less a matter of human relationships between man and man than social relationships between one large organization and another. This new impersonality of economic relations brought with it new social tensions."[15] The world of finance displayed exactly the same combination of organizational growth and impersonality.

The growth of the Limited Liability Company and municipal trading had important consequences. Such large, impersonal manipulation of capital and industry greatly increased the numbers and importance of shareholders as a class, an element in the national life representing irresponsible wealth detached from the land and the duties of the landowner; and almost equally detached from the responsible management of business.[16]

And the gradual erosion of laissez-faire by governmental interference, bringing with it a "great and increasing accumulation of public business,"[17] plus the ever-increasing complexity of every department of modern life, necessitated more and more bureaucratic structures. One can see this organizational ten-

[15] *England in the Nineteenth Century* (Penguin Books, 1950), pp. 151–152.

[16] Trevelyan, *English Social History* (London: Longmans, 1948), p. 573.

[17] *The General Report on the Civil Service*, commissioned by Gladstone, quoted in Asa Briggs, *Victorian People* (London: Odhams Press, 1954), p. 117.

dency at work even in the world of philanthropy, with its Charity Organization Society, Exeter Hall, Bands of Hope, and so on. As we shall see later, Dickens' realization of this gave him the power to add more than one level of significance to his concept of the Court of Chancery.

In the first instance, however, it provided him with an instrument for the delineation of money and its effects on those characters who are linked by it in a web of greed and ruin. The inner circle is composed of Rick, Gridley, and Miss Flite, and their stories form a beautifully contrasted parable of the human waste and suffering generated by the Court. The dissolution of Rick's youthful promise, the frenetic rage by which Gridley attempts to retain his sanity, and Miss Flite's madness are all touchingly, and sometimes powerfully, conveyed; but only Miss Flite is totally innocent. She is the true victim, caught up in a system she is unable either to understand or to resist. With Gridley, although to a very minor extent, and, much more important, with Rick, there is a question of moral failure as well as external pressure. Rick is unable to find the strength to resist the lure of an easy fortune, for he has no reserves of character with which to face the temptations it presents.

Richard had a carelessness in his character that quite perplexed me—principally because he mistook it in such a very odd way, for prudence. It entered into all his calculations about money. (IX)

But Dickens understands the sources of the corruption in his personality too well to view him with anything other than the compassion he feels, and makes us feel, for all the many victims of Chancery. Its pervasive power is such that only the most resolute have a chance of escaping its evil influence: "The uncertainties and delays of the Chancery suit had imparted to his nature something of the careless spirit of a gamester, who felt that he was part of a great gaming system" (XVII). In a brilliant stroke, however, Dickens makes us understand that a heavy price is exacted even from those who *have* the strength to resist it. Esther explains to Rick that Mr. Jarndyce is untainted by the suit because "his is an uncommon character, and he has resolutely kept himself outside the circle" (XXXVII), and yet the effort to combat the evils by which he is surrounded has led him into an "eccentric gentleness" (VI), which however lovable is still eccentricity.

He had taken two or three undecided turns up and down while uttering these broken sentences, retaining the poker in one hand

and rubbing his hair with the other, with a good-natured vexation.
(VI)

Although Mr. Jarndyce understands Chancery for the mirage
of fruitless hopes that it is, he is just as much the victim, in
another direction, as Rick himself, of the confusion of appearance and reality which is such an important strand in the book.
His confusion is such that he can be taken in by the apparent
ingenuousness of Harold Skimpole, an ingenuousness that
masks a ruthless financial dependence on others, and by the
rapacious hypocrisy of the philanthropists. Harold's "charming"
ability to rob even such innocents as the young Rick, and Mrs.
Jellyby's insatiable pursuit of money for her good causes, are
personal manifestations of a sickness that pervades the world
of *Bleak House*. And their success in deceiving Mr. Jarndyce
is of real significance: it makes clear that he is no exception to
T. S. Eliot's dictum that none of us can "bear too much reality."
Mr. Jarndyce has triumphed in his encounter with the evil
reality of Chancery, but the violence of the struggle has ir-
retrievably damaged his personality. It has led to the eccentricity I have already mentioned and to an unwillingness to face
evil in areas of life other than that of Chancery itself. This is
another example of a theme that is to be of continuing interest
throughout Dickens' later career, the power of a hostile environment to taint the deepest levels of the individual's inner
life. Mr. Jarndyce is enmeshed in a society that distorts his
natural goodness by making claims on him that no one should
be asked to bear: "It seemed to Ada and me that everybody
knew him, who wanted to do anything with anybody else's
money" (VIII). And so we can see that even John Jarndyce
illustrates, if in a negative way, Humphry House's view that
Dickens frequently organizes his characters "around an attitude to money."[18] His attitude is one of horror and revulsion,
but it does, nevertheless, help to form some of the most important aspects of his character. This complexity of response
helps to expose the falsity of the often-repeated view that
Dickens' benefactors are all essentially of the same kind. Despite his attractiveness, Jarndyce is very far from Mr. Pickwick's world of gay inconsequentiality or the rather more
dubious benevolence of Mr. Brownlow and the Cheerybles.
Their generosity is a given, an integral, part of their personality,

[18] *Dickens World*, p. 58.

while that of Mr. Jarndyce has, we feel, been formed in a harsh
school of suffering.

This deepening, and darkening, of attitude from an earlier
book to a later can be seen if we turn to another group of
characters, this time on the fringes of Chancery. The Smallweeds are built around an approach to money of a much simpler
kind than that of Mr. Jarndyce. And Chick, the noble bread-
winner of that happy family, surely reminds us of another
"town-made article, of small stature," of Young Bailey, in fact.
Chick's genius—"He stands precociously possessed of centuries
of owlish wisdom" (XX)—is very much akin to that of Bailey,
"an abstract of all the stable-knowledge of the time."[19] But the
differences between them are even more startling than their
similarities. Bailey's stature is the perfect reflection of a spirit
of Napoleonic resource, while Chick's is the barren inheritance
of generations of money-grubbers reinforced by the dry lusts
of his own mean soul. His mental powers are devoted to the
single object of getting cash, but Bailey is a poet, a creature
of the imagination, as his insistence on a mock shave from
Poll Sweedlepipe so magnificently showed. As Poll said, "It
was all his fun,"[20] but there is precious little fun to be got out
of Chick or his family. The humor to which they give rise is
grotesque and horrible; it is a just index of the bitter hatred
with which Dickens views them. They make a terrifying picture of human greed in his best vein of vividly externalized
detail. They are creatures who know joy of neither soul nor
body: "Everything that Mr. Smallweed's grandfather ever
put away in his mind was a grub at first, and is a grub at last.
In all his life he never bred a single butterfly" (XXI).

Grubbing away like moles in their filthy underworld of
greed and selfishness, the Smallweeds are blind to all those
qualities that make for a truly human life. They cannot see that
their conception of living is dehumanized, and this moral
blindness makes them a part of that theme of the confusion of
appearance and reality which, as I said earlier, is so important in
Bleak House. It is, for example, an integral part of the story
of those philanthropic ladies Mrs. Jellyby and Mrs. Pardiggle,
and is symbolized by Mrs. Jellyby's "handsome eyes," which
"had a curious habit of seeming to look a long way off. As
if . . . they could see nothing nearer than Africa!" (IV). In

[19] *Martin Chuzzlewit*, chap. xxvi.
[20] *Ibid.*, chap. xlix.

them, concern for individuals has been replaced by concern for some abstract idea of humanity. This is ruthlessly exposed in Mrs. Pardiggle's approach to the brickmakers, where human contact is eschewed in the interests of some general notion of how the poor should be dealt with. Esther sums up her approach:

We both thought that Mrs. Pardiggle would have got on infinitely better, if she had not had such a mechanical way of taking possession of people. . . . We both felt painfully sensible that between us and these people there was an iron barrier. . . . Even what she read and said, seemed to us to be ill chosen for such auditors if it had been imparted ever so modestly and with ever so much tact.(VIII)

Dickens is not, as some of his contemporaries seemed to think, attacking philanthropy as such in passages like these or, indeed, slyly intimating the belief that woman's true place is in the home. He did, after all, give practical support to the real-life philanthropist on whom Mrs. Jellyby was based. It is the exclusiveness of a vision that fails to see the validity of claims that lie nearer home, both in the private and the public sphere, as well as the lack of an unpatronizing understanding of the poor, which he finds so reprehensible. He hates the romanticism of that false philanthropy which could ignore Jo, the representative of thousands of suffering poor, because he "is not one of Mrs. Pardiggle's Tockahoopo Indians; he is not one of Mrs. Jellyby's lambs; being wholly unconnected with Borrioboola-Gha; he is not softened by distance and unfamiliarity; he is not a genuine foreign-grown savage; he is the ordinary home-made article" (XLVII).

This failure of characters to understand the facts of their environment is repeated again and again throughout the book, amongst the generously honest just as much as the selfishly hypocritical. Skimpole and Mr. Turveydrop project self-delusory conceptions of themselves which take in Mr. Jarndyce, on the one hand, and Caddy and her husband, on the other. Sir Leicester understands neither Lady Dedlock nor Mr. Tulkinghorn. Miss Barbary and Chadband confuse, in their different ways, the true nature of religion. Mr. Snagsby finds himself surrounded by mysteries on all sides, for he "cannot make out what it is that he has to do with. Something is wrong, somewhere; but what something, what may come of it, to whom, when, and from which unthought-of and unheard-of quarter, is the puzzle of his life" (XXV). And his mystification reaches a comic climax when Allan Woodcourt comes to take him to the dying Jo:

"At it again, in a new direction! A certain person charges me, in the solemnest way, not to talk of Jo to any one, even my little woman. Then comes another certain person, in the person of yourself, and charges me, in an equally solemn way, not to mention Jo to that other certain person above all other persons. Why, this is a private asylum! Why, not to put too fine a point upon it, this is Bedlam, sir!" (XLVII)

But the tragic climax of all this alienation from reality occurs with Rick, who, at the height of his obsession with the Chancery suit, mistakes even the true nature of Mr. Jarndyce: "I do declare to you that he becomes to me the embodiment of the suit; that, in place of its being an abstraction, it is John Jarndyce; that the more I suffer, the more indignant I am with him." (XXXIX)

What does all this confusion and mystery mean? We must seek for its meaning, because it is too persistently present throughout *Bleak House* to be fortuitous. The answer lies, I think, in the fact that it is Chancery that has brought about Rick's downfall, and in trying to understand this the truth of my earlier statement that the suit makes up the real organizing crux of the novel will perhaps become clearer. For is not the Court of Chancery itself a huge structure of unreality, a vast maze in which the selfish, greedy, or often merely victimized wander hopelessly in search of money or, with even less chance of success, justice? Its falsity is only too obvious when it is juxtaposed with the facts of human life:

To see everything going on so smoothly, and to think of the roughness of the suitors' lives and deaths; to see all that full dress and ceremony, and to think of the waste, and want, and beggared misery it represented. . . . There seemed to be no reality in the whole scene, except poor little Miss Flite, the madwoman. (XXIV)

Although Chancery as an institution with any real social function is as illusory as the dreams of those who chase money in the hope of being able to buy happiness, it is not as pointless as it might at first sight appear to its victims or to outsiders; for "the one great principle of the English law is, to make business for itself. . . . Viewed by this light it becomes a coherent scheme, and not the monstrous maze the laity are apt to think it" (XXXIX). From this center of social anarchy swirl mysteries and confusions to engulf in a corrupting fog those who are only remotely connected with it. If even the single case of Jarndyce and Jarndyce can spread evil far and wide, one can imagine the sum total of evil caused by the whole Court of Chancery.

> Shirking and sharking, in all their many varieties, have been sown broadcast by the ill-fated cause; and even those who have contemplated its history from the outermost circle of such evil, have been insensibly tempted into a loose way of letting bad things alone to take their own bad course, and a loose belief that if the world go wrong, it was, in some off-hand manner, never meant to go right. (I)

So far removed from reality itself, so much of a monstrous game, it infects with its unreality almost all those who come in contact with it. Its pervasiveness and dominance are such that those influenced by it are forced to view at least part of their world through its distorted and cloudy mirror.

The question naturally presents itself of what Dickens was about, ultimately, in the creation of this dreamlike amalgam of hopes and fears, greed and madness. John Butt has shown how much agitation for Chancery reform was in the air at the time *Bleak House* was being written.[21] Is Dickens, then, simply launching a limited attack on an institution within which people can lose themselves in an exhausting and deranging search for wealth? Or does not my earlier point that the large-scale organization is a characteristic feature of nineteenth-century society suggest that his purpose was rather deeper than this? In the first place, Chancery enables Dickens to bring forward some of the scattered themes of his earlier books from the private into the public sphere. It is obvious enough, for example, that it provides a perfect setting for the delineation of the many problems raised by money and its worship. And the concrete embodiment of this money worship is achieved through the enlargement of one of the elements of popular melodrama, the mystery surrounding a will, which Dickens had used a great deal in his early novels. Examples are the destruction by Monk's mother of the will proving Oliver's parentage in *Oliver Twist*, the will benefiting Madeline Bray which is in the possession of Arthur Gride in *Nicholas Nickleby*, and Anthony Chuzzlewit's will, which exerts such a powerful influence over his son Jonas. The case of Jarndyce and Jarndyce comes into this category, for it was "about a Will when it was

---

[21] *"Bleak House* in the Context of 1851," *Nineteenth Century Fiction,* X (1955), 3–7.

about anything. . . . A certain Jarndyce, in an evil hour, made a great fortune, and made a great Will" (VIII); but its scope and significance are obviously of a different order from these previous examples. The great suit itself is far-reaching enough to take on an almost public meaning, but over and above this, it is embedded in a structure whose major concern is with wills in a way that takes its influence into every last corner of the country. Again, Mr. Jarndyce's benevolence is more than a matter of helping isolated individuals. It is extensive enough to bring him into contact with many forms of charity and to raise moral problems of a kind that would never have occurred to Mr. Pickwick: the problem, for example, that giving aid to Mrs. Jellyby's causes is a way of increasing the miseries of her unfortunate children. But it is, perhaps, above all in the theme of the relationship between character and environment that Chancery is seen to have its greatest social import. Indeed, for Richard Carstone it does, in a sense, form the society in which he is enveloped from his earliest years: "Jarndyce and Jarndyce was the curtain of Rick's cradle" (XXXV). If this is so, then the function that Dickens intends the Court to fulfill within the complex of *Bleak House* is a very important one.

I have already pointed out that the Court of Chancery is not as senseless a system as it appears to those whom it has in its grasp or to mere outsiders. It is not a world in complete anarchy. There are those who, fearing what they think of as a Marxist view of social conspiracy or withdrawing from a vulgar imputation of motive, would prefer to think of it as the reflection of a society for whose state no one could reasonably be blamed. But such is not Dickens' view. For him, the Court gave "to monied might, the means abundantly of wearing out the right" (I). If nineteenth-century society did consist of two classes, the exploiters and the exploited, then surely Chancery is a paradigm of that society. Conversation Kenge may use that "*most* respectable man" Mr. Vholes as a means of defending the excesses of the system, but we have a pretty shrewd idea that it is not Mr. Vholes' well-being with which he is mainly concerned.

"Repeal this statute, my good sir?" says Mr. Kenge, to a smarting client, "repeal it, my dear Sir? . . . Alter this law, sir, and what will be the effect of your rash proceedings on a class of practitioners very worthily represented . . . by the opposite attorney in the case, Mr. Vholes?" (XXXIX)

Money is just as much the motive force of this society in miniature as it is of capitalist society as a whole. Greed and necessity
are the twin gods of the world of Chancery, and lawyer and
client, like employer and worker, are indissolubly bound together by them. As nineteenth-century capitalists fought bitterly the attempts to lessen their untrammeled freedom, so the
lawyers struggle with equal pertinacity to retain their own
positions:

The respectability of Mr. Vholes has even been cited with crushing
effect before Parliamentary committees . . . In a word, Mr. Vholes . . .
is continually doing duty, like a piece of timber, to shore up some
decayed foundation that has become a pitfall and a nuisance.
(XXXIX)

If we consider the whole body of Dickens' work it seems
obvious that he regarded English society as a series of interlocking systems, each held together by the power of money,
each bent on maintaining its status and privilege: Parliament,
the law, the church, the civil service, manufacturers and merchants, financiers, doctors, philanthropists, all pursuing their
self-contained and limited aims, but all finally forming into a
vast complex of social, political, and economic oppression.
Beneath this structure lies the mass of unorganized men and
women on whom it battens. It is part of the greatness of *Bleak
House* that Chancery both contains within itself, as I have
tried to show, the essence of society viewed as a single entity
and yet is also seen as a system linked to other crucially important systems. This is brought out, for example, by the
juxtaposition of the consecutive chapters "Attorney and Client"
and "National and Domestic" (XXXIX, XL). They are concerned with the retention of power, and the worlds they describe are remarkably similar. The winnings of the legal game
circulate among the same group of players, and if one is more
successful today then it will probably be the turn of "the opposite attorney in the case" tomorrow. The benefits of political
rule are divided in the same way, for "Lord Coodle would go
out, Sir Thomas Doodle wouldn't come in, and there being
nobody in Great Britain (to speak of) except Coodle and
Doodle, there has been no Government" (XL). As the winnings here amount to much more than those of the legal game,
so the stakes are correspondingly higher, and it is necessary
for Doodle to throw "himself in an auriferous and malty shower"
(XL) on the country; but at last the coup is achieved and "Sir

Thomas Doodle has not only condescended to come in, but has done it handsomely, bringing in with him all his nephews, all his male cousins, and all his brothers-in-law" (XL). And that happy swing of the pendulum so characteristic of English political life will no doubt next time bring in Coodle instead.

This linking of one segment of society with another and, within society as a whole, individual with individual is crucial to the organization of *Bleak House*. Dickens himself makes this clear when he writes of Jo's effect on Mr. Jarndyce and Allan Woodcourt: "both thinking, much, how strangely Fate has entangled this rough outcast in the web of very different lives" (XLVII). Such a passage has overtones of melodrama, for bringing the unlikeliest people into close contact was a favorite device of popular fiction. But there is nothing of the fortuitous, of mere mystification for its own sake in the role that Jo has to play within the novel. He is, of course, part of the machinery of the plot, but he is also the characteristic product of Tom-all-Alone's and the cruelty, oppression, and neglect that has gone to make Tom's what it is. Tom is allowed to go to rack-and-ruin in his own way, but "he has his revenge" and Jo is the unwitting agent of that revenge:

There is not a drop of Tom's corrupted blood but propagates infection and contagion somewhere. . . . There is . . . not one obscenity or degradation about him, not an ignorance, not a wickedness . . . but shall work its retribution, through every order of society, up to . . . the highest of the high. (XLVI)

This passage is not simply propaganda for better drainage facilities for the poor. It cuts below the sense of isolation and alienation of modern society to expose the substratum of connection that exists between class and class, man and man. Unlike the connections of an idealized feudal society, however, with its ties of duty as well as obligation, the relationship here is something dark and fearful. The "cash nexus" is the cement of this society, holding capitalist and laborer, upper class and lower in an embrace of mutual hatred. And through it all, as always in Dickens, runs the ground swell of that theme of the inevitability of the revenge that must eventually engulf those who live comfortably while Tom dies of starvation. The ultimate tragedy is that the upheaval will destroy the good and evil alike. It is the innocent Esther whose beauty is destroyed by Jo, the helpless social victim, in the very act of trying to aid him. It is not enough to attribute their sufferings to the vagaries of life itself. They are the effects of an evil social system whose evil could be ameliorated by the application af energy, intelligence, and goodwill.

As Jo is linked to Esther, so Tom's is linked to Chancery. Tom-all-Alone's is, in Humphry House's words, the "moral type of a London slum,"[22] and as we should expect, "this desirable property is in Chancery" (XVI). In it, the evil and misery of the Court are given a physical reality, for the filth and horror that it contains both stem from and reflect the vileness of Chancery itself. Death, madness, and decay unite them and the society of which they are the type:

Twice, lately, there has been a crash and a cloud of dust, like the springing of a mine, in Tom-all-Alone's; and, each time, a house has fallen. These accidents have made a paragraph in the newspapers, and have filled a bed or two in the nearest hospital. . . . As several more houses are nearly ready to go, the next crash in Tom-all-Alone's may be expected to be a good one. (XVI)

Beneath their superficially different exteriors Chancery and Tom's are seen to be structures of the same kind, and so, in the same way, are the Lord Chancellor and Krook, that "dirty hanger-on and disowned relation of the law" (V). In this novel of appearance and reality the "respectable" institution is mirrored in the grotesque fantasy that is its only adequate form of representation. Krook himself says "I go to see my noble and learned brother pretty well every day. . . . There's no great odds betwixt us. We both grub on in a muddle" (V). Krook and his establishment are not, as they might first appear to be, a fantastic parody of Chancery. In its insane inhumanity that institution is not susceptible of such treatment. Its workings are simply being transferred to another area of society in a way that helps to illuminate, still further, its true nature and convince us of its all-pervasive influence. As Krook says, "And I have so many old parchmentses and papers in stock. And I have a liking for rust and must and cobwebs. And all's fish that comes to my net. And I can't abear to part with anything I once lay hold of . . . or to alter anything, or to have any sweeping, nor scouring, nor cleaning, nor repairing going on about me" (V). He also exemplifies the theme of false-seeming in a very direct way. His unavailing attempts to learn to read mean that the documents by which he is surrounded remain

[22] *Dickens World*, p. 193.

almost unintelligible to him, and so he can never fully grasp their meaning. Finally, his death, the fantastic nature of which can only be justified by its symbolic value, takes the form of a prophetic retribution, the doom that will overtake all evil institutions: "it is the same death eternally—inborn, inbred, engendered in the corrupted humours of the vicious body itself" (XXXII).

I have tried to show that Chancery enabled Dickens to undertake, in Edgar Johnson's words, "nothing less than an anatomy of modern society."[23] The large-scale organization was, as I have already pointed out, a new and characteristic feature of nineteenth-century life, but Dickens chose one that was of peculiar relevance to his own age. For Cardinal Newman, the "especial political evils of the day" stemmed from "that principle, which St. Paul calls the root of all evil, the love of money."[24] The power of Chancery to show that evil at work, both in the public and private sphere, is obvious enough. Again, that concern with unrealities and false appearances which lies at the heart of the Court and with which those who come into contact with it are so easily infected is part of another crucial aspect of modern society. It mirrors that sense of alienation which the great Victorian critics, including Carlyle, saw as something new in human life:

In no time, since the beginnings of Society, was the lot of those same dumb millions of toilers so entirely unbearable as it is even in the days now passing over us . . . to be heart-worn, weary, yet isolated, unrelated, girt-in with a cold universal laissez-faire.[25]

The bewilderments and impersonality of Chancery are those of the great world outside and, specifically, of Dickens' symbol of an alienated society, the great city as it first presents itself to Esther: "We drove slowly through the dirtiest and darkest streets that ever were seen in the world (I thought), and in such a distracting state of confusion that I wondered how the people kept their senses" (III). As Hillis Miller remarks, Dickens sees the world as a totality of separate identities, and "the concrete embodiment of this totality is the great modern commercial city, made up of millions of people all connected to one another without knowing it, and yet separated from one

[23] *Charles Dickens: His Tragedy and Triumph*, II, 743.
[24] *Apologia Pro Vita Sua* (London: Everyman's Library, 1912), p. 175.
[25] *Past and Present*, ed. A. D. M. Hughes (Oxford: Clarendon Press, 1918), p. 190.

another and living in isolation and secrecy."[26] An example of this is little Charley, forced into adulthood by her father's death, leaving her brother and sister locked in their room while she goes off to earn their living. Despite some help from neighbors, she is a figure of complete isolation: "I don't know where she was going, but we saw her run . . . through a covered way at the bottom of the court; and melt into the city's strife and sound, like a dewdrop in an ocean" (XV). But, as Miller realizes in the passage quoted above, such individuals are connected with each other although they do not know it, and finally, Chancery enables Dickens to show this also. For the members of a modern capitalist society are held together in a vastly complex web of economic interdependence. The necessity and the desire for money are the driving forces of such a society and without them it would collapse in upon itself, for it has no other system of humanized or spiritualized social values by which it might be sustained. And so Dickens stresses this unity beneath a seeming disparity again and again. The worlds of the law, government, philanthropy, and religion; Bleak House, the place in Lincolnshire, and Tom-all-Alone's; individuals from Sir Leicester down to Jo—all are brought together through the working of money in Chancery.

Perhaps, now, it may be possible to attempt an answer to the question I posed earlier in this study: what kind of novel is it whose primary interest does not lie in the presentation of the inner life of its one or two major characters? My analysis of the role of Chancery in *Bleak House* has, I hope, clarified this point somewhat. Our attention is held here by characters rather than by character itself, but the word characters does not deserve to be enclosed by quotation marks. We are not dealing with a set of unreal grotesques, aimlessly jigging about in an empty universe. There may not be much psychological subtlety in Esther, Mr. Jarndyce, and the rest, but they are real enough to engage our sympathy. And the setting in which they are embedded lives triumphantly through the concreteness of its detail, while involving us emotionally and intellectually in the layers of its social and symbolic meanings. What I wish to argue, in fact, is that *Bleak House* is a novel that draws its suggestiveness not so much from any significance that may inhere in its characters, but rather from the fact that these characters are enclosed in a significant setting.

[26] *Charles Dickens: The World of his Novels* (London: Oxford University Press, 1958), p. xv.

My meaning may be made clearer by the example of Rick. His corruption and death does, I think, impress us as a tragedy, but this sense of tragedy hardly arises from the contemplation of his character alone. He is conventionally gay, handsome, and brave, but without any of that depth of personality which would make him interesting in his own right. His death gains its force from the reality of the circumstances with which he becomes involved. We see his bright, emblematic figure constantly in *relationship* to other things: to the lowering presence of Chancery, to Miss Flite—never thinking "what a fatal link was riveting between his fresh youth and her faded age" (XXIII)—to, perhaps most memorably of all, Mr. Vholes:

I never shall forget those two seated side by side in the lantern's light; Richard, all flush and fire and laughter . . . Mr. Vholes, quite still, black-gloved, and buttoned-up, looking at him as if he were looking at his prey and charming it. I have before me the whole picture . . . and the driving away at speed to Jarndyce and Jarndyce. (XXXVII)

Rick, however, is no more important than half-a-dozen other characters who gain their main interest from their relationship to each other and the world of the novel which they inhabit. It is this inclusiveness and the reservation of the deepest levels of insight for a setting rather than for individuals which gives *Bleak House* its claim to be called a true social novel.

CHAPTER SIX

The Darkening World

"We admit that Mr. Dickens has a mission, but it is to make the world grin, not to recreate and rehabilitate society." The writer who expressed this opinion in the *Saturday Review* of July 4, 1857,[1] was voicing a complaint, in this instance of *Little Dorrit*, which was made with great force and frequency of Dickens' novels from *Bleak House* onward. Such a view of Dickens' later work could be adopted for more than one reason. Many were disappointed by what they thought of as an almost willful abandonment of that vein of high-spirited fun which constituted, for them, his true genius. The Jamesian insistence of others on the purity of the novel form and their dislike of its being used as a vehicle of didacticism were often based on nothing more than a hatred of the ideas that were being propagated. For, as G. H. Ford has pointed out,[2] with creations such as Mrs. Jellyby and the Court of Chancery, Dickens was capable of enraging liberals and conservatives in the course of a single book. But perhaps most important of all was the feeling that such criticism was no longer necessary. The social novels of the Hungry Forties had no doubt been useful in bringing many gross abuses to light, but the worst evils of that period had been overcome and England was becoming a much more prosperous country. The fact that between 1851 and 1871 more than a million people were employed as domestic servants is convincing proof of the prosperity of the middle classes, although we may be permitted a passing thought for the standard of life of the servants themselves, a far from negligible proportion of the country's population. Whatever the true facts, there was a widespread feeling among those social classes fortunate enough to be sharing in it that England had entered on a new era of wealth and well-being.

[1] IV, 15.
[2] *Dickens and His Readers* (New York: The Norton Library, 1965), p. 100.

It is worthwhile, however, to look at a few points that help to make our picture of the period a little darker than it probably appeared to some of its luckier contemporaries. Between 1851 and 1871, for example, there was a rise in the death rate, and the same twenty years saw an increase in other social evils. In *Das Kapital* Marx discusses the case of a railway disaster—reported in *Reynolds' Newspaper* of January, 1866—which was "attributed to negligence on the part of the railwaymen concerned. These testified unanimously to the effect that till ten or twelve years before they had worked for only 8 hours a day. During the last 5 or 6 years, their working time had been screwed up to 14, 18, and even 20 hours."[3] There was a large section of the community which remained relatively untouched by the new prosperity. The condition of the more highly skilled and self-conscious members of the working class did improve and with this improvement came respectability. By the 1860's their unions had begun to acquire a reputation for responsibility, but as one economic historian has pointed out, the position of the poorest was very different. When they struck, "their strikes were broken in detail. . . . They subsisted darkly and violently in the slums of the cities, which for all Chadwick's battles were still squalid and insanitary."[4] Chadwick's famous sanitary report was presented in 1842, but it was not until six years later, in 1848, that the Public Health Act for which it had called was passed, and this was only "a poor shadow of the measure Chadwick and other 'sanitary' reformers had worked for."[5] My earlier point of the importance of London in forming the creative Victorian's view of his own society is relevant here. Most of its industries, such as piecework tailoring, were not susceptible to union organization, and there is real evidence that sections of the capital's life underwent no radical improvement throughout the nineteenth century. This was the conclusion of Booth's *Life and Labour of the People of London,* based on statistics gathered between 1881 and 1891, as summed up by Beatrice Webb.

The authoritative demonstration—a fact which could not be gainsaid after the publication of Charles Booth's tables—that as many as 30

---

[3] *Das Kapital* (London: Allen and Unwin, 1928), p. 256 n. 1.

[4] Edith Batho and Banamy Dobrée, *The Victorians and After* (London: Cresset Press, 1938), p. 139.

[5] *The Sanitary Condition of the Labouring Population of Gt. Britain,* ed. M. W. Flinn (Edinburgh: University Press, 1965), p. 1.

per cent of the inhabitants of the richest as well the largest city in
the world lived actually at or beneath the level of bare subsistence—
came as a shock to the governing class.[6]

With the pages of Booth's report, we seem to be transported
back into the world pictured by the documentary agitation of
the 1840's.

Further than this, an official return, made in 1889, gives over 40,000
children in the London Board Schools, or nearly 10 per cent of the
number on the roll, as habitually attending in want of food, to which
the number returns from Voluntary schools add about 11,000 in the
same condition. . . . Puny, pale-faced, scantily clad and badly shod,
these small and feeble folk may be found sitting limp and chill on
the school benches in all the poorer parts of London.[7]

Perhaps we should be grateful for the fact that these children
were shod, however badly, and were to be found sitting on
school benches rather than roaming wild in the streets, but this
is a consolation to the coolly objective observer, not to the passionately humanitarian participator in life that Dickens was.
Every year that passed without radical social change was another year of suffering for countless thousands, a suffering
made real to Dickens by his never-ending concern for the
individual.

The comfort of Dickens' life could not insulate him from
the world about him. His restless nocturnal wanderings, his
fascination with the darker aspects of city life, his philanthropic
zeal and intense sympathy for human misery, all combined to
prevent him from succumbing to a complacent view of his society. But as he grew older, although he lost none of his anger
at particular examples of suffering and injustice, Dickens became more concerned with the general ethos of his period. Even
if we admit, as we must, that the balance of poverty and riches
had changed since the 1840's, there was still much that Dickens
came to hate in the spirit of the fifties and sixties. He was fully
alive to facts that to the average man were either obscured by
prosperity or neutralized by indifference.

The prisons, the asylums, the coffin-ships . . . the curiosities of City
finance, the crisis of 1857, the Overend and Gurney scandal of 1866,
the perpetual and unsavoury bankruptcies, odd little episodes such as
that in which the financial editor of *The Times* became involved in
the meshes of "Baron" Grant, and the Thunderer found itself in the

[6] *My Apprenticeship* (London: Longmans, n.d.), p. 247.
[7] *Ibid.*, p. 248 n. 1.

cats-paw of a shady financier. In so golden an age, these things passed, censured, but rarely amended.[8]

Dickens came more and more to view his society as a muddle of greed, selfishness, snobbery, and bungling inefficiency, and this feeling came to a head with the series of administrative scandals that emerged from the conduct of the Crimean War. These scandals induced widespread emotions of shame and indignation, but it is surely a tribute to the ingrained privilege and complacency of Victorian society that they did not shake it to its foundations. After all the sound and fury of public rage, the Report of Roebuck's Select Committee on the condition of the army before Sebastapol was, in the words of Asa Briggs, "not as damning a document as it might have been, for Roebuck's draft was turned down and a far more gentle document by Seymour accepted in its place."[9] In fact, no really new action emerged from the committee's work. Even if it had, it would have met, as Dickens knew, "the resistance of all the phalanx, who have an interest in corruption and mismanagement . . . the resistance of a struggle against death."[10] Dickens himself admitted that he was "full of mixed feelings about the war" and he was not entirely free of certain jingoistic desires "to cut the Emperor of Russia's throat," but he saw with "something like despair" how "the old cannon-smoke and blood-mists obscure the wrongs and sufferings of the people at home."[11] Important as this setback was, he saw beyond it to how the conduct of the war revealed to him the true nature of English society. It was a reality that he transmuted, in art, into the sinister farce of the Circumlocution Office and which, in life, evoked those great letters to Forster on the Condition of England Question:

A country which is discovered to be in this tremendous condition as to its war affairs; with an enormous black cloud of poverty in every town which is spreading and deepening every hour, and not one man in two thousand knowing anything about, or even believing in, its existence; with a non-working aristocracy, and a silent parliament, and everybody for himself and nobody for the rest; this is the prospect, and I think it a very deplorable one.[12]

[8] *The Victorians and After*, p. 138.
[9] *Victorian People* (London: Odhams Press, 1954), p. 87.
[10] Letter to W. C. Macready, June 30, 1855, in *Letters*, ed. Walter Dexter (London: Nonesuch Press, 1938), II, 675.
[11] Letter to Hon. Mrs. Richard Watson, Nov. 1, 1854, in *Letters*, II, 603.
[12] April 27, 1855, in *Letters*, II, 655.

The seriousness with which Dickens regarded the situation is shown by the support he gave to the Administrative Reform Association, which he joined in 1855. He usually regarded his work as his main field of action, but he felt, for a time, that the gravity of his country's problems was such that they demanded some more direct form of participation. And he also felt that his reformism was demanded directly of him by the temper of the times. In a letter to Miss Coutts of May, 1855, he expresses both his view that the people will not bear their injustices much longer and his desire to "interpose something between them and their wrath":

For this reason solely, I am a Reformer heart and soul. I have nothing to gain—everything to lose (for public quiet is my bread)—but I am in desperate earnest, because I know it is a desperate case.[13]

Dickens always remained too socially committed to regard despair and withdrawal in the face of difficult problems as anything other than a nerveless reaction, but despite his attempts to take some kind of practical steps, the political difficulties of this time often reduced him to a condition very close to hopelessness:

I really am serious in thinking . . . that representative government is become altogether a failure with us, that the English gentilities and subserviences render the people unfit for it, and that the whole thing has broken down since that great seventeenth-century time, and has no hope in it.[14]

At the time he was writing *Little Dorrit* we find Dickens in a state of great distress at the social and political faults of his society. But, combined with the stress of this dissatisfaction with the outside world, Dickens had to bear the weight of acute personal problems. I have already pointed out the peculiar intimacy between Dickens' inner life and that of his times. I have suggested that his experience in the blacking factory was a paradigm of the experience of thousands of people caught up in the blind forces of industrial capitalism. And now we find him again being forced to endure a psychological crisis that did, nevertheless, through its painful results enable him to understand at a more conscious level some of the deepest psychic stresses of the period of upheaval in which he lived.

---

13 In *Letters*, II, 660.
14 Letter to Forster, Sept. 30, 1855, in *Letters*, II, 693.

"We call it a Society; but go about professing openly the totallest separation, isolation."[15] This is Carlyle's dramatic judgment of his period, but the words he uses to describe the sufferings of the modern worker caught up in this system are an equally accurate description of Dickens at this climactic period of his life: "heart-worn, weary, yet isolated, unrelated."[16] How did the great Dickens, famous and surrounded by friends, come to be in such a condition? The restless unhappiness that began to be a marked feature of his character in the early fifties arose from a variety of causes. For one thing, the facts of the world in which he found himself were enough to cause at least dissatisfaction to a man as socially conscious as Dickens. Again, although the pain may have been muffled by the exciting years of early fame, it is doubtful if he ever fully recovered from the psychological shock of the blacking-factory episode. The evidence for the intensity with which Dickens always regarded this experience is too well-known to need detailed recounting here. It remained completely unknown to Dickens' family and intimate friends until its revelation, after his death, in Forster's biography. And the tone of the autobiographical fragment in which he told the story to his only confidante, Forster, in 1847 is amazingly bitter so many years after the event: "It is wonderful to me how I could have been so easily cast away at such an age. . . . No words can express the secret agony of my soul as I sunk into this companionship. . . . My whole nature was so penetrated with the grief and humiliation of such considerations that, even now—famous and caressed and happy— I often forget in my dreams that I have a dear wife and children—even that I am a man—and wander desolately back to that time of my life."[17] But now, with the knowledge that "the skeleton in my domestic closet is becoming a pretty big one,"[18] that he and his wife were basically unsuited to each other, he had an adult and rational reason for serious unhappiness. The combined weight of these public and private troubles seemed sometimes intolerable, as the question we find him asking in a letter to Forster of January, 1855, clearly shows: "Why is it, that as with poor David, a sense comes always crushing on me now, when I fall

[15] *Past and Present*, ed. A. D. M. Hughes (Oxford: Clarendon Press, 1918), p. 132.
[16] *Ibid.*, p. 190.
[17] See Forster's *The Life of Charles Dickens* (London: Everyman's Library, 1948), Vol. I, chap. ii, "Hard Experiences in Boyhood."
[18] Letter to Forster, 1856, in *Letters*, II, 765.

into low spirits, as of one happiness I have missed in life, and one friend and companion I have never made?"[19]

A letter he was to receive a month later provides part of the answer. That letter was from Mrs. Winter, who, as Maria Beadnell, had been the great love of Dickens' early manhood. As the Crimean War had brought to a climax his involvement with public affairs, so this reestablishment of such an important relationship caused a crisis in his personal life. That his unhappy love affair with Maria Beadnell was one of the crucial experiences of Dickens' life is made clear by the state of almost hysterical excitement into which her letter threw him. Whatever may be true of his art, in his life Dickens strove constantly to keep the wildness of his nature in check by the exercise of self-discipline and common sense, or to channel it into high spirits and strenuous outside activity. His common sense reasserted itself in the way in which he kept Mrs. Winter at bay, firmly yet kindly, after the shattering of his dreams involved in their first meeting. But for the moment he was beside himself, and the man of forty-three indulged in the romantic fancies of a boy. That the memories of that youthful time had continued to haunt Dickens in the midst of his fame and fortune is shown by an early letter to Mrs. Winter:

And I have gone over that ground within these twelve months hoping it was not ungrateful to consider whether any reputation the world can bestow is repayment to a man for the loss of such a vision of his youth as mine.[20]

Our knowledge of his passionate character, burning ambition, and youthful feeling of insecurity would be enough to tell us what this affair must have meant to Dickens; but it is probably best described in the words of his rebuke to Forster:

I don't quite apprehend what you mean by my over-rating the strength of the feeling of five-and-twenty years ago. If you mean of my own feeling, and will only think what the desperate intensity of my nature is . . . then you are wrong, because nothing can exaggerate that. . . . To see the mere cause of it all, now, loosens my hold upon myself.[21]

It seems unlikely that Maria would ever have been capable of rising to such intensity of emotion, but whether she could

[19] *Letters*, II, 620–621.
[20] Feb. 22, 1855, in *Letters*, II, 634.
[21] Letter to Forster, *ca.* Dec., 1855, in *Letters*, II, 716.

or not is beside the point, for at her family's instigation, the relationship was broken off. And so Dickens felt himself to be the victim of another bitter rejection of whose social overtones he was this time conscious. His dismissal for purely personal reasons would have been a painful enough blow to his self-esteem, but that the trivia of class and money should have been allowed to interfere with the purity of his affection must have seemed the cruelest of irrelevancies. The inhuman had triumphed over the human, and what was to be one of the great themes of his art had once again made itself felt with terrible force in his life. But self-control asserted itself, and it seems as though Dickens, even at that very early age, was capable of putting away that side of life almost in the way that Arthur Clennam was to do. He was undoubtedly fond of his wife at the time of their marriage, and for many years afterwards, but Edgar Johnson has pointed out the difference in tone between the humorous and reasonable love letters he wrote to Catherine and the passionate outpourings evoked by Maria. Such feelings, however, had to find some outlet if they were denied their proper means of expression, and it seems impossible to doubt that they played a significant part in causing the restlessness and that aching sense of loss which overtook Dickens more and more in his maturity:

However strange it is to be never at rest, and never satisfied, and ever trying after something that is never reached, and to be always laden with plot and plan and care and worry, how clear it is that it must be. . . . It is much better to go on and fret, than to stop and fret. As to repose—for some men there's no such thing in this life.[22]

Can we not detect in this the authentic note of a specifically modern disorientation, the despair that cannot find at least some ease in the contemplation of an externally justified social or religious good? The personal misery of a Swift or Johnson, for example, is never that of a total isolation from God or man. What I am trying to suggest is that the facts of his life impressed upon Dickens a feeling of deep inner loneliness and that this gives him the status of a representative modern figure. The ceaseless rush of his activities—his philanthropic work, his theatricals, his public readings (significantly, the first of these took place shortly after the upheavals I have been discussing)—has all the marks of Arnold's "strange disease of modern life."

[22] Letter to Forster, April, 1856, in *Letters*, II, 765.

A sense of terror seems to lurk behind so much action. The great Victorian critics return so frequently to the themes of social responsibility and class solidarity that we begin to suspect they did so partly because they realized how much the greed and selfishness of their civilization had made them already lost causes. And, similarly, we suspect in Dickens a fleeing from the emptiness he felt yawning within him. It was in 1854, Forster tells us, that he first made use of a description from *David Copperfield* to characterize his own life: "the so happy and yet so unhappy existence which seeks its realities in unrealities, and finds its dangerous comfort in a perpetual escape from the disappointment of heart around it."[23] Does not the phrase seeking "its realities in unrealities" sum up the condition of the soul of man under capitalism?

In a broadcast talk given some fifteen years ago, E. M. Forster advised those of his listeners who did not form part of that tiny minority to whom their work was a joy to heed the claims of leisure. The politicians exhort those who turn a screw every ten seconds in a factory or add up rows of figures at an office desk to turn yet more screws and add up yet more rows of figures. But to do so at the cost of making in-roads into reserves of vitality is to court a stagnation far worse than a purely economic one. To follow Forster in his basic creed, one that is difficult to justify on any philosophic or religious grounds, it seems that for modern man the end of life must be sought in personal relations. The complexities of the outside world make social and political involvement a perilous exercise. But the very triumphs of industrial capitalism militate against human contact. Mass production floods our lives with a host of cheap and sometimes useful gadgets that frequently threaten to overwhelm them. The question, as Matthew Arnold realized, is one of means and ends.[24] The car and the television set are pieces of Machinery, things to be used by us for what should always be specifically human purposes. The pursuit of the object or, as in Dickens' day, of money for its own sake reduces life to a mechanical exercise that "seeks its realities in unrealities." The evil inherent in such dehumanization is, of course, a major theme of Dickens. We find it exemplified in Mr. Dombey, Merdle, the Veneerings, and a host of other characters who

[23] *Life of Charles Dickens*, II, 196.
[24] See *Culture and Anarchy*, ed. J. Dover Wilson (Cambridge Paperback, 1963), chap. i, "Sweetness and Light."

seek happiness in the externals of wealth, power, social success, and self-aggrandizement. John Forster shows that the fundamental health of Dickens' nature made his fevered existence unsatisfactory to him: "Not his genius only, but his whole nature, was too exclusively made up of sympathy for, and with, the real in its most intense form."[25] It is the tension arising from his own conflict which gives Dickens the power to chart the confused wanderings of the soul of man through the maze of modern society in search of the true nature of reality.

This is the background of public and private events from which the novels of Dickens' last period will emerge. There is a continuity of the outer and inner life here which is surely remarkable. Social, political, and personal factors weld outer and inner reality into a predominantly somber unity of thought and feeling. Didacticism and creative autonomy, life and art, will now operate together. Out of Dickens' grappling with his society and with himself will come an art with the beauty of self-containment whose self-consistent world will yet anatomize modern life. His struggle could never belong to himself alone; its significance made it the property of the nineteenth century, and the depth of its roots in the life of his time allowed it to find expression in symbolism, poetry, and mythology. We will not be surprised to find, I think, that this symbolism, poetry, and mythology will usually be dark and foreboding.

[25] *Life of Charles Dickens*, II, 200.

CHAPTER SEVEN

The Years of Achievement

Little Dorrit

The profundity and complexity of *Little Dorrit* is such that it does not easily yield the depth of its meaning. The conjunction of seemingly inexplicable absolutes of good and evil is liable to delude us into the belief that we are dealing with a world of melodrama. But this apparent simplicity is only the oblique reflection of that dramatic confrontation of moral forces whose subterranean life forms part of the book's motive power. Once we realize this, the scope of the dilemmas with which it deals is clearly so wide that the difficulty of uncovering a final core of unifying truth seems immense. The universe of its moral fable seems too vast to be held in the mind in all its multifarious detail. The parts may be grasped, but the whole seems to escape us. Edgar Johnson, for example, calls his critical chapter on this work "The Prison of Society,"[1] while for Lionel Trilling its significance lies more on the personal or religious plane. For him, Little Dorrit's physical smallness is the sign that "she not only is the Child of the Marshalsea . . . but also the Child of the Parable."[2]

Little Dorrit resists the easy formulation and the snap judgment, as does life itself, but I would suggest that the chief memory it leaves is of a sense of overwhelming loneliness. That loneliness does, at any rate, afflict almost all the novel's characters can be shown by these few examples. For Blandois and Miss Wade it is a self-adopted sign of their perverse rejection of social contact. Blandois is against any society, and his final self-justification is, in Lionel Trilling's words, "the classic social rationalization: Society has made him what he is; he does in

[1] *Charles Dickens: His Tragedy and Triumph* (London: Gollancz, 1953), II, 883.
[2] "Little Dorrit," *Kenyon Review*, XV (Autumn, 1953), 590.

his own person only what society does in its corporate form
and with its corporate self-justification."[3] Miss Wade's determination to misinterpret every kindness offered her is set out
in detail in her own tale, which Dickens mentions in a letter to
Forster:

> With Miss Wade I had an idea, which I thought a new one, of
> making the introduced story so fit into surroundings impossible of
> separation from the main story, as to make the blood of the book
> circulate through both.[4]

This is an interesting comment on technique, but it also does
something to corroborate the view I am putting forward here.
Flora and Mr. F.'s Aunt are meant to be comic expressions of
the same isolation. For Angus Wilson, Mrs. Finching passes
the "great test of divine madness in Dickens' world—the use of
the English language to express a solitary, cut-off universe, the
mark of Mrs. Gamp or Flora Finching or Mrs. Nickleby."[5] But,
apart from one or two superb flights, she does not seem to be
in the same class as Mrs. Gamp as far as humor is concerned,
although she is not far behind her in terms of alienation
from reality. And Mr. F's Aunt is perhaps the most frightening
example of complete solitude that Dickens ever created. Little
Dorrit is lonely in her love for Arthur Clennam; Mr. Dorrit is
trapped in his own self-approval; while Mrs. Clennam inhabits
a physical as well as a mental prison:

> "Look round this room. If it is any compensation for my long con-
> finement within these narrow limits . . . that while I am shut up from
> all pleasant change, I am also shut up from the knowledge of some
> things that I may prefer to avoid knowing, why should you, of all
> men, grudge me that relief?" (Bk. 1, XV)

If I am correct in my belief that spiritual loneliness, lack of
communication, is an organizing force in *Little Dorrit*, then the
importance of Arthur Clennam's role in the novel becomes clear.
When we look at him with this theme in mind, we see with
what illuminating power the "blood of the book" flows through
him. He lives in his own right, but his relationship with the fictional universe of which he is a part is similar to that of Dickens
and the nineteenth century as a whole. There is an identity

[3] *Ibid.*, pp. 583–584.
[4] Dated 1856, in *Letters*, ed. Walter Dexter (London: Nonesuch Press,
1938), II, 776.
[5] "Charles Dickens: A Haunting," in *The Dickens Critics*, ed. G. H.
Ford and Lauriat Lane (Ithaca: Cornell University Press, 1961), p. 377.

between the psychic life of the men and the period which gives them both the stature of representative figures. Clennam is the chief wanderer on that painful journey that Dickens now sees— in one of those groups of images which is such a distinctive feature of the style of *Little Dorrit*—as summing up the nature of human existence: "climbing the dusty hills and toiling along the weary plains . . . move all we restless travellers through the pilgrimage of life" (Bk. 1, II).

The subtlety with which Arthur is formed for his part makes it impossible for us not to perceive this more than personal significance. Even the external details of his life work toward the creation of a strong sense of isolation. His twenty years of solitary exile in China and his return to a strange London are used by Dickens to make his actual journeyings symbolic of his inner state. Thus, when he is asked by Mr. Meagles if he has made up his mind where to go next, now that they are free of their imprisoning quarantine, he replies, "Indeed, no. I am such a waif and stray everywhere, that I am liable to be drifted where any current may set" (Bk. 1, II). He is as solitary a figure in the great city as he ever was abroad.

Clennam was left alone at the corner of Barbican. He had no inten- tion of presenting himself in his mother's dismal room that night, and could not have felt more depressed and cast away if he had been in a wilderness. (Bk. 1, XIII)

Arthur is the child of nineteenth-century greed and materialism, cloaked under a veil of religious repression. His parents' re- ligion was "a gloomy sacrifice of tastes and sympathies that were never their own, offered up as a part of a bargain for the se- curity of their possessions" (Bk. 1, II). As such, he is a victim, a something to be used from his earliest years. His human worth is slighted in the disregard of his individuality, and he is treated as nothing more than a pawn in a terrible game of hatred and revenge. His first adult attempt to assume his own personality by falling in love with Flora is crushed, and he is sent into an exile that is as much spiritual and emotional as physical. The system under which he has been brought up cannot make room for the free play of love. The stunted creatures who fit them- selves onto its Procrustean bed feel threatened by any full development of human character. Either this flowering of per- sonality in their enemies must be crushed or they must be banished.

The external forces that shape Clennam's life are almost enough to submerge his individuality. He would, presumably, have endured his banishment for much more than twenty years if his father's death had not released him, and by the time he is given his freedom, his power of choice is almost completely eroded. And yet he still retains an element of personal worth.

It had been the uniform tendency of this man's life—so much was wanting in it to think about, so much that might have been better directed and happier to speculate upon—to make him a dreamer after all. (Bk. 1, III)

The man of deep emotion who feels himself to be part of a society concerned only with means rather than ends may retreat from the impossibility of meaningful collective action into a world of private relationships as the only way of keeping his sense of identity alive. The inhuman constraint of Arthur's existence has excluded even this possibility. If the ideal human life consists of the interaction of subjective expression, personal relations, and social connection, then Arthur is at the farthest remove from reality. He inhabits a world of fantasy because "he was a man who had, deep-rooted in his nature, a belief in all the gentle and good things his life had been without" (Bk. 1, XIII). Denied objective expression, these emotions would wither and die were they not nourished by the springs of imagination. Profoundly unsatisfactory as such a mode of being is, it still remains superior to the way of life that rejects the claims of feeling altogether. But it is an index of the evil of a materialistic society that the human spirit is put to such shifts in order to preserve some part of itself.

The stratagems that enable the spirit to win its bitter triumphs constitute for Dickens one of the deepest mysteries of existence. That its triumphs often are bitter is shown by the price exacted from Arthur for his "inner immigration." His withdrawal into a world of dreams is both a reality and an unreality: a reality in the sense that he knows of no other method of keeping the springs of his personality pure, and an unreality in that he is obviously divorced from the world about him. And so when he comes to give objective form to the love that he has such a profound need to express, his choice falls on the romantic figure of Pet Meagles, and he is blind to what Little Dorrit feels for him. Clennam's pilgrimage is that of a man moving slowly away from fantasy—his love for Pet, his idea that he can defeat the Circumlocution Office, his ultimate delusion by the power of money—into the clear light of reality by means of suffering. The last stage of this journey comes when he fully understands Little Dorrit's love, the knowledge of which is given to him as an act of grace by John Chivery. The realization of his own blindness completes his necessary expiation, and it is only then that the chains of his bondage to a world of phantoms are completely loosened.

This ability of the human soul to hold fast to some essential piece of self-truth is connected with the mysterious relationship, of as great an interest as ever to Dickens, between character and environment. It is doubtful if Dickens' intellectual position on this question changed much over the years. What did change, and develop, was his artistic power of embodying his insights. In *Little Dorrit* we find characters who exemplify absolutes of good and evil and those who respond to the pressures of their outside world. Blandois and Little Dorrit herself form the antipodes of the novel's moral universe, and neither is intrisically altered by the good and bad influences that form part of their environment; although it is worth noticing that Dickens does introduce, at two points, a darker note into the drawing of his heroine's character. One is at that moment when she cannot repress her instinctive dislike of John Chivery's attentions: "It was but a momentary look, inasmuch as she checked it. . . . But she felt what it had been, as he felt what it had been; and they stood looking at one another equally confused" (Bk. 1, XVIII). The other occurs when she hears of her father's good fortune and feels that it is hard that he should have to pay his debts after all his years in prison.

The prison, which could spoil so many things, had tainted Little Dorrit's mind no more than this. Engendered as the confusion was, in compassion for the poor prisoner, her father, it was the first speck Clennam had ever seen, it was the last speck Clennam ever saw, of the prison atmosphere upon her. (Bk. 1, XXXV)

They represent, on the one hand, part of the generally gloomy tone of the book, and on the other, the result of a fairly rigorous self-criticism. The second is obviously an attempt to mitigate the unreality, if such it be, of too perfect a goodness. Similarly, it has been pointed out that the Patriarch is a parody of all Dickens' benevolent old gentlemen, and Dickens also makes an effort to exorcise some of the father-child aspects of the relationship between Arthur and Amy. The thought of her marriage is made more acceptable by the fact that when Little Dorrit returned from abroad she "looked something more womanly than when she had gone away, and the ripening touch of the Italian sun was visible upon her face" (Bk. 2, XXIX). And the kiss Arthur remembers having given her when she had fainted is rather unlike that given to Mr. Jarndyce by Esther when she agrees to be his wife. He asks himself if it were "quite as he might have kissed her, if she had been conscious? No difference?" (Bk. 2, XXVII).

The passage about the one speck Clennam ever saw in Little Dorrit is all of a piece with, for example, that questioning of motive which is such a distinctive feature of *Little Dorrit*. Clennam's first visit to Flora is made under the pretext of aiding Little Dorrit, but "it is hardly necessary to add, that beyond all doubt he would have presented himself at Mr. Casby's door, if there had been no Little Dorrit in existence; for we all know how we all deceive ourselves—that is to say, how people in general, our profounder selves excepted, deceive themselves—as to motives of action" (Bk. 1, XIII). This is nowhere seen more significantly than in the connection Dickens clearly establishes between the faults of the generally amiable Mr. Meagles (who in any earlier book would surely have been nothing more than a good and simple man) and the evils of his society.

Clennam could not help speculating . . . whether there might be in the breast of this honest, affectionate, and cordial Mr. Meagles, any microscopic portion of the mustard-seed that had sprung up into the great tree of the Circumlocution Office. His curious sense of a general superiority to Daniel Doyce, which seemed to be founded, not so much on anything in Doyce's personal character, as on the mere fact of his being an originator and a man out of the beaten track of other men, suggested the idea. (Bk. 1, XVI)

Nevertheless, Blandois and Little Dorrit are essentially unchanged by the forces in the world about them. Dickens seems to imply that the inner reality of such people is too strongly marked to be encroached on by external influences. They are so deeply fulfilled by their commitment to either evil or good that to act at the behest of any other command would seem a kind of self-destruction. It is those who inhabit the no-man's-land of character who are most susceptible to the distracting pull of the contrary impulses that make up their little world. The most important of these hollow men is, of course, William Dorrit, flickering continually from one point to another on his moral compass. The formlessness of his character when he enters prison—in every difficulty the "irresolute fingers fluttered more and more ineffectually about the trembling lip" (Bk. 1, VI)—gradually hardens under its influence. His sentimentality, snobbery, selfish love of others, and sense of personal dignity are directed by nothing stronger than a fondness for his own comfort, and this makes him an easy prey to the debilitating influence of the Marshalsea. As we watch his deterioration, displayed in scenes of great comic and pathetic power, we are likely to recall the destruction of Rick by Chancery. With this comparison in mind, we realize what an advance in artistry *Little Dorrit* marks. Nothing in Rick's story can match Mr. Dorrit's protectiveness toward the brother he ruined, his patronage of Old Nandy, and, most subtle of all, his hint to Little Dorrit that she should not rebuff Young John's advances too harshly. The movement within this last scene begins from the pathetic attempt to clothe his intention in an anecdote; he was "so conscious all the time of that touch of shame, that he shrunk before his own knowledge of his meaning." He passes through "dead silence and stillness" and anger with his dinner, "laying down his knife and fork with a noise, taking things up sharply, biting at his bread as if he were offended with it," to the final "catch in his breath that was not so much a sob as an irrepressible sound of self-approval, the momentary outburst of a noble consciousness" (Bk. 1, XIX). This represents one of the great achievements of Dickens' art; but, as always, there remains that feeling of mystery in the face of human complexity: "Only the wisdom that holds the clue to all hearts . . . can surely know to what extent a man, especially a man brought down as this man had been, can impose upon himself" (Bk. 1, XIX).

It is obvious that the whole tendency of this discussion is to bring out the importance of character in understanding *Little Dorrit*. But it is character in a sense that is usually thought of as being un-Dickensian. The novel may lack the almost overwhelming presence of a Micawber or a Gamp, but it also lacks characters as flatly emblematic as Rick or Esther. The richly observed surface detail of Mr. Micawber is so comically satisfying that we grant him fullness of life out of our own pleasure. His reality stems from a kind of confidence trick. His physical presence and verbal opulence lie before us on the page, but the collaboration of our laughter is needed to bring him completely alive. William Dorrit may not have the immediate force of obsessive detail, but there is ample compensation to be found in the dramatic presentation of his inner conflicts. The self-deceit of Mr. Micawber is an eccentricity, and so merely comic; but that of William Dorrit is more than just one piece among many in an externally conceived jigsaw puzzle. It lies at the heart of his personality, and its subtle exploration gives it a pathetic, almost a tragic, power.

The acceptable goodness of Little Dorrit forces us to ask how it is that the impression she makes on us is so different from that of Esther Summerson. At first sight, there would seem to be a great similarity in their function as embodiments of selfless love and in their role as "little mother" to their respective circles. I have already pointed out that as part of the general somberness of *Little Dorrit*, Dickens is prepared to take a much tougher line than formerly with even his good characters, and this certainly helps to prevent his heroine from sharing Esther's cloying sweetness. The difference in their circumstances is important also. Esther is truly the "kind of domesticated fairy" (Bk. 1, XXII) that Clennam is so fearful of making of Little Dorrit, while Little Dorrit's struggle to help her family survive is waged against such desperate odds that it moves out of the realm of the domestic into that of the heroic. Again, as Esther trips about Bleak House, jingling the keys in her little basket, we feel that she has no organic connection with the world of which she is a part. She is a figure lifted from stock, a household goddess, and when tragedy strikes her in the destruction of her beauty we are moved, if at all, by the circumstances of the event rather than by anything more personal. We remain unoffended by Little Dorrit's physical smallness, not merely because, as Lionel Trilling shows, it is the outward sign of her spiritual grace, but also because it is explained in a way that connects her with her social world: Dickens describes "the retiring childish form, and the face in which he [Clennam] now saw years of insufficient food, if not of want" (Bk. 1, VIII).

She is, moreover, connected with her fictional universe in a way that is even more important than this. She shares, to a bitter degree, the loneliness that lies at the heart of the book, for she knows that her love is imprisoned by her family's selfishness and Clennam's ignorance. Until her final liberation in Arthur's love for her, she can never know the joy of being accepted for what she is rather than for what she does; and it is only then that the strength with which she is capable of feeling for others is given its full value. Yet it is her behavior in the face of neglect which makes Little Dorrit such a moving figure. Like many other Victorian heroines, Esther Summerson *stands for* the ideal of selfless domestic love, but Little

Dorrit *embodies* moral purity in a world whose evil is so great that it imparts a dignity to her solitary struggle. She has, indeed, the force of Plato's perfectly just man, a being fated—until her ultimate release—never to be truly understood.

The constant effort of this study is to show how, in his later novels, Dickens is continually striving to elaborate a form that will enable him to encompass as many of the private and public aspects of his society as possible. In *Dombey and Son,* he attempts to depict the opposition of material and spiritual values through the interplay of two large-scale characters, while *Bleak House* is fundamentally a novel of social organization. Its perhaps too rigidly composed structure depends mainly on the role of Chancery as a method of holding the characters in significant juxtaposition. The difficulties of this task may have absorbed too much of Dickens' creative energy, for the characters have not much interest in their own right. It is the weaving of external incident rather than personal psychology that holds our attention. I have already said enough to show that this is not at all true with *Little Dorrit.* Comparison with *Bleak House* may help to explain why.

My analysis of *Bleak House* shows, I think, that its plot tends to fall into several sections. There is a discontinuity between the theatrical elements, which seem to deal in mystery-making for its own sake, and the meaningful organizing structure of the Court of Chancery. It is from that central core that the book's true meaning emerges, but when we search for something similar in *Little Dorrit* we find it in the Circumlocution Office. And while it is true that the world of Chancery *is* the world of *Bleak House,* the Circumlocution Office constitutes only a part of the other novel. Chancery is a masterful device for bringing a great number of people together in fruitful relationships, but despite the spiritual and psychological effects it has on individuals, it remains something external, the great web in which the innocent and guilty alike are trapped. And, similarly, the fog symbolism has no organic connection with what it infects. The Court, the fog, and the people do not become more than disparate aspects of a total reality. Fog creeps into the heart of Chancery, the Court destroys the human heart and spirit; but both seem imposed, as brilliant intellectual conceptions, from the outside.

The meaning of that loneliness which I have stressed as such a vital theme in *Little Dorrit*—and the consequent importance this gives to character—may now begin to emerge. It presents us with one of the most profound examples of Dickens' constant transposition of social reality into the material of art. For him, this loneliness is nothing more nor less than the malaise of a whole society. Just before his triumphal attack on the Patriarch, Pancks describes what his existence has been as his employee:

"Neither will you find in Grubbers like myself, under Proprietors like this, pleasant qualities. I've been a Grubber from a boy. What has my life been? Fag and grind, fag and grind, turn the wheel, turn the wheel! I haven't been agreeable to myself, and I haven't been likely to be agreeable to anybody else. (Bk. 2, XXXII)

The mechanical imagery of this passage of rhetoric on behalf of the underprivileged makes it almost a dramatic equivalent of an analysis of the Marxist concept of alienation:

Men living in capitalist society are faced by a social order that, although it results from what they do, exerts a senseless constraint over them as if it were something purely physical presented to their senses.[6]

This state of spiritual desolation, which springs from specific causes, infiltrates the entire social world of *Little Dorrit*. The third chapter—ironically titled "Home"—depicts a complete identity between Clennam's inner condition and the London that he sees on a Sunday evening from the window of a coffee-house on Ludgate Hill. The physical horrors of the place are bad enough: "Fifty thousand lairs surrounded him where people lived so unwholesomely, that fair water put into their crowded rooms on Saturday night, would be corrupt on Sunday morning" (Bk. 1, III). But the inhuman restriction of men within an eternal cycle of "Fag and grind, fag and grind" seems even worse:

Everything was bolted and barred that could by possibility furnish relief to an over-worked people. . . . Nothing to see but streets, streets, streets. Nothing to breathe but streets, streets, streets. . . . Nothing for the spent toiler to do, but to compare the monotony of his seventh day with the monotony of his six days, think what a weary life he led, and make the best of it—or the worst, according to the probabilities. (Bk. 1, III)

[6] H. B. Acton, *The Illusion of the Epoch* (London: Cohen and West, 1955), p. 226.

Just as the American scenes of *Martin Chuzzlewit* transmute an observed reality into a self-consistent world of the imagination, so *Little Dorrit* is both an autonomous creation and a vision of the society from which it sprang. Its artistic power and the suggestiveness of its social criticism arise from the same cause: the fusion of its sense of public isolation and private loneliness, a fusion effected by the dominant prison image. It would be tiresome to give a complete catalog of the subtle ways in which Dickens keeps the idea of imprisonment so constantly before the reader's mind. The novel opens in the Marseilles prison and moves on to the scenes in quarantine before we get to the Marshalsea itself. Calais, the ruins of Rome, and the Convent of St. Bernard all have a prison-like air. The image recurs constantly, both in tiny personal details, such as Mr. Merdle clasping his wrist as though he were taking himself into custody, and in the widest social contexts: that, for example, of the kind of life lived by the Dorrits after their rise to fortune, when "it appeared on the whole, to Little Dorrit herself, that this same society in which they lived, greatly resembled a superior sort of Marshalsea" (Bk. 2, VII). Beyond this again we find, in a description of the sun, a comment on the very nature of life itself in this fictionalized universe: "For aslant across the city, over its jumbled roofs, and through the open tracery of its church towers, struck the long bright rays, bars of the prison of this lower world" (Bk. 2, XXX).

In *Little Dorrit*, prison is the physical setting both literally and metaphorically, a description of the characters' inner state and, uniting them in a totality of meaning, a symbol. We have seen how the Court of Chancery affected people spiritually, but from the outside. Externality of relationship is Dickens' method in *Bleak House*, an externality reflected in the complexities, sometimes mere complications, of its plot. The characters of *Little Dorrit*, on the other hand, are a microcosm of their social world, for each carries his own prison within him. In the world of the novel, enslavement in some degrading relationship or to some inhuman ideal almost seems to be man's inevitable fate. The desire for money and social position, self-aggrandizement, snobbery, false piety, the crushing weight of uncongenial labor, all play their part in breeding delusion and in destroying the flow of human sympathy.

An escape from this world, darkened everywhere by the shadow of the prison, is possible for only a very few, those who are free from the evil desires that permeate society. And it is

Dickens' constant intention throughout *Little Dorrit* to reveal the sheer extent of this corruption, as it clarifies itself in the general attitude toward Merdle:

All people knew (or thought they knew) that he had made himself immensely rich; and, for that reason alone, prostrated themselves before him, more degradedly and less excusably than the darkest savage creeps out of his hole in the ground to propitiate, in some log or reptile, the Deity of his benighted soul.

Nay, the high priests of this worship had the man before them as a protest against their meanness. The multitude worshipped on trust—though always distinctly knowing why—but the officiators at the altar had the man habitually in their view. They sat at his feasts, and he sat at theirs. There was a spectre always attendant on him, saying to these high priests, "Are such the signs you trust, and love to honour; this head, these eyes, this mode of speech, the tone and manner of this man? You are the levers of the Circumlocution Office, and the rulers of men. . . . if you are competent to judge aright the signs I never fail to show you when he appears among you, is your superior honesty your qualification?" (Bk. 2, XII)

With the figure of Merdle we again find Dickens working within the popular tradition, for this character is clearly based upon such figures as Hudson the Railway King, who first appeared in a fictional form in Robert Bell's *The Ladder of Gold*, published in 1850. But the superiority of Dickens' creation is made clear if we compare him with even the finest of these attempts, the character of Melmotte from Trollope's *The Way We Live Now*, published in 1875. The similarity of name and artistic function in these characters seems to warrant the assumption that Trollope must have drawn some of his inspiration from that novel, and it should be of interest to those who claim that Dickens was always out of date in his satirical rendering of contemporary types that his novel was the earlier by almost twenty years. Both are personifications of that rootless, money-worshipping, unprincipled spirit that seemed to their creators inseparable from the growth of laissez-faire capitalism. But Trollope, although he obviously disapproves of Melmotte, paints him in the crude, bold colors of the high-powered captain of industry. The man is harsh and overbearing, and these very qualities help to give him some positive force as a character. This may be true to life, but is it true to the effect that Trollope wishes to achieve within the artistic scheme of his work? Dickens' great man is very different.

He did not shine in company; he had not very much to say for himself; he was a reserved man; with . . . that particular kind of dull red colour in his cheeks which is rather stale than fresh. (Bk. 1, XXI)

Except in the power that derives from his wealth he is an entirely negative figure and lacks even the coarse, almost sensual pleasure in the consciousness of his own position which is enjoyed by Melmotte. He is the fitter symbol, in his drab joylessness, of the life-destroying pursuit of money which both writers are attacking. Dickens cuts below the fleshy surface of the typical merchant adventurer because he understands more profoundly than Trollope the utter worthlessness, both for the individual and society, of the values incarnated in such a figure. The depth of Dickens' understanding of the forces with which he is dealing is shown by the way in which Merdle's symbolic function is reinforced by every detail of his private and public life. Melmotte, for example, turns up in London with the kind of wife that any adventurer might have acquired on his travels. Madame Melmotte is neither interesting in her own right nor does she contribute anything to the scheme of the novel. Merdle, on the other hand, has a partner who is symbolized by her most important function.

This great and fortunate man had provided that extensive bosom, which required so much room to be unfeeling enough in, with a nest of crimson and gold some fifteen years before. It was not a bosom to repose upon, but it was a capital bosom to hang jewels upon. Mr. Merdle wanted something to hang jewels upon, and he bought it for the purpose. (Bk. 1, XXI)

The complete perversion of human values inherent in money worship is expressed here with an exactness and force of language that is quite beyond Trollope.

The public activities of both men have disastrous effects on the many people connected with them; but Trollope can only *tell* us about these activities, while Dickens is capable of embodying his social insights in a fully realized artistic form. On our first meeting with Mr. Merdle we learn that he may be suffering from some mysterious and vague illness:

Mr. Merdle's complaint. Society and he had so much to do with one another in all things else, that it is hard to imagine his complaint, if he had one, being solely his own affair. Had he that deep-seated recondite complaint, and did any doctor find it out? (Bk. 1, XXI)

Whenever he appears in the book, hints of this complaint hover behind him like a dark shadow, and they grow stronger and stronger until, with his suicide, we realize that his sickness is the expression of Mr. Merdle's complete moral and spiritual nullity. And with that comes the knowledge that his sickness is the sickness of a whole society, whose feverish pursuit of wealth can be seen as an attempt to escape from self-hatred and the fear of death. Again, there is a crucial difference in the inclusiveness of the visions in which Trollope and Dickens attempt to embody the evil aspects of their respective societies. This is made clear by Trollope's description of those who attended Melmotte's banquet for the Emperor of China.

The existing Cabinet was existing, and though there were two or three members of it who could not have got themselves elected at a single unpolitical club in London, they had a right to their seats at Melmotte's table. (XXXV)

He obviously wishes us to feel that this is the strongest possible condemnation he can make of such unsavory characters, but he fails to realize that in other parts of the novel he shows us the very members of such clubs displaying the greed, selfishness, and snobbery of the world he is trying so hard to criticize. Trollope's artistic and personal conception of society is fragmented. In the midst of all the cupidity and materialism of his world there are still institutions, as opposed to merely individuals, which manage to maintain some sense of decency and human values. Such self-contradictory admissions weaken the all-embracing force of the novelist's world. In *Little Dorrit*, the angle of Dickens' denunciatory vision is wide enough to include all but a few of the humblest and simplest of individuals. His description of a dinner given in Merdle's Harley Street Establishment forms an apt example of this:

There were . . . magnates from the Commons and magnates from the Lords, magnates from the bench and magnates from the bar, Bishop magnates, Treasury magnates, Horse Guard magnates, Admiralty magnates,—all the magnates that keep us going, and sometimes trip us up. (Bk. 1, XXI)

Dickens understands that the infection with which he is dealing in *Little Dorrit* is contagious and that its effects cannot be isolated in one section of society alone. He would have seen Melmotte's banquet table and clubland as merely two views of the same social reality.

Perhaps this brief discussion justifies the point that Merdle should not be seen primarily as a man, but as the specific realization of a general social disease.

He, the uncouth object of such wide-spread adulation, the sitter at
great men's feasts, the roc's egg of great ladies' assemblies, the sub-
duer of exclusiveness, the leveller of pride, the patron of patrons,
the bargain-driver with a Minister for Lordships of the Circumlocution Office, the recipient of more acknowledgement within some ten
or fifteen years, at most, than had been bestowed in England upon
all peaceful public benefactors, and upon all the leaders of all the
Arts and Sciences, with all their works to testify for them, during two
centuries at least. (Bk. 2, XXVI)

Merdle represents, in fact, that rage for wealth which, as we
have seen, was taken to be the dominant fact of their age by
most of the best minds of the nineteenth century, and through
him Dickens is able to show society's imprisonment by the desire for money at every level. If we understand Merdle in this
way, we can perceive that his hold on government, which is
presented in the novel through the insanity of a single representative institution, is not a matter of personal control. The
Circumlocution Office is not the victim of the conspiratorial
view of public affairs. This wonderful fantasy whose richness
of detail makes it, for me, at once funnier and more serious than
the allegorical structures of Kafka is corrupted by the personal
evil of its own members. When Merdle and Treasury meet we
are involved not in the simple bribing of one individual by
another, but in the participation of an evil that seems to
Dickens to be of the very nature of society as it exists in a capitalist world.

It is only total innocence or supreme willpower that can escape this evil, but even they are subjected to severe strains in
the process. Lionel Trilling argues that Daniel Doyce and Little
Dorrit are free because they represent "the nonpersonal will in
which shall be our peace."[7] But for all the power that stems
from her selfless love for others, Little Dorrit's environment is
perverted enough to prevent her from enjoying the pure air of
complete reality. She has to draw on fantasy, however innocent
it may be, to enable her to play her part in the Marshalsea: "I
never was at a party in my life. . . . I hope there is no harm
in it. I could never have been of any use, if I had not pretended
a little" (Bk. 1, XIV). And her new life of wealth and travel
only accentuates the phantom aspects of her existence.

All that she saw was new and wonderful, but it was not real. . . . The
more surprising the scenes, the more they resembled the unreality of

7 "Little Dorrit", p. 590.

her own inner life. . . . Even the old mean Marshalsea was shaken to its foundations, when she pictured it without her father. (Bk. 2, IV)

It is only when her love is met on equal terms by that of a Clennam purified by suffering that she is able finally to shake them off.

The pressures of the external world can be overcome, but not by means of social change. The personal nature of their salvation is symbolized as Little Dorrit and her husband walk "out of the church alone. They paused for a moment on the steps of the portico, looking at the fresh perspective of the street in the autumn morning sun's bright rays, and then went down." They went down "into a modest life of usefulness and happiness," but one in which "as they passed along in sunshine and shade, the noisy and the eager, and the arrogant and the froward and the vain, fretted, and chafed, and made their usual uproar" (Bk. 2, XXXIV).

Great Expectations

Most men feel the need to justify their lives to themselves. The great artist is perhaps an exception to this: the reason for his existence lies so obviously in the works that he is driven to create. Dickens honored his creative demon as much as any Lawrence in his determination to allow his work to take precedence over every other aspect of his life. We can discover him taking an almost ivory-towered delight in the technical difficulties that he sets himself. Yet the work itself was never enough. It had to be read, and so give Dickens' acute social consciousness the assurance that it fulfilled an objective function. Entertainment, social amelioration, the sustenance of the imaginatively deprived, these all played their part in giving point to his labors. But at this distance in time the books seem to divulge another, and perhaps more serious, layer of meaning. They form a monument to a great and twofold struggle for understanding. From *Martin Chuzzlewit* onward, we see Dickens grappling with his age in the attempt to analyze and then present it in its essence, and with *Little Dorrit* begins the most conscious stage of the battle for self-knowledge, transposed into imaginative terms. Society, self, literary form, are the major ingredients in this process, and they change ceaselessly in their complex relationship to each other. With a

writer such as Dickens, who is always trying something new,
each novel is both complete in itself and part of the process
of unfolding a view of society and human life. We have seen
Dickens' first social attempt in the American scenes of *Martin
Chuzzlewit*; the partial failure, in *Dombey and Son*, to write a
novel of character; and in *Bleak House* and *Little Dorrit* the
opposition and then reconciliation of character and society.
The task of this study is to illuminate the specific genius of
Great Expectations as a part of this changing process.

In a review that gives definitive expression to a continuing
judgment of Dickens' early work as well as an estimate of
Great Expectations, The Times presented the plea of many of
his contemporary readers.

Give us back the old *Pickwick* style, they cried, with its contempt
of art, its loose story, its jumbled characters, and all its jesting that
made us laugh so lustily. . . . Mr. Dickens has in the present work
given us more of his earlier fancies than we have had for years.[8]

Great Expectations may be considered a return to the past in
the sense that, like *Dombey and Son*, it is concerned with the
presentation of a single major character (although in *Dombey*,
Florence becomes at least as important as her father); but
apart perhaps from the simplicity of the opening humor, it is
not a return in any other way. It lacks the formlessness of a
Nicholas Nickleby. Indeed, its qualities of "serious purpose,
consistent plot, finished writing," are just those that *The Times*
claimed Dickens' modern readers were prepared to dispense
with. But these qualities are as evident in *Little Dorrit*. The
importance of *Great Expectations* is that in writing it Dickens
steps into the central tradition of the European novel which I
have discussed earlier in this work. Like Raskolnikov, Pip
makes an inner, spiritual pilgrimage—one that never loses touch
with a particular, and yet generalized, social reality. We see the
social meaning inhering in the changes wrought in one individual. Pip *is*, in a sense, *Great Expectations*, and so a large
part of this study is concerned with his character.

This is all the more necessary because it may provide a
way into the understanding of a book whose complexity defies
a tidy approach to its discussion. How can one disentangle and
discuss separately plot, character, and meaning when all are

[8] Thurs., Oct. 17, 1861, p. 6.

so intimately bound up together? As I suggested in the discussion of *Little Dorrit*, the highly wrought structure of a unified work of art may prove deceptive. Its unity of plot and character, language and symbol, may be so great that it will wear an air of simplicity. Such works, however, leave us not merely with the particularities of person, time, and place, but also with the sense of a larger meaning. And when we return to them we find that this meaning leads its existence below the apparently straightforward surface. This may account for the lack of understanding of *Great Expectations* among contemporary readers. The review in *The Times* is evidence of this failure of apprehension, and we also find Carlyle, who ought to have known better, doing no more than laughing at the "Pip nonsense."[9] Underneath the "Pip nonsense" we can discern yet another variation of Dickens' major theme, and I hope to show that it is the especial greatness of the book that this theme of greed for money and class consciousness has never before been worked out in such purely personal terms. For the *novel* itself as the battleground for the opposing forces of good and evil, Dickens has substituted the individual human soul.

When these forces come into conflict within the compass of an artistic whole, we are less concerned with their personal than with their symbolic embodiment. If they can represent effectively the good and evil that we feel to be present in the universe, then we may be prepared to accept a certain melodramatic sketchiness of outline. This is certainly true of Blandois, and we may also feel that a greater degree of psychological complexity would only detract from Little Dorrit's strength of purity. But if the moral dialectic is to be played out within one man, power of impression at the expense of psychological realism will not be enough. In the young Pip's agonizings over Magwitch we see Dickens' recognition, for the first time in a character who is to carry the novel's entire moral weight, of a kind of original sin.

I was too cowardly to do what I knew to be right, as I had been too cowardly to avoid doing what I knew to be wrong. I had had no intercourse with the world at that time, and I imitated none of its many inhabitants who act in this manner. Quite an untaught genius, I made the discovery of the line of action for myself. (VI)

[9] See G. H. Ford, *Dickens and his Readers* (New York: The Norton Library, 1965), p. 90.

Pip, then, is to be no Oliver, but neither is Joe to be a Toots. Ingenuous as he is, there is nothing idiotic in his goodness; in his treatment of his wife, for example.

"And last of all, Pip—and this I want to say very serious to you, old chap—I see so much in my poor mother, of a woman drudging and slaving and breaking her honest heart and never getting no peace in her mortal days, that I'm dead afeerd of going wrong in the way of not doing what's right by a woman, and I'd fur rather of the two go wrong the t'other way, and be a little ill-conwenienced myself." (VII)

This goodness stems as much from observation and moral principle as simple good nature. And just as consciousness of choice bestows dignity upon the human personality, so the acceptance of a personal evil that is neither melodramatically exaggerated nor simply socially conditioned implies a respect for the tragic potential of the human soul which is not always evident in Dickens.

Such an attitude to character, with its interest in the vagaries of a changing human presence, is much closer to that of George Eliot or Henry James than to the more usual Dickensian mixture of physical detail and psychological eccentricity. In an art of this kind, the general can only be reached through the particular. We must feel the beating heart of a character before we can accept its larger meaning. Esther Summerson's reaction to Mr. Guppy's proposal of marriage, or her sorrow over her lost beauty, may command our belief and sympathy, but that side of her personality which simply incarnates a Platonic form of domestic goodness is incredible. And, despite their symbolic roles, Blandois and Little Dorrit must, in the first instance, impose their presence upon us. Pip's reality is established by the absolute truth we feel to exist in the presentation of his childish mind and sensibility. His soul is laid bare to us, and because we recognize what is familiar, we accept what is strange in him. We can, in fact, follow the consistency between what he shares with humanity at large and what is idiosyncratic. We believe in Pip's particular reality and so we can believe in his representative force. This is strengthened by that respect for human complexity which I have just mentioned. They combine to make Pip, unlike Mr. Dombey, a character who is "big" enough to bear the social significance of the snobbery and money worship that is created in him. Pip's character, background, and expectations all interact in a richness of significance that allows the following passage to comment, however unobtrusively, upon a whole society as well as upon an individual.

"I was a blacksmith's boy but yesterday; I am—what shall I say I am—today? . . . When I ask what I am to call myself today, Herbert . . . I suggest what I have in my thoughts. You say I am lucky. I know I have done nothing to raise myself in life, and that Fortune alone has raised me; that is being very lucky. And yet . . . I cannot tell you how dependent and uncertain I feel, and how exposed to hundreds of chances." (XXX)

Great Expectations contains many examples of the humanly destructive effects of money. Pip's reaction to Joe's visit to London is an index of the extent of his corruption by it; he confesses, "if I could have kept him away by paying money, I certainly would have paid money" (XXVII). But the novel's major theme, its particular variation of Dickens' constant subject, is that of money as the key to gentility. We see in this yet another example of his understanding of his age. Asa Briggs has pointed out that "in the battle between the self-made man and the gentleman, the self-made man won in England only if he became a gentleman himself."[10] This was, of course, a process that had begun very early in the industrial revolution, and Dickens himself had treated it before. The reservation of its full-scale treatment until the early sixties seems peculiarly apt, however, when we remember that the naked struggle for economic domination which characterized the thirties and forties had been replaced by superficially more responsible attitudes. Capitalism might still be red in tooth and claw, but it was thought politer not to mention the fact. The descendants of the first generation of fortune hunters were now established in good society and were unlikely to wish to have their financial background too harshly characterized. Pip's position was identical with that of those whose wealth had come from a father rather than from a mysterious benefactor, for Jaggers told Mr. Pocket "that I was not designed for any profession, and that I should be well enough educated for my destiny if I could 'hold my own' with the average of young men in prosperous circumstances" (XXIV). This theme of gentility is a constantly felt presence in the book. Magwitch is obsessed with it in his attitude to Compeyson: "He's a gentleman, if you please, this villain. Now, the Hulks has got its gentleman again, through me" (V). And we find it more lightheartedly in Pip's ingenuous

[10] *Victorian People* (London: Odhams Press, 1954), p. 144.

question to Herbert about brewers: " 'Yet a gentleman may not keep a public-house; may he?' said I. 'Not on any account . . . but a public-house may keep a gentleman' " (XXII).

In the world of *Great Expectations*, it is Dickens' continual effort to work out his themes in personal terms. His lasting concern is with the destructive effects of the material upon the spiritual, but the Court of Chancery, for example, is a public embodiment of evil forces in the nineteenth century. Now we see Dickens merging the motif of money and gentility with the most intimate of human emotions, that of love. At this point it may be as well to stop and consider his general treatment of love in the novel, for it is here that Dickens' own inner problems emerge most clearly. It would be untrue to say that his delineation of passion in *Great Expectations* is something completely new in his fiction. Rosa Dartle and Miss Wade showed the power with which he could depict intense longing. But these are minor and, more important, in some sense evil characters. What is new and what gives one a kind of shock is to realize that Miss Havisham's definition of love applies to the love that Pip, the character who commands most of our interest and sympathy, feels for Estella.

"I'll tell you . . . what real love is. It is blind devotion, unquestioning self-humiliation, utter submission, trust and belief against yourself and against the whole world, giving up your whole heart and soul to the smiter." (XXIX)

David and Agnes, Prince and Caddy, Herbert Pocket and Clara, constitute what we think of as the authentically Dickensian paradigms of love as it effects the good. Based upon mutual admiration and respect, their affection is quietly domestic, and perhaps its strongest characteristic is its rationality: each deserves the love that he receives. The infantile play of David and Dora, and Nancy's fidelity to Bill Sikes, are attempts to portray some of the more directly emotional aspects of love, but neither is very interesting. Only under the pressure of his relationship with Ellen Ternan was Dickens able to create those two great cries of anguish that break from Pip when he thinks and then speaks of what Estella means to him.

The unqualified truth is, that when I loved Estella with the love of a man, I loved her simply because I found her irresistible. Once for all; I knew to my sorrow, often and often, if not always, that I loved her against reason, against promise, against peace, against hope, against happiness, against all discouragement that could be. Once for all;

I loved her none the less because I knew it, and it had no more influence in restraining me, than if I had devoutly believed her to be
human perfection. (XXIX)

"You are part of my existence, part of myself. You have been in every
line I have ever read, since I first came here, the rough common boy
whose poor heart you wounded even then. You have been in every
prospect I have ever seen since—on the river, on the sails of the ships,
on the marshes, in the clouds, in the light, in the darkness, in the
wind, in the woods, in the sea, in the streets. . . . Estella, to the last
hour of my life, you cannot choose but remain part of my character,
part of the little good in me, part of the evil." (XLIV)

Nowhere else in mid-Victorian fiction, except in the Brontës, do
we find love treated with this degree of abandonment. There
is a disruptive element in this acceptance of a human need
that must be given its free play which is antipathetic to the
Victorian ideal of domesticity. Tennyson attempts the delineation of a similar kind of intensity in *Maud*, but the irredeemable
sentimentality of his love lyrics destroys the embodiment of
that part of his morbid vision. And Thackeray shies away from
frankness almost always, except in the character of the con-
fessedly evil Becky.

Love in *Great Expectations* is almost to be feared for the
commanding power it exerts over the human soul, and this
destructive element is intimately bound up with the forces
that do so much to damage Pip's character. In fact, his love for
Estella is the prime motivation of his downfall.

Truly it was impossible to dissociate her presence from all those
wretched hankerings after money and gentility that had disturbed
my boyhood—from all those ill-regulated aspirations that had first
made me ashamed of home and Joe . . . . In a word, it was impossible for me to separate her . . . from the innermost life of
my life. (XXIX)

Never before in Dickens has love itself been the corrupting
factor. We have seen Rick's love for Ada obscured by selfishness
and greed, but only as part of a whole process of personal degradation. Here, with such a subtle weaving of character and
situation that it is almost impossible to categorize the forces at
work, we are made to see that the very source of all that is
most life-giving is tainted. Pip's plasticity of temperament and
his ability to be so easily influenced, Estella's upbringing and
strength of purpose, the mysterious otherness of Miss Havisham,
all combine to render him helpless. Pip shares the desire of

every lover to be worthy of his beloved, but his desire is con-
centrated on purely external things. In the final analysis, he
does not wish to be morally or spiritually better; to be fit for
Estella, it is enough for him to be wealthy and a gentleman.
Her inability to arouse any higher kind of aspiration in Pip is
connected with Estella's upbringing. She is more than the
product of a melodramatic hatred of men. Miss Havisham's
secret emotions were violated in a purely materialistic way:
her love was betrayed by greed for money. Estella is as much
the spiritually dead product of a money society as Edith
Dombey, who is hawked around before her marriage to the
highest bidder. But, in keeping with the novel's intention, her
fate is worked out in completely personal terms. The meanings
of *Great Expectations* emerge from the interplay of individual
action and reaction, and yet these personal effects mirror the
social influences of the outside world. The Circulocution Office
may be a method of presenting an analysis of certain aspects
of nineteenth-century society, but it is still in terms of the
public institution. Miss Havisham and Estella constitute a true
microcosm, in that they encompass a whole range of social pressures within a single relationship.

In Estella we find exposed one of the book's major connections of plot and meaning. The device of having her related to
Magwitch stems directly from the field of popular melodrama,
but Dickens is now capable of transforming such a device into a
vehicle for his own purposes. It makes possible a masterly irony
at the expense of Pip's love.

Why should I pause to ask how much of my shrinking from Provis
might be traced to Estella? Why should I loiter on my road, to compare the state of mind in which I had tried to rid myself of the stain
of the prison before meeting her at the coach-office, with the state
of mind in which I now reflected on the abyss between Estella in her
pride and beauty, and the returned transport whom I harboured?
(XLIII)

With unsparing realism, Dickens has contrived his tale so
that even Estella is made a part of those expectations that turn
to dust and ashes for Pip. He loves her partly because his
imagination is fired by her beauty, but also because, having
inspired him with a sense of his own social inferiority, he sees
her as the exquisite representative of a higher kind of life. But
this higher mode of living is seen only in class terms, and the
truth is that Estella is as much a creature of the mire as Mag-

witch and Molly. Insofar as Pip does love her for the wrong reasons, he is doomed to a disappointment similar to that which he feels when he discovers the source of his good fortune (although he was quite content to be made a gentleman at Miss Havisham's expense).

The more one feels one's way into the heart of the book, in fact, the more important becomes the connection between Pip's love for Estella and his love for the externals of wealth and position. He is imprisoned by his desires, and this lack of freedom forms a constantly reiterated motif of language and symbolism.

I consumed the whole time in thinking how strange it was that I should be encompassed by all this taint of prison and crime; that, in my childhood out on our lonely marshes on a winter evening I should have first encountered it; that, it should have reappeared on two occasions, starting out like a stain that was faded but not gone; that, it should in this new way pervade my fortune and advancement. While my mind was thus engaged, I thought of the beautiful young Estella, proud and refined, coming towards me, and I thought with absolute abhorrence of the contrast between the jail and her. (XXXII)

It is loving Estella rather than helping Magwitch which forms the crucial action of Pip's life, for it is the personal corruption engendered by the one that determines his attitude to the other.

All the truth of my position came flashing on me; and its disappointments, dangers, disgrace, consequences of all kinds, rushed in in such a multitude that I was borne down by them and had to struggle for every breath I drew. (XXXIX)

We sympathize with this reaction at the moment it occurs, but the second great conjunction of plot and meaning, triggered by the convict's return, reveals the final truth of Pip's personal degradation. The mystery of his expectations is seen to have a function far beyond the creation of suspense or uncertainty. It leads irresistibly to the moment of irony when Pip soliloquizes on his fate.

But, sharpest and deepest pain of all—it was for the convict, guilty of I knew not what crimes, and liable to be taken out of those rooms where I sat thinking, and hanged at the Old Bailey door, that I had deserted Joe. (XXXIX)

Would it then, one cannot avoid asking, have been quite permissible for Pip to have deserted Joe for Miss Havisham? The

hollowness of his remorse is made clear by the fact that it
stems only from his social fear of Magwitch. It is not the *fact*
of having deserted his old friends for money or having been
given a position he has done nothing to earn which worries
Pip; it is only the *way* in which it has been done. The revelation that Miss Havisham was his benefactor could have done
nothing to impair his all-important status.

There is a strand of pure snobbery in Pip's reaction to Magwitch, as in his dislike of his heavy grubbing, but this is a
fairly trivial aspect of their relationship. It does contain elements of a terrible and serious humor, in Magwitch's hideous
playfulness on the subject of "bright eyes," for example: "There's
bright eyes somewhere—eh? Isn't there bright eyes somewheres,
wot you love the thoughts on? . . . They shall be yourn, dear
boy, if money can buy 'em" (XXXIX). It is, however, in their
roles as the possessed and the possessor that we see the novel's
complexities working with their greatest power. Pip fears Magwitch as only the insecurely established parvenu can fear the
criminal outcast. Despite his veneer of culture and poise, his
class position is so uncertain that it can be threatened by the
merest taint of the socially unacceptable. The nouveau riche's
fear of the skeleton in his cupboard must have been an important social reality to have found its way so often into fiction.
One remembers Mr. Bounderby and his myth of being a self-
made man, and Mr. Bulstrode's self-righteous peculation. But
Pip's terror of exposure embodies the shame of a whole society,
not just that of the new men. There is no exaggeration in the
view that Victorian prosperity rested upon a substratum of
fearful poverty and exploitation. The source of Pip's wealth
which seems, when it is first made known to him, to be something evil, is of the same kind as that of his society. A similarity
exists between their expectations, its effects upon them, and
the way in which they were brought to fruition. In a personal
sense there is something genuinely hateful in Magwitch's
ownership of Pip: "I says to myself, 'If I ain't a gentleman, nor
yet ain't got no learning, I'm the owner of such. All on you
owns stock and land; which on you owns a brought-up London
gentleman?'" (XXXIX). Yet this is the inescapable price that
must be paid by those who sacrifice their humanity for money
and position. In a real sense Pip does belong to the convict, for
everything that he most values in his life has been brought into
being by Magwitch (even Estella's very existence). In the
same way, the leisured classes were in thrall to those who

made that leisure possible, although, perhaps fortunately, the exploited never fully realized to what extent the exploiters depended upon them.

Great Expectations is a comment on both a man and a period. It exhibits Dickens' ability to penetrate the surface of his age to the relations that determined its being and to create a world that would display them in purely personal terms. But the novel is more than a mere display. It edges toward a solution of sorts, and it is this that gives it its radical quality. I am not using the word "radical" with any narrowly political meaning, but rather to suggest that the book gives one a sense of being utterly out of sympathy with its time. I hope I have already shown that this is true of its attitude to love, but it can be seen in various other ways. Nowhere in Dickens, for example, is the antipathy of child and adult made so explicit: "However, they were grown up and had their own way, and made the most of it" (XIII). It can be felt, again, in the death-sentence scene with its concentration on "civic gewgaws and monsters, criers, ushers, a great gallery full of people—a large theatrical audience" (LVI). Its most powerful presentation is after the interruption of the Christmas dinner.

As I watched them while they all stood clustering about the forge, enjoying themselves so much, I thought what terrible good sauce for a dinner my fugitive friend on the marshes was. They had not enjoyed themselves a quarter so much, before the entertainment was brightened with the excitement he furnished. And now, when they were all in lively anticipation of "the two villains" being taken, and when the bellows seemed to roar for the fugitives, the fire to flare for them, the smoke to hurry away in pursuit of them, Joe to hammer and clink for them, and all the murky shadows on the wall to shake at them in menace . . . the pale afternoon outside almost seemed in my pitying young fancy to have turned pale on their account, poor wretches. (V)

One's final estimate of this aspect of the novel depends, of course, on where one locates its center of feeling. Humphry House is representative of most critics when he says that at the end Dickens "takes Pip's new class position as established, and whisks him off to the East."[11] And so avoids, naturally enough, any facing up to unpleasant realities. But this seems to me to be entirely beside the point. If Pip were to return to his past he could only, within the texture of the novel, return

[11] *The Dickens World* (London: Oxford Paperbacks, 1960), p. 66.

to the forge, and the marriage of Joe and Biddy makes that impossible. Again, would it have been sensible in terms of any recognizable social reality known to Dickens, to have made someone with Pip's education into a laborer?

The true and radical center of the book lies, for me, in the development of Pip's relationship with Magwitch, which is one of the most interesting in the whole of Dickens. Here, above all, one can see the working of that respect for human complexity which I discussed earlier. The two individuals, and the friendship that gradually grows up between them, are presented simply as they are, with no mitigating sentimentality. The return of Magwitch reveals how far gone in selfishness and snobbery Pip is, despite his fundamental good-heartedness, while the convict's fierceness and glee in possession of his gentleman makes him at first a terrifying figure. The slow change in Pip's attitude is managed with psychological skill, and the realism of his relationship with Magwitch is characterized by Dickens' avoidance of all cheap effects, even when Magwitch is on his deathbed.

I sometimes derived an impression, from his manner or from a whispered word or two which escaped him, that he pondered over the question whether he might have been a better man under better circumstances. But he never justified himself by a hint tending that way, or tried to bend the past out of its eternal shape. (LVI)

As we understand more of Magwitch, so we come to sympathize with and even to love him; yet the moment of Pip's final identification with him comes not in one of his softer moods, but when he may finally have managed to murder Compeyson.

For now my repugnance to him had all melted away, and in the hunted wounded shackled creature who held my hand in his, I only saw a man who had meant to be my benefactor, and who had felt affectionately, gratefully, and generously, towards me with great constancy through a series of years. I only saw in him a much better man than I had been to Joe. (LIV)

This is the true end of Pip's enforced journey toward self-knowledge: his recognition of the human worth of this complete outcast of society as the wheel turns full circle and he feels once again with the "pitying young fancy" of the child who suffered in the forge.

His cleaving to Magwitch is the beginning of Pip's moral and spiritual regeneration, and yet there is another meaning here,

one that takes us very close to what seems like a complete rejection of society. This seems to contradict my earlier observation concerning Dickens' "acute social consciousness," but a
letter of 1858 to Wilkie Collins may help to make clear a
distinction that is of great importance to these last novels. He
is discussing a story of a person who tries to escape from the
world, but for whom everything shows "beyond mistake that
you can't shut out the world; that you are in it, to be of it; that
you get into a false position the moment you try to sever yourself from it."[12] The question is what Dickens means by the
"world" here. I would suggest that it is something like humanity
at large rather than society in any organized sense. Dickens
never gave mankind up in despair, but there is a great deal of
evidence that he felt more and more hopeless about society.
Although it is not worked out in explicit terms, there is a
moment of absolute choice for Pip in this novel. His decision to
stay with, and help, Magwitch—"when I took my place by
Magwitch's side, I felt that that was my place henceforth while
he lived" (LIV)—is one that surely would cut him off completely from polite society. His being "whisked off" to the
East, far from being a device to avoid commitment, is rather a
recognition of how far Pip has placed himself outside the pale
of English society.

   The sadness of *Great Expectations* is all-pervasive. It cannot
be affected by the revised ending, for once we know the
original conclusion it takes its place in the imagination as the
only possible one. Pip's inner journey is not fully completed
until Joe and Biddy are married, but the description of his state
before he hears of the wedding is true of what his life will be
in the future: "My heart was softened by my return, and such a
change had come to pass, that I felt like one who was toiling
home barefoot from distant travel, and whose wanderings had
lasted many years" (LVIII). Sympathy isall that Pip has
gained from his great expectations; the love and understanding
that comes from the painful recognition of error. The balance
of culpability in the society and the individual was even.
Society offered false gods to be worshipped; Pip chose to worship them, and the inevitable price for his confusion of appearance and reality had to be paid.

[12] Dated Sept. 6, in *Letters*, III, 51.

CHAPTER EIGHT

The Final Years:
Our Mutual Friend

One of the biggest disappointments in literature occurs in *Our Mutual Friend* at the moment when we discover that Boffin's moral degeneratation has been nothing but a well-intentioned sham. The extent of the shock that this induces is, perhaps, a tribute to Dickens' ingenuity, but it casts, for a time at least, a damaging blight upon the whole work. The seriousness of the portrayal of Boffin seems matched by its subversiveness. He may lack the stature of William Dorrit, but the progress of his apparent corruption by money is managed with skill, and his depiction seems to constitute a radical piece of self-criticism on Dickens' part. Boffin belongs to the tradition of Dickens' genially eccentric old benefactors, and yet we feel convinced that Dickens is prepared to sacrifice him in the interests of artistic truth. His failure to do so is damaging, as I have said, to our response to the entire novel, but it makes nonsense of the earlier scenes in which we have watched Boffin's breakdown. These passages can never be read again with patience. Our resentment might be contained if we felt that this particular "mystery" enclosed a special meaning, but the reason for Boffin's absurd pretence is as disappointing as the pretence itself.

"This brings up a certain confabulation regarding a certain fair young person; when Noddy he gives it as his opinion that she is a deary creetur. 'She may be a leetle spoilt, and nat'rally spoilt . . . by circumstances, but that's only on the surface! . . .' Then says John, 'Oh, if he could but prove so!' Then we both of us ups and says, that minute, 'Prove so!' " (Bk. 4, XIII)

I have contended that in *Great Expectations* Dickens displayed a new respect for the total complexity of character, but he seems here to have reverted to that almost contemptous dealing in deception at the expense of human feeling which was so evident in Mr. Jarndyce's trifling with Esther on the subject of their marriage. Such manipulation of people, in life or in art, is at once arrogant and frivolous.

It cannot be denied that the weakness of the Boffin strand seriously undermines the novel's artistic unity. We sense in it a failure of nerve, and yet we would lose much by rejecting the book out of hand. Dickens' greatness demands critical responsibility, and when that is given it will be seen that *Our Mutual Friend* has much to offer. It is my task in this chapter to attempt to evaluate the degree of success and failure in the work and so to understand its meaning within the framework of Dickens' creative effort.

The novel's most significant figure is Bradley Headstone. He haunts the imagination in all his guises—as individual, as social portent, as self-projection of his creator. The age of the concentration camp can even endow him with a universal force. His violence is partly that of the individual trapped by restrictive, and ultimately meaningless, social gestures.

Tied up all day with his disciplined show upon him, subdued to the performance of his routine of educational tricks, encircled by a gabbling crowd; he broke loose at night like an ill-tamed wild animal. (Bk. 2, XI)

But it is in his particularity that he first impresses himself upon us. His "decent" clothes become him, for very different reasons, almost as ill as Joe Gargery's Sunday best. Joe's uneasiness is an index of his moral worth, while Bradley's displays the warring impulses of his soul. The sheer doggedness by which he has won his way, and his never-ending struggle to hold on to what he has gained, would make him pathetic were it not for the force of the passion that exists so close to the surface of his character. This gives a memorable power to all the scenes in which he appears, but especially to his rejection by Lizzie when he struggles so desperately for self-control until the final moment of defeat.

"Then," said he, suddenly changing his tone and turning to her, and bringing his clenched hand down upon the stone with a force that laid the knuckles raw and bleeding; "then I hope that I may never kill him!" (Bk. 2, XV)

There is no melodrama here.

Bradley is also interesting as an embodiment of social change. Accounts of middle-class advance are common enough—in fact, it sometimes seems as though the middle classes have been "rising" since at least 1066—but we are shown here the

painful struggle toward respectability of the lowest of the
low. Respectability is the key word in Headstone's scheme of
values, as gentility was in that of Pip, a fact that is fully appreciated by Rogue Riderhood.

"Yours is a 'spectable calling. To save your 'spectability, it's worth
your while to pawn every article of clothes you've got, sell every
stick in your house, and beg and borrow every penny you can get
trusted with." (Bk. 4, XV)

Once again we can only marvel at Dickens' almost uncanny
awareness of the subtly changing patterns of his own age.
More and more efforts were being made to educate the poorest
sections of the population, and at the very moment when the
products of the training colleges were beginning to be felt
as a distinctive force, Dickens not only describes them but
also makes them a living part of his critique of nineteenth-
century society. Some critics have expressed surprise that
Dickens, who supported the Ragged Schools so generously in
his life, should have painted such an unflattering portrait of
them, and of their successful pupils, in his fiction. But this is to
mistake the import of a work such as *Our Mutual Friend*. To
touch on a point that I later develop more fully, Dickens is
not concerned here with short-term ends: Headstone and
Charley Hexam are being weighed, and found wanting, on a
much more important scale than that of mere utilitarianism.

Again, we cannot fail to see that Bradley contains several
important elements of his creator's character. His sense of
insecurity, his passionate nature, his self-divisiveness, even
his nocturnal wanderings, all echo Dickens at this unhappy
stage of his life. The most important connection lies, of course,
in the love he feels for Lizzie, which is expressed in language
as passionate as that of Pip. But here Dickens goes even further
in the direction of self-projection, for he makes Bradley give
expression to what he himself had felt regarding his own wife.
When Lizzie asks him why he has not married someone of
his own class, Bradley replies: "The only one grain of comfort
I have had these many weeks is, that I never did. For if I had,
and if the same spell had come upon me for my ruin, I know
I should have broken that tie asunder as if it had been thread!"
(Bk. 2, XV). The pessimism that was so deep a part of Dickens'
life and art at this period makes him say of Riderhood's attempts to recover from drowning, "like us all, every day of
our lives when we wake—he is instinctively unwilling to be

restored to the consciousness of this existence, and would be left dormant, if he could" (Bk. 3, III); and it is this pessimism that finds such powerful expression in Bradley's death. It is, surely, a fulfillment of Dickens' desire to escape from the complexities of his existence, but it has other, related meanings. There is a sense of the ineluctable power of the forces of anarchy to drag down into the slime even such a fundamentally misguided attempt at self-development as Bradley's. The impossibility of the coexistence of classes as close to each other as those of Riderhood and Headstone is made clear by their self-destructive embrace. Its most important significance is, however, the personal one. In their confrontation, Bradley comes face to face with the objectified form of his own truest nature and can do nothing but destroy it.

Headstone is a figure to be feared, but there are some occasions when he does arouse our sympathy, as in the scene of his encounter with Eugene Wrayburn when he accompanies Charley Hexam on his attempt to dissuade Eugene from seeing his sister. It would be difficult to conceive of two more dissimilar characters than the tortured, incoherent schoolmaster and the handsome, indolent man-about-town, but Dickens achieves both with masterly force. Eugene's careless attitude toward women is exposed with economy in two revealing moments. On Riderhood's talking of having a daughter we find: "'Incidentally mentioning, at the same time, her age?' inquired Eugene" (Bk. 1, XII). And on hearing that Charley has left the fatherless Lizzie: "'Will she be left alone then?' asked Eugene. 'She will be left,' said Mr. Inspector, 'alone'" (Bk. 1, XIII). Another aspect of Eugene's personality, his ironic humor, is suggested with an equal lightness of touch. When Riderhood first visits the two friends in order to inform on Hexam he insists on being sworn by "Lawyer Lightwood."

"I tell you, my good fellow," said Lightwood, with his indolent laugh, "that I have nothing to do with swearing."
"He can swear *at* you," Eugene explained; "and so can I. But we can't do more for you." (Bk. 1, XII)

That "explained" brings Eugene before us as a living presence. And there is an illuminating frivolity in his remark to Mortimer just after Headstone has left them: "The man seems to believe that everybody was acquainted with his mother!" (Bk. 2, VI).

The passage in which this occurs is a fine example of the

dramatic power of Dickens' art. Mortimer and even Charley Hexam, who should be a major force in the encounter, are mere lay figures. They form a background to an often unspoken exchange of cool disdain on the one hand and savage hatred on the other.

Very remarkably, neither Eugene Wrayburn nor Bradley Headstone looked at all at the boy. Through the ensuing dialogue, those two, no matter who spoke, or whom was addressed, looked at each other. There was some secret, sure perception between them, which set them against one another in all ways. (Bk. 2, VI)

Character is exposed continually, in facial expression and gesture just as much as in speech; in Bradley's pride at Charley's weakly selfish speech in defense of his sister, for example, and in Eugene's repeated blowing of the ash from his cigar. And when speech is used it is without any interference from an omniscient author.

"But I am more than a lad," said Bradley, with his clutching hand, "and I *will* be heard, sir."
"As a schoolmaster," said Eugene, "you are always being heard. That ought to content you." (Bk. 2, VI)

It is impossible not to sympathize with Bradley at this moment, as he writhes helplessly in the grasp of a Eugene who has never seemed more hateful. The respect Dickens denies to Boffin and Bella is given in full measure to the living complexities of these two creations. With a far-reaching realism he accepts the shifting patterns of good and evil in them, and with consummate artistry he makes us respond to their changes as we would in life. We are being presented here with a microcosm of class struggle, a mass antagonism worked out in a personal way, and the ambiguities of feeling that form the scene's meaningful undercurrent stem from the depth of Dickens' understanding of his material. We realize, once again, that he is the perfect interpreter of this clash, for Dickens himself was both Bradley and Eugene. He knew the insecurity that comes from the knowledge that one has been in the abyss, and yet he had achieved the savior faire of the man of the world. Dickens himself had lived through one of the crucial tensions of his age, important not only in social but also in personal terms because of its legacy of rankling injustice to the lower classes and effortless superiority to the upper.

Again, Dickens shows his respect for character in the absence of sentimentality in Eugene's pursuit of Lizzie, with its mixture of indolence, selfishness, and desire. It is only his wit, the gaiety hiding beneath the ironic gravity of his exterior, which saves Eugene from being a hollow man. His moral universe is not completely neutral, but he seems dead to the possibilities of action within it: "He looked at her with a real sentiment of remorseful tenderness and pity. It was not strong enough to impel him to sacrifice himself and save her, but it was a strong emotion" (Bk. 4, VI). And his laziness is often stirred by no more than a sense of emotional mastery which is perverse because it is external, as when he realizes that she has brought tears to his eyes.

And his next [thought] struck its root in a little rising resentment against the cause of the tears.
"Yet I have gained a wonderful power over her, too, let her be as much in earnest as she will!" (Bk. 4, VI)

This is the titillation of sexual power rather than the mutual involvement of love. Dickens' analysis of the progress of Eugene and Lizzie's relationship is in keeping with this exploration of genuine motive. Its romantic, Cophetua and the beggar-maid aspect is ignored, and we have in its place a recognition of such factors as the mixture of desire and real kindness in Eugene's wishing to help the illiterate girl, and Lizzie's pride in being loved by a "gentleman." They both, Lizzie especially, have a core of what might be called absolute love for each other, but Dickens is not afraid to trace the fluctuations wrought in such deep feelings by the momentary chances of life and fleeting, unrecognized emotions.

And going on at her side so gaily, regardless of all that had been urged against him; so superior in his sallies and self-possession to the gloomy constraint of her suitor, and the selfish petulance of her brother; so faithful to her, as it seemed, when her own stock was faithless; what an immense advantage, what an overpowering influence were his that night! (Bk. 2, XV)

Such a passage reminds one of George Eliot's description of the growth of Dorothea's love for Casaubon.

Lizzie herself fits reasonably well into this framework of psychological and social realism. Indeed, considered simply as a woman she is a successful creation, far removed from the puerilities of many of Dickens' heroines. The conflict in her feelings toward Eugene is particularly well managed. One must, of course, have reservations about her in her "social" aspect. Language is again a major problem here (although

Dickens makes some attempt to introduce a few harmless
solecisms into her speech in the earlier parts of the book), and
her moral awareness is perhaps a little too refined for the
daughter of Thames-side scum. But there is absolutely no
balking at her social *position* as the child of such a father. Although the river does not, in my view, carry a unifying symbolic weight in *Our Mutual Friend*, it is, nevertheless, convincingly a thing of horror. And when Lizzie protests her
hatred of it, her father reminds her of a few of the facts of her
existence.

> "As if it wasn't your living! As if it wasn't meat and drink to you!
> . . . The very fire that warmed you when you were a baby, was
> picked out of the river alongside the coal barges. The very basket
> that you slept in, the tide washed ashore. The very rockers that I put
> it upon to make a cradle of it, I cut out of a piece of wood that
> drifted from some ship or another." (Bk. 1, I)

What, then, are we to say of the union of this girl, who exists
beyond the pale of even respectable lower-class society, and
her upper-class lover? Whatever else it may be, we can be sure
it is not intended as a Disraelian solution to the Condition of
England problem. There has been much discussion of how
truly radical this marriage is in effect, but such argument seems
to me to be beside the point. That it is not, at any rate, reac-
tionary is very clear. There is a somewhat legalistic exactitude
in Mortimer's denial that Lizzie was ever a "female waterman,
turned factory girl" (Bk. 4, XVII), but Mr. Twemlow's use of
the word "gentleman" in "the sense in which the degree may
be attained by any man," and Eugene's passing thought of
escaping to the Colonies, make it clear that the couple can
never hope to find themselves socially acceptable. Pessimism,
not radicalism, is the operative word here. The marriage of
Little Dorrit and Clennam has some small residue of social
meaning. If nothing else they will create some happiness for
others in the tiny personal society of which they will form the
heart. But the meaning of the union of Lizzie and Eugene is to
be sought in its despairing romanticism. Theirs is the solidarity
of figures who are otherwise in utter isolation, and their marriage is without content except on the personal level. Eugene is
as much an orphan in spirit as Lizzie is in fact, and neither has
any meaningful connection with a wider social reality. Nothing
could be more significant than the novel's ending. The last
section, called distinctively "Chapter The Last," is concerned
not with any summing-up, but exclusively with "The Voice of

Society." A little stirring of hopefulness is aroused in Mortimer, and the reader, by Mr. Twemlow's plucky intervention; and yet after he has spoken, Mortimer does not ask himself if his is the Voice of Society. This is not, surely, because he believes that it may be, but because he realizes that Twemlow's stand is a personal one. Indeed, by placing his plea for humanity in the mouth of such an ineffectual vessel, Dickens only emphasizes the enormity of the forces ranged against that humanity.

In view of such riches as these, my earlier reservations about the novel may seem mere quibbling. The passages I have been discussing far from exhaust the book's genius. The Lammles, for example, are in a very different style from those characters I have already mentioned, but they are achieved with equal brilliance. They seem to occupy a middle ground between the psychological reality of Wrayburn and Headstone and the caricature of Podsnap and the Veneerings. They possess both inner consistency and a simplified sharpness of outline, with neither carried to its point of fullest development, but drawing a satisfying sense of idiosyncrasy from their mingling. Like savage birds of prey they wage continual war on mankind, and the savagery of their economic individualism is tempered only by Sophronia's occasional twinges of conscience.

"Restraining influence, Mr. Twemlow? We must eat and drink, and dress, and have a roof over our heads. Always beside him and attached in all his fortunes? Not much to boast of in that; what can a woman at my age do?" (Bk. 2, XVII)

They fight, not for riches, but for the necessities of life, like any other animal. In a scene of almost Strindbergian intensity we watch them, on their honeymoon, rend and tear each other at the discovery that neither has the fortune the other expected. This revelation forms part of one of the greatest moments in later Dickens, remarkable for its economy of description and dialogue. The mood is set perfectly at our first sight of them.

Mr. and Mrs. Lammle have walked for some time on the Shanklin sands and one may see by their footprints that they have not walked arm in arm, and that they have not walked in a straight track, and that they have walked in a moody humour; for the lady has prodded little spirting holes in the damp sand before her with her parasol, and the gentleman has trailed his stick after him. As if he were of the Mephistopheles family indeed, and had walked with a drooping tail. (Bk. 1, X)

So they pass on, through rage to the bitter quietness of their pact against mankind—"We agree to keep our own secret, and

to work together in furtherance of our schemes . . . any scheme
that will bring us money"—and to the coda of husband escort-
ing wife in "the light of the setting sun to their abode of bliss."
The greed and selfishness of a society are again here presented
in personal terms.

Nevertheless, such brilliancies do not constitute the whole
of *Our Mutual Friend*. They would be enough to make the
reputation of any lesser writer, but with Dickens we have *Little
Dorrit* to act as a touchstone of merit. By the standard of that
work of supreme genius the later novel is seen to fall short.
Perhaps the defining characteristic of *Little Dorrit* is its in-
divisibility of artistic achievement and social critique. Its
people, events, and institutions combine, whatever their origin
in the world of observed reality, to form a criticism of the
quality of nineteenth-century life which moves far beyond an
attack on specific social or political abuses. The world of the
novel constitutes a created and self-consistent universe that
is parallel to, rather than identical with, the human life with
which it is nevertheless connected. The Circumlocution Office
is only part of a larger imprisonment that afflicts the individual
human soul. The nature of the attack that the book mounts
upon modern civilization is characterized, in a distinction I
have already made, by pessimism rather than radicalism. The
novel displays to us its own dark world; it cannot offer us any
limited solutions outside the realm of the personal. *Our Mutual
Friend* is, if anything, even more pessimistic than *Little Dorrit*,
but we must differentiate in it between that quality and artistic
unity. This may best be done by comparing its symbolism of
dust and dustheaps with the prisons of the earlier novel. In a
sense the first is the more radical. Writers such as Humphry
House have clarified this by pointing out the contemporary relevance of the dust, how sweeping is Dickens' condemnation of
the whole paraphernalia of capitalist money-making.[1] But,
compelling as it is, this symbol can say nothing to us of *human*
interest, and try as he may, Dickens cannot invest it with the
pervasive, unifying force of the prison.

The grating wind sawed rather than blew; and as it sawed, the sawdust whirled about the sawpit. Every street was a sawpit, and there
were no topsawyers; every passenger was an under-sawyer, with the
sawdust blinding him and choking him. (Bk. 1, XII)

[1] *The Dickens World* (London: Oxford Paperbacks, 1960), pp. 166–
167.

Such passages only emphasize the externality of the notion. Similar ones were to be found in *Little Dorrit*, but there they were a reinforcement of the profound human truth that was being created. In *Our Mutual Friend* they cannot hold the structure together as a consistently interrelated and meaningful whole.

This is a failure of artistic creation; yet it is not, I think, farfetched to connect it with the psychological and narrative failure contained in Boffin's revelation of his make-believe. In neither is Dickens' involvement with form and content sufficiently strong to allow his deepest insights to come to the surface. His uneasiness is betrayed by the falsely ludicrous behavior of Mrs. Boffin.

At this Mrs. Boffin fairly screamed with rapture, and sat beating her feet upon the floor, clapping her hands, and bobbing herself backwards and forwards, like a demented member of some Mandarin's family. (Bk. 4, XII)

Behind the hysteria of the character there lies the unsure creator's lack of control. We find in this the direct expression of a tiredness that runs through a great deal of the novel, a tiredness that makes itself felt in trivial as well as in important ways. In Venus, for example, we hear echoes of Dick Swiveller and other Dickensian lovers.

"Mr. Wegg. . . . There are strings that must not be played upon. No, sir! Not sounded, unless in the most respectful and tuneful manner. Of such melodious strings is Miss Pleasant Riderhood formed." (Bk. 4, XIV).

This stale repetition of the past is not important in itself, but it does contribute to a general feeling of creative flatness. More significant is Dickens' ineffectual attempt to tack his alienation theme onto the sterotyped comic figure of Wegg.

"And this, sir . . . was once Our House! This, sir, is the building from which I have so often seen those great creatures, Miss Elizabeth, Master George, Aunt Jane, and Uncle Parker"—whose very names were of his own inventing—"pass and repass!" (Bk. 2, VII)

His tiresomeness is only increased when we compare him with Wemmick, the perfect representative of the alienated modern man, whose slow transitions from domestic warmth to business efficiency are both psychologically convincing and socially meaningful. Again, it is impossible not to notice that Rokesmith, with his pretence of being dead and of burying himself, is little but a weaker version of Arthur Clennam and that the Veneering's stylized guests are all, with the exception of Lady Tippins, better done in *Little Dorrit*.

There is evidence in the book of self-indulgence and lack of nerve as well as tiredness. Eugene does marry Lizzie, but this is to some extent balanced by Dickens' treatment of Bella. The warring impulses of her character are conveyed well in the earlier part of the novel, and her desire, after her marriage, to be fully adult is quite convincing: "I want to be something so much worthier than the doll in the doll's house!" (Bk. 4, V). But Dickens condemns her to domestic fairyhood from what we can only think of, if we bear Estella in mind, as capitulation to his own personal difficulties. And the clue to the fact that she is doomed to the doll's role can be charted exactly. It comes with the abrupt change in the style of Dickens' presentation of her after Boffin's final mock attack on Rokesmith: " 'I hate you!' cried Bella, turning suddenly upon him, with a stamp of her little foot" (Bk. 3, XV). Only a domestic fairy could be the possessor of a "little foot." And only failure of nerve can account for the fact that Bella's blind devotion to Rokesmith in his gratuitous mystery-making, the reverse of understanding between mature adults, is rewarded in a way that runs counter to the book's ostensible spirit: "And on Bella's exquisite toilette table was an ivory casket, and in the casket were jewels the like of which she had never dreamed of" (Bk. 4, XIII). The desire for riches was one of the very things that Boffin's absurd plot had been designed to cure in Bella: "I love money, and want money—want it dreadfully. I hate to be poor, and we are degradingly poor, offensively poor, miserably poor, beastly poor" (Bk. 1, IV). There is a timidity here which complements the fear noticed by Edmund Wilson: "It comes to us as a disturbing realization that Dickens is now *afraid* of Podsnap."[2] Dickens can still create his Iagos, but he no longer takes delight in them. Hatred has replaced the shared joy of moments such as Mr. Pecksniff's appearance on the landing at Mrs. Todgers'. There is a sense in which Podsnap is too serious a figure ever to be treated in this way.

Our Mutual Friend marks the end of Dickens' struggle to comprehend himself and his age. The conclusion is, in many ways, a sad one, for the flawed genius of that work betrays the personal exhaustion and artistic defeat that were his ultimate

[2] "Dickens: The Two Scrooges," in *The Wound and the Bow* (Boston: Houghton Mifflin, 1941), p. 78.

fate. His later silence and the emptiness of *Edwin Drood* serve to confirm this, and a letter to Forster of March 29, 1864, reveals remorselessly the decline in his creative vitality.

I have grown hard to satisfy, and write very slowly, and I have so much—not fiction—that *will* be thought of when I don't want to think of it, that I am forced to take more care than I once took.[3]

Yet it would be impertinent to dwell too much on this theme. To care ceaselessly, even too much, is a noble fault. There is much to censure in Dickens' relationship with Ellen Ternan, but his primary motivating force was, surely, a passionate desire to know love. His unceasing concern with the state of his society was a reflection of his love of humanity. Even the desire for money which drove him so relentlessly in his last years stemmed partly from a too acute sense of personal responsibility. Our final feeling must be one of admiration for the courage, the passion, and the gaiety with which Dickens tackled his crushing personal and public problems.

[3] *Letters*, ed. Walter Dexter (London: Nonesuch Press, 1938), III, 384.

CHAPTER NINE
Conclusions

Poetry and the Social Novel

Where is Dickens to be placed in the tradition of the English novel? An answer to this question necessitates some general statement of the specific nature of his fictional achievement, and I think this can best be done by comparing Dickens and George Eliot. In terms of creative vitality sustained over a long period, variety of form, and richness of imagination, Dickens is a greater novelist than George Eliot, but it seems to me that *Middlemarch* must force its claim upon us as the defining touchstone of Victorian fiction. If we keep Dickens in mind, I think it is true that this greatness is most immediately apparent in the realm of characterization. People such as Dorothea and Lydgate have a depth of interest that characters in Dickens' work approach only once or twice and never equal. When Dorothea receives her letter of proposal from Mr. Casaubon, for example, George Eliot takes us into those recesses of her personality where character and circumstance combine to effect the decisive action. Dorothea hopes to aid Mr. Casaubon in what she thinks is his great work, but her identification with him, although cerebral, is not bloodless, as Eliot shows in summing up this sequence of events.

This hope was not unmixed with the glow of proud delight—the joyous maiden surprise that she was chosen by the man whom her admiration had chosen. All Dorothea's passion was transfused through a mind struggling towards an ideal life; the radiance of her transfigured girlhood fell on the first object that came within its level. The impetus with which inclination became resolution was heightened by those little events of the day which had aroused her discontent with the actual conditions of her life. (V)

George Eliot here dissolves the crystallized moment of choice and displays the elements out of which it has fused.

In the same way we are made to understand how the inter-

action of character, society, and chance bring about the marriage of Lydgate and Rosamund. Unlike Heathcliff and Catherine, who gaze at each other with a mutual absorption that
admits of no interference from the outside world, Lydgate and
Rosamund do not exist for each other alone. By a variety
of friendships and enmities each is linked to an outside world
whose claims and pressures are as strong as those of their love.
Such diverse influences as the need for money and the desire
for social prestige impinge upon their world of sensual passion.
Lydgate reserves his most serious attention for the realm of
intellectual discovery and accepts unquestioningly his knowledge of the complexities of love and marriage, "these being
subjects on which he felt himself amply informed by literature,
and that traditional wisdom which is handed down in the genial
conversation of men" (XVI). In doing so he displays an almost
tragic flaw in his character.

Lydgate's spots of commonness lay in the complexion of his prejudices, which, in spite of noble intentions and sympathy, were half
of them such as are found in ordinary men of the world: that distinction of mind which belonged to his intellectual ardour, did not penetrate his feeling and judgement about furniture, or women, or the
desirability of its being known (without his telling) that he was
better born than other country surgeons. (XV)

In a subtle way society has even helped to determine the very
fact that Lydgate and Rosamund fall in love with such disastrous results. Those "spots of commonness" in Lydgate's character with regard to women have not been refined by any
different, and higher, social ideal. His concept of what a woman
should be is in perfect harmony with that of his society. The
discriminations of a finer civilization could not have failed to
affect a sensibility of such potential as Lydgate's. Similarly, her
society only confirms Rosamund in her greatest moral failing:
her perfect self-satisfaction has never been disturbed by an
education capable of moving beyond superficial "accomplishments."

In writing of *Great Expectations*, I claimed that it took its
place in the tradition of European fiction together with such
novels as *Crime and Punishment* and *Middlemarch*. But with
that standard of comparison before us, we must admit that Pip
has neither the stature of Raskolnikov nor the psychological
interest of Lydgate. In those realms of character which are
his own, Dickens is supreme. Mrs. Gamp is an absolute crea-

tion in the sense that it is meaningless to try to imagine how she could be bettered. The highest levels of wildness and complexity, were, however, beyond Dickens' reach. Pip is a passionate creature, but he lacks the compelling strangeness of Dostoevsky's hero; and the part played by social pressure in forming his character is, if we think of these other writers, a shade too mechanically arranged on the side of society. And there is a final absence of fully adult interest even in him. In following the agonizing course of Lydgate's career, George Eliot shows us the subtle impingements of the external world on human character and conscience, but her chosen field for this marvelous display remains the individual soul. The complex of forces that go to make up Lydgate the man is always, in the last analysis, the center of interest. The equivalent center of serious interest in *Great Expectations* is, I would suggest, the meaning of Pip's expectations for Victorian society as a whole rather than the psychological exploration of Pip's moral breakdown. Traces of a pale boyishness cling irredeemably to Pip when he is compared with a figure such as Lydgate. His desires are too much those of *l'homme moyen sensual* to ever acquire a tragic dimension. But there is strength as well as weakness in his callowness. We must admit, I think, that Pip suffers as a character from Dickens' lack of intellectuality. Part of Eliot's triumphant success with Lydgate is to compel a total belief in the validity of his intellectual pretensions. His downfall involves us in a degree of genuinely tragic suffering because we are convinced that a brilliant mind has been destroyed, a mind deeply engaged in a serious area of human experience. Dickens cannot invest Pip with this kind of seriousness because of the limitations of his own mind, but he attempts to give him a fully adult complexity in another way, by means of a transmutation of personal experience into art that can only be called heroic. Pip's relationship with Estella is surely a reenactment in fiction of the last, crushing unhappiness of Dickens' life, as Edgar Johnson suggests.

It is inevitable that we should associate Pip's helpless enslavement to Estella with Dickens' desperate passion for Ellen Lawless Ternan. . . . The tone of Dickens' unhappy letters to Collins and Forster during all the time between the last night of *The Frozen Deep* and the time of the separation discloses an entirely new intensity of personal misery far exceeding the restlessness of years before.[1]

[1] *Charles Dickens: His Tragedy and Triumph* (London: Gollancz, 1953), II, 991.

Unlike the manipulation of Bella Wilfer in *Our Mutual Friend* into the role of the doll in the doll's house—a manipulation contrived, we feel, for personal rather than artistic reasons, for it runs counter to the ostensible tenor of the novel—Pip and Estella mark Dickens' attempt to grapple with an adult emotional reality. Instead of using art for the vicarious solution of his own problems, he objectifies personal experience in a relationship of great power. And yet it is difficult to follow Edgar Johnson unreservedly in his view that while Dickens' youthful letters to Maria Beadnell reveal the suffering of a boy, "Pip's is the stark misery of a man."[2] There seem to me three reasons that argue against the acceptance of this view. First, although we may agree that it is in keeping with the passivity and plasticity of Pip's temperament, his "helpless enslavement" smacks too much of boyish infatuation to convey any general insight into the nature of mature masculine passion. We remember that Lydgate is also helplessly enslaved, but this is brought about in him by an unconscious appeal to his protective tenderness, not by an almost masochistic submission to an ideal of gentility that is as false as it may appear beautiful. Second, the clouds of melodrama that Estella trails after her, however faintly, in the form of an icy and statuesque restraint are seriously damaging to the psychological realism that Dickens is aiming for here. Thematically brilliant as her relationship with Miss Havisham is, she is in the line of Edith Dombey and Lady Dedlock; the all-too-human bitchiness of Rosamund, rather than echoes of the tragedy queen, was what Dickens needed for Estella's characterization. Last, it is perhaps necessary to point out that Pip and Estella never, in fact, have a relationship in the true sense of the word. It is not, of course, necessary that they should be married or be lovers, but we should be made to feel (for the purposes that Dickens obviously had in mind) that some kind of developing personal dialogue exists between them. But, however much we may see a movement in Pip's character, his love for Estella is a constant from the beginning, and the only change in their involvement occurs as the novel's impossible happy ending. Their meetings amount to a fairly simple repetition of Estella's cold rejections and Pip's desperate longings (however passionately these may be expressed on occasion).

But these failings are the obverse side of one of the novel's greatest virtues. The strength of Pip's callowness, the sheer

2 *Ibid.*, p. 992.

ordinariness of his desires, makes him a pathetically believable representative of a large and significant area of human life: he is a perfect example of that obsession with Machinery, the confusion of means and ends, which Matthew Arnold saw as typical of his own century, and which is hardly unfamiliar to our own. Pip is the antihero of man's deluded involvement with money in capitalist society, and in creating him Dickens pushed himself, with an effort wholly admirable, in a direction away from the main current of his genius. The obsessive physical detail, the vivid externalization, is put to one side (do we ever have any clear idea of what Pip looks like?) in favor of a searching examination of an individual soul. Here Dickens is prepared to explore the human mystery, whereas more typically, he is content to display it with as great a richness of evocative detail as he can muster. One of Dickens' most satisfying statements of this sense of mystery is to be found in *Hard Times*.

So many hundred Hands in this Mill; so many hundred horse Steam Power. It is known, to the force of a single pound weight, what the engine will do; but, not all the calculators of the National Debt can tell me the capacity for good or evil, for love or hatred, for patriotism or discontent, for the decomposition of virtue into vice, or the reverse, at any single moment in the soul of one of these its quiet servants, with the composed faces and the regulated actions. There is no mystery in it; there is an unfathomable mystery in the meanest of them, for ever. (XI)

This external rather than analytical approach to human character is entirely successful in *Hard Times* because it is deeply related to one of the book's major themes. The novel mounts a brilliantly satirical attack on those moral arithmeticians who feel convinced of their ability to probe the deepest recesses of the human personality, and Dickens' presentation of personal complexity in action provides an implicit commentary on their shallowness.

And yet I do not think it has been sufficiently realized how extraordinary this approach is for a *novelist*. Examples occur in the present study in the course of discussing other matters, and it would be useful to recall them to mind at this point. There was the porter of the Anglo-Bengalee in *Martin Chuzzlewit*: "Whether he was a deep rogue, or a stately simpleton, it was impossible to make out" (XXVII). And Mr. Tulkinghorn's pursuit of Lady Dedlock in *Bleak House*.

It may be that he pursues her doggedly and steadily, with no touch of compunction, remorse, or pity. It may be that her beauty, and all the state and brilliancy surrounding her, only gives him the greater zest for what he is set upon, and makes him the more inflexible in it. . . . Whether he be any of this, or all of this . . . (XXIX)

But no answer is given to the implied question. Such a view of character is obviously linked with Dickens' predeliction for the eccentric. There *is* a mystery in eccentricity, often of a quite uninteresting kind, in its bizarre and apparently unmotivated behavior, but this is not the material from which the greatest fiction is made. One of the most rigorous of Dickens' many acts of self-criticism can be seen in his attempts to overcome his easy manipulation of oddity in favor of subtler methods of characterization. I have glanced at one of these in my discussion of Pip, where Dickens grapples with the problems of a full-scale study in psychological realism. More typically, he capitalizes with superb insight on his gift for the external, as in a scene that Dr. Leavis singles out for praise (although not much analysis) in his justly famous essay on *Hard Times*.[3] This is the moment when Mr. Gradgrind tells his daughter that Mr. Bounderby wishes to marry her.

Mr. Gradgrind . . . had no need to cast an eye upon the teeming myriads of human beings around him, but could settle all their destinies on a slate, and wipe out all their tears with one dirty little bit of sponge. To this Observatory, then: a stern room, with a deadly statistical clock in it, which measured every second with a beat like a rap upon a coffin-lid; Louisa repaired on the appointed morning. A window looked towards Coketown; and when she sat down near her father's table, she saw the high chimneys and the long tracts of smoke looming in the heavy distance gloomily . . .

"Louisa, my dear, you are the subject of a proposal of marriage that has been made to me." . . .

Again he waited, and again she answered not one word . . .

"Well! . . . you are even more dispassionate than I expected, Louisa. Or, perhaps, you are not unprepared for the announcement I have it in charge to make?"

"I cannot say that, father, until I hear it. Prepared or unprepared, I wish to hear it all from you. I wish to hear you state it to me, father."

Strange to relate, Mr. Gradgrind was not so collected at this moment as his daughter was. He took a paper-knife in his hand,

3 F. R. Leavis, *The Great Tradition* (Penguin Books, 1962), pp. 260–262.

turned it over, laid it down, took it up again, and even then had to
look along the blade of it, considering how to go on. . . .

Silence between them. The deadly statistical clock very hollow.
The distant smoke very black and heavy.

"Father," said Louisa, "do you think I love Mr. Bounderby?"

Mr. Gradgrind was exceedingly discomfited by this unexpected
question. "Well, my child," he returned, "I-really-cannot take upon
myself to say."

"Father," pursued Louisa in exactly the same voice as before, "do
you ask me to love Mr. Bounderby?"

"My dear Louisa, no. No. I ask nothing."

"Father," she still pursued, "does Mr. Bounderby ask me to love
him?" (XV)

Almost everything here is achieved from the outside, by dialogue and action, and when narrative occurs it is used not for
analysis, but for an evocation of scene that can only be called
poetic. What we get in this passage is not the dense particularity
of a social moment, but the suggestive directness of symbol
combined with a sensuous exactness that prevents any limiting
schematization of the richness of life. The "deadly" clock with
its beat like "a rap upon a coffin-lid" suggests perfectly the
spiritual and moral death that is the substance of the scene,
and the unobtrusive reminder of Coketown ("The distant smoke
very black and heavy.") establishes the link between Mr.
Gradgrind's treatment of Louisa and the suffering of thousands
in a society dominated by utilitarian values. It does not seem
farfetched to suggest that there is a Jamesian richness here, a
demand made upon the reader to imply for himself the under-
tones of human conflict that vibrate between father and daughter with such a wealth of unspoken meaning.

It is James, perhaps, who provides the solution to the problem
of "showing" and "telling" which can encircle one so relentlessly in discussing George Eliot and Dickens. Is it critically
valid to censure the lack of drama in Eliot's analyses of character when they convey such a profound understanding of the
springs of human motive, or to censure Dickens' limitations of
understanding when he conveys such an overwhelming sense
of the surface of life? There is nothing to censure, as I have
tried to suggest, in the passage from *Hard Times*, but that is
unusual in its masterful ability to suggest psychological depths
by means of the external. Is it not often true, as in the great
scene from *Little Dorrit* where William Dorrit tries to persuade
his daughter not to be cold to the advances of young John
Chivery, that we feel a twinge of disappointment at Dickens'

failure to make the final descent into the core of the human mystery?

Only the wisdom that holds the clue to all hearts . . . can surely know to what extent a man, especially a man brought down as this man had been, can impose upon himself. (Bk.1, XIX)

The Jamesian "moment," in its ability to combine the deepest levels of human understanding with a total impression of life's vitality, may be allowed to act as the touchstone in this argument. But, to return to the comparison of Eliot and Dickens, if we prefer her greater insight into character, it is necessary to remember that scenes such as that from *Little Dorrit* are presented with a dramatic force, a spareness of narrative, and a significance of dialogue that belong to Dickens alone. We may understand more of the inner life of Bulstrode, but is he ever quite so real to us as Dorrit?

There is another basis of comparison between Eliot and Dickens which may, ultimately, throw some light on the precise nature of his genius. I think it is possible to argue that the Victorian novel, with the exception of a work such as *Wuthering Heights*, is a genre concerned with the realization of character *in society*, but it might be more accurate to say of George Eliot that she presents society *through* character. In discussing Dickens' career, I have pointed out that in certain works he makes a strenuous effort to express his general sense of society in personal terms, but nowhere does he achieve the insistent working-out through character alone that is the triumph of *Middlemarch*. Beatrice Webb's autobiography provides convincing proof of how deep a strand of Victorian life Eliot touched on in her presentation of Dorothea. This passage, on her mother's death, is from her manuscript diary.

When I work with many odds against me, for a far distant and perhaps unattainable end, I think of her and her intellectual strivings which we were ready to call useless, and which will yet be the originating impulse of all my ambition, urging me onward towards something better in action and thought.[4]

The sense of a mind desperately seeking to express itself is heartbreakingly present in the opening chapters of *My Apprenticeship*, and we find Dorothea up against exactly the same obstacles—imperfect education, conventional prejudice, and limited social opportunity; but her story is never presented in

---

[4] *My Apprenticeship* (London: Longmans, n.d.), p. 17.

abstract or even symbolic terms. She is delighted when Mr. Casaubon intervenes on her side in a dinner-party conversation and dreams of him as a "man who could understand the higher inward life, and with whom there could be some spiritual communion."

Dorothea's inferences may seem large; but really life could never have gone on at any period but for this liberal allowance of conclusions, which has facilitated marriage under the difficulties of civilization. Has anyone ever pinched into its pilulous smallness the cobweb of pre-matrimonial acquaintanceship? (II)

Dorothea is caught at that point where private personality and public pressure cross, the point at which character can be seen in its richest complexity. Her desire for the finest possible kind of life, the limitations of her intellectual environment, her emotional needs, and the narrowness of her social circle all combine to make Mr. Casaubon appear in a transfiguring light. And so the general significance of her predicament is always subsumed under the most personal actions of her private experience.

The smallness of Victorian prematrimonial acquaintanceship is an important cause of the disasters that overtake both Dorothea and Lydgate. This transmutation of a public theme into a private concern is seen most clearly in Lydgate's whole story. It is embodied in his marriage, in the probings of his conscience after the death of Raffles, and in his difficulty in deciding whom to support for the chaplaincy of Bulstrode's hospital. His respect for Farebrother clashes with his desire for freedom to work as he chooses, and so we find that "for the first time Lydgate was feeling the hampering threadlike pressure of small social conditions, and their frustrating complexity" (XVIII). He is defeated by the combination of his own character and his circumstances, but these circumstances are never rendered in an abstract fashion. Once again, it is character, composed of the interaction of public and private, which is of primary importance: there is a sense in which the externals of Lydgate's life are breathed in so deeply that they become a part of his personality.

The difference between Dickens' and Eliot's sense of society can be seen in the discussion concerning the chaplaincy which takes place before the arrival of Lydgate and Bulstrode. Eliot seizes this as an opportunity to depict in some detail a cross section of influential Middlemarch society. We have the doctors: "Dr. Minchin . . . soft-handed, pale-complexioned, and of rounded outline, not to be distinguished from a mild clergyman in appearance. . . . Dr. Sprague . . . superfluously tall"; "old Mr. Powderell, a retired ironmonger of some standing"; Mr. Frank Hawley, lawyer and town clerk, "whose bad language was notorious in that part of the county"; and various others (XVIII). By means of this device, which she uses more than once—to convey the opinion of the lower orders as to Lydgate's medical skill, for example—Eliot builds up a social picture that is thick with realistic detail. Each character has his own peculiarities and each his own opinion in the matter of the chaplaincy. Dickens' method in this respect is very different. When he wishes to convey the sweep of a social group, with its views and prejudices, he usually assembles the kind of party we find at Merdle's dinner table in *Little Dorrit*. There "Bar" and "Bishop," "Horse Guards" and "Treasury," replace the respected ironmonger and the town clerk. It is in intention, however, rather than in effect that these personifications differ. This description, for example, could surely belong to either writer: "Mr. Hackbutt, a rich tanner of fluent speech, whose glittering spectacles and erect hair were turned with some severity towards innocent Mr. Powderell." (Although this may only be, we suspect, because Eliot has the benefit of the Dickensian influence here.) Schematic as they are, Dickens' figures are at least as vivid as those of Eliot, but it is their satirical force not their personal idiosyncrasy which accounts for this.

Surely the goods of this world, it occurred in an accidental way to Bishop to remark, could scarcely be directed into happier channels than when they are accumulated under the magic touch of the wise and sagacious, who, while they knew the just value of riches (Bishop tried here to look as if he were rather poor himself), were aware of their importance, judiciously governed and rightly distributed, to the welfare of our brethren at large. . . . Bishop then—jauntily stepping out a little with his well-shaped right leg, as though he said to Mr. Merdle "don't mind the apron; a mere form!"—put this case to his good friend. . . . Whether . . . his good friend . . . would shed a little money in the direction of a mission or so to Africa? (XXI)

George Eliot uses her irony at the expense of human nature, while Dickens is concerned to mount an attack against individuals as representatives of social and institutional forces rather than directly as members of the human race.

Despite her concern with the "social air in which mortals begin to breathe" and her belief that "there is no creature whose

inward being is so strong that it is not greatly determined by
what lies outside it" (Finale), we feel finally that George Eliot
is interested in the effect society *in itself* has upon individuals.
I mean by this that it is not the *specific* quality of nineteenth-
century life that compels her attention so much as the complexities of attempting a personal and public life in *any* social
setting. Of course, the facts of her period mean that she deals
with evangelical religion, the education of women, and some
aspects of capitalism, but only as a reflection of the external
factors that must exist in any form of society. I would argue
that these facts constitute the subject matter, but not the theme
of *Middlemarch*. Eliot's deepest specific involvement with her
age is in the realm of ideas, as her early period of strenuous
intellectual activity showed, but I have tried to demonstrate
that Dickens' grasp of his century cuts below the play of ideas
to more crucially determining features. She has no characters
like Pip, Arthur Clennam, and Bradley Headstone, who, though
they may lack the total complexity of life, achieve the status of
significantly modern men. There is a distinction to be made
here between "manners," in Lionel Trilling's sense, and what I
would call themes. When Eliot says of Mrs. Cadwallader that
"a much more exemplary character with an infusion of sour
dignity would not have furthered their comprehension of the
Thirty-nine Articles, and would have been less socially uniting"
(VI), she is dealing with what Trilling calls a "culture's hum
and buzz of implication":

I mean the whole evanescent context in which its explicit statements
are made. It is that part of a culture which is made up of half-
uttered or unuttered or unutterable expressions of value.[5]

Dorothea and Lydgate are caught up in the pressures of Victorian life, while Dickens' characters exist at its moment of
crisis. Dickens' major interest is the theme: Pip's desire for
gentility, Clennam's sense of alienation, Headstone's social insecurity—all facets of the nineteenth-century at breaking point.
    The implication of this distinction between manners and
theme and, indeed, of my whole argument in this section might
be summed up in the following way: *Middlemarch* is the
prose epic of man's life as it is lived in inescapable relation
with others; Dickens' greatest novels are the poetic epics of

    [5] "Manners, Morals, and the Novel," in *The Liberal Imagination* (New
York: Doubleday Anchor Books, 1953), p. 200.

nineteenth-century society. George Eliot's meanings, her com-
passionate yet objective understanding of human nature, demand and are forged from a style of intellectual, ironic wit:

Having made his clerical toilette with due care in the morning he
[Mr. Casaubon] was prepared only for those amenities of life which
were suited to the well-adjusted stiff cravat of the period, and to a
mind weighted with unpublished matter. (XX)

Apart from that, however, her style is without graces; it is an
instrument of analysis, not of imaginative creation. Her literari-
ness: Mr. Casaubon as a "learned provincial clergyman is accustomed to think of his acquaintances as of 'lords, knyghts,
and other noble and worthi men, that conne Latyn but lytille'"
(III); her paucity of dialogue; the summaries, rather than embodiment, of what happened at Dorothea's early meetings with
Mr. Casaubon; the straightforward realism of her description
of Mr. Casaubon's house (IX), which has none of the symbolic
power of Dickens' imaginative descriptions—all combine to give
her work a certain air of prosaicness. And her use of the web
and pier-glass images is without any of the consistency or richness to be found in the verbal and symbolic structure of *Little
Dorrit*. This flatness of tone and her authorial interpolations
have the effect, as they are perhaps designed to do, of bringing
one back to the "real" life in which she is interested, whereas
the dense verbal texture of *Little Dorrit* is a major factor in the
creation of a world whose imaginative force keeps it distinct
from the contemporary life that helped give it birth. In other
words, Eliot reflects reality with as much attention to sober
detail as possible, while the created worlds of Dickens possess
an aesthetic autonomy because his reflection is distorted by
creative insights into a new whole whose often violent exaggeration and melodrama is capable of exposing the roots of
modern life.

This is, in my view, the final justification of Dickens' method,
and serves also, perhaps, as an answer to the Dickens' problem.
I began this book by pointing out how extraordinary is the conjunction of social concern and, for want of a more precise word,
poetry in Dickens. And in this section I analyzed some of the
limitations of his vivid grasp of the external in the creation of
character. But it is not enough simply to belabor Dickens for
his failings. He was sufficiently aware of them himself to attempt self-criticism, as the creation of Pip shows, but we can
surely guess that he realized these faults were only the other

side of his overwhelming genius, his ability to embody the spirit
of the nineteenth century in a concrete realization of its pressures and institutions. And this realization was transmitted not
through the subtle exploration of major characters, but by
means of a direct embodiment of the institutions themselves
and their influence on figures whose complexity was limited,
but not destroyed, by their necessary contribution to an overall
pattern of significance. Poetry is of the essence of Dickens'
method, as analysis is of George Eliot's, because only poetry
could combine the sensuous particularity of detail and the
generalized weight of implication that make up the echoing
realities of the Court of Chancery and the Circumlocution
Office. The poetry of Dickens, which expresses itself most obviously in a verbal evocation of externality, is not finally to be
separated from the deeply symbolist nature of his genius. The
worlds of the great novels of his last period are symbolic trans-
mutations of Victorian life; and within the novels as a whole,
character, setting, and action are insistently imbued with symbolic meaning. The link between externality and symbolism
lies, of course, in the fact that however inner-directed may be
its implications the symbol is always solidly rooted in the world
of mundane actuality. The "circus animals" of the poet's imagination exist in terms of surface detail as well as subterranean
meaning, and the way to Dickens' insight into the nature of
nineteenth-century society is by means of the symbolic surface
in which it is embodied.

One final example may serve to place the direction of this
argument. The social novel, the novel of character *in* society
or of society *through* character, could find no place for the
Wemmick of *Great Expectations*. As he returns with Pip from
the excursion to Walworth he gradually "got dryer and harder
as we went along, and his mouth tightened into a post-office
again. At last, when we got to his place of business and he
pulled out his key from his coat-collar, he looked as unconscious
of his Walworth property as if the Castle and the drawbridge
and the arbour and the lake and the fountain and the Aged,
had all been blown into space together by the last discharge of
the Stinger" (XXV). This, we protest, is not human character,
but Dickensian eccentricity, the manipulation of oddity; Wemmick is a mechanical puppet rather than a living being. But as
soon as the protest is registered, we realize its limitations and,
simultaneously, the extent to which Dickens is capable of wid-
ening the scope of his most well-tried technical devices. Wem-

mick is a mechanical character because an inhuman dichotomy is the key, symbolic reality of his nature. He is a schematic and limited, but poetic, embodiment of the utterly alienated man of modern capitalist civilization. He explains to Pip that Jaggers has never seen Walworth and never "heard of it. Never seen the Aged. Never heard of him. No, the office is one thing, and private life is another. When I go into the office, I leave the Castle behind me, and when I come into the Castle, I leave the office behind me"; and when he has crossed his drawbridge into the Castle at night "I hoist it up—so—and cut off the communication" (XXV). Walled impenetrably in the private world of the Englishman's castle, Wemmick can gratify normal human impulses in his bizarrely tender relationship with the Aged P; but in the world of business he is a sinister scavenger, willing to take his last possession from a man who stands condemned to death.

It is extraordinary that a novel containing the psychological realism of Pip's delineation (thus making *Great Expectations* the closest of Dickens' works to a social novel in the conventional Victorian sense) could successfully accommodate a figure of such a very different kind as Wemmick. The secret of this success is to be explained, I think, in three ways. First, Wemmick is brilliantly integrated within the novel's thematic structure. He forms a subsidiary, and reinforcing, expression of the book's organizing principle, the corrupting power of money. In keeping with his position in the social hierarchy, Wemmick's desire for money stems not from the ambitions of gentility, but simply as part of a process of economic survival. "Portable property" for him will mean, eventually, complete retirement behind the Castle's fortifications and the full assumption of a semblance of human life. But in the process of accumulating his portable property Wemmick is continuously eroding the possibility of attaining a recognizable humanity. He has worked out a strategy for defeating the system of which he is a part, but the strategy operates by means of the existing social values and these cannot possibly lead to the end Wemmick has in view. Wemmick is trying to overthrow the system from within, and as Dickens continually shows, this may be possible in personal terms, but only at the expense of spiritual fragmentation. Perhaps the clearest example of Wemmick's fundamental corruption is his reaction to Magwitch's death and the loss of his fortune, a reaction that is, significantly, given to Pip in his "private and personal capacity":

". . . I assure you I haven't been so cut up for a long time. What I
look at is, the sacrifice of so much portable property."

"What *I* think of, Wemmick, is the poor owner of the property."

"Yes, to be sure. . . . Of course there can be no objection to your
being sorry for him, and I'd put down a five-pound note myself to
get him out of it. But what I look at, is this . . . the portable property
certainly could have been saved. That's the difference between the
property and the owner." (LV)

The confusion between means and ends here is total, and
this leads to the second point I want to make about the success
of Wemmick's characterization: his personal schizophrenia reveals with masterly insight the perilous situation of man under
the conditions of industrial capitalism. His lack of integration
is symbolized by almost every detail of his appearance, actions,
and the setting in which he figures, but Dickens' understanding
of his social implications can be illustrated by a point I do not
think has been made before. Wemmick's Castle is his own
creation in every detail:

"At the back, there's a pig, and there are fowls and rabbits; then I
knock together my own little frame, you see, and grow cucumbers;
and you'll judge at supper what sort of a salad I can raise. So,
sir . . . if you can suppose the little place besieged, it would hold out
a devil of a time in point of provisions." (XXV)

I am, he says, "my own engineer, my own carpenter, and my
own plumber, and my own Jack of all Trades," and we can
see in this a desperate attempt to preserve the sanctity of an
inner life against the hostility of an inhuman outside world.
Both Wemmick and his Castle are, in fact, besieged, and his
response to this reveals him as a significant modern type, the
do-it-yourselfer seeking escape from division of labor in an attempt to recapture the lost wholeness of creative work. But,
once more, the pressures of a hostile environment corrupt the
strategy at its source, and Wemmick is gripped in the eccentricity of an *idée fixe*: "Then at the back . . . out of sight, so
as not to impede the idea of fortifications—for it's a principle
with me, if you have an idea, carry it out and keep it up"
(XXV). At the back, out of sight, Wemmick keeps his cannon,
the Stinger; and the description of what happens to the Castle
when it is set off shows clearly the shakiness of the very foundations of Wemmick's solution to his problem: it "went off with
a bang that shook the crazy little box of a cottage as if it must
fall to pieces, and made every glass and teacup in it ring"

(XXV). Like Arthur Clennam, Wemmick tries to defend himself against the incursions of a hostile society, but in this unequal struggle the enemy must secure its hostages if even a hope of victory is to be attained. Clennam retreats from a dreamlike fog of hypocrisy and evil into dreams of his own, a stratagem that involves a limiting loss of mature adulthood; Wemmick seeks to avoid a mechanical world, but can do so only by becoming a mechanism himself, and his Castle is precarious in its flimsiness, lunatic in its dissociation from normal human life.

Many readers might grant the validity of the points I have been making in this discussion and yet still argue that Wemmick is an unsatisfactory character; my third point may answer their objections more conclusively. There is no sense in denying that Wemmick is a schematic figure, but I would argue that his symbolic and thematic importance are an artistic success because they are embodied in a language of poetic precision and suggestiveness. Wemmick's courtship of Miss Skiffins is a wonderful example of this:

As Wemmick and Miss Skiffins sat side by side, and as I sat in a shadowy corner, I observed a slow and gradual elongation of Mr. Wemmick's mouth, powerfully suggestive of his slowly and gradually stealing his arm round Miss Skiffins's waist. In course of time I saw his hand appear on the other side of Miss Skiffins; but at that moment Miss Skiffins neatly stopped him with the green glove, unwound his arm again as if it were an article of dress, and with the greatest deliberation laid it on the table before her. . . . if I could have thought the act consistent with abstraction of mind, I should have deemed that Miss Skiffins performed it mechanically. (XXXVII)

This is far from being a simple example of Dickensian humor or the cheap manipulation of aimless eccentricity. It *is* amusing, of course, but it has a sinister quality also. We feel that we are observing the mating gestures of two puppets and are reminded, perhaps, that Miss Skiffins possesses a fair amount of portable property. The thought of their eventual lovemaking is hardly capable of penetrating one's consciousness; but however much they may violate our sense of fictional character, they are presented to us with an evocative accuracy that impresses the whole scene upon the imagination with indelible intensity.

This, then, is the specific nature of Dickens' fictional achievement: the creation of a new form in literature, the social novel refined into a sharpness of thematic brilliance by the combination of prophetic social insight and a poetic use of language. I

have already explained Dickens' commitment to the social concern by means of those features of Victorian civilization which
led most of the century's best minds to a similar involvement;
in Dickens' writing they were reinforced by the events of his
own life. Is it possible, one wonders, to suggest an explanation
of his equally profound commitment to the poetic? No doubt
its roots lie too deep for critical analysis, but it may be valid to
point out that there is a unity of content and style at work
here. Dickens' vision of his world was conditioned by what he
saw as the degrading power of money and the personal alienation that stemmed from it, and the implications of this for his
view of human character have been interestingly postulated
by Dorothy Van Ghent.

Dickens' intuition alarmingly saw this process [the reduction of
people into things] in motion, a process which abrogated the primary demands of human feeling and rationality, and he sought an
extraordinary explanation for it. People were becoming things, and
things . . . were becoming more important than people. People were
being de-animated, robbed of their souls, and things were usurping
the prerogatives of animate creatures—governing the lives of their
owners in the most literal sense.[6]

It is certainly true that Dickens regarded the degradation of
human spontaneity into a mechanical rigidity of personality as
one of his society's constant threats to the individual, and this
degradation was usually embodied in an imagery that mirrored
the character's mechanization; Wemmick is only the most intense example of this creative peculiarity. Moreover, as Mrs.
Van Ghent points out, this view of humanity seems to have
exerted a powerful attraction over Dickens at all times; Dickens
told John Forster that "he was always losing sight of a man in
his diversion by the mechanical play of some part of the man's
face, which 'would acquire a sudden ludicrous life of its own.' "[7]
If a writer's primary concern is with the psychological exploration of character, as is George Eliot's, there is the possibility
that the language of analysis may replace that of direct imaginative involvement. In a writer whose grasp of the world
depends on the "thingness" that symbolizes for him the pro-
foundest determining pressures of that world, we are likely to
find his creative struggle centered on embodying this thingness
in a language of sensuous plasticity. Dickens himself does this,

6 *The English Novel* (New York: Harper Torchbooks, 1961), p. 128.
7 *Ibid.*, p. 130.

a fact that makes him a poet, for the poet's main object is almost always to convince us of the "reality" of his work's surface in order that we will accept the spiritual or abstract meanings that it conveys. Dickens saw the triumph of Machinery as the fate progressively overtaking the nineteenth century, and it was this insight that gave him his almost abnormal awareness of his society's flux hardening into a mechanical arrangement of things. Rooted together with this social insight in the depths of Dickens' creative personality was the desire to body forth this arrangement in a language vibrant with symbolic meaning.

Didacticism and Creative Autonomy

I hope the preceding section has thrown some light on the relationship that exists in Dickens between realist and poet, and "in his work between didacticism and poetry."[8] Some further discussion may bring it to a final conclusion.

This problem has presented itself in a variety of ways. We can accept Dickens' estimate of Wackford Squeers as little more than a representative type, but his view of Mrs. Gamp seems grossly out of harmony with the facts. Indeed, there is something truly alien in the mind that could talk in this way about one of the great characters of fiction. We can combine with Dickens' judgment in this respect the progress of his concern with social, political, and institutional abuses from his earliest works onward. Even *Pickwick* contains an attack on legal chicanery and the evils of the debtors' prison, and from then on the examples are too many to be numbered. Yorkshire schools, the Poor Law, Chancery, the shame of illegitimacy, greed, snobbery, and hypocrisy are only some of the few that come most readily to mind. From this short list, an unprejudiced reader who knew nothing of Dickens might fairly conclude that he is the crudest of polemical writers, especially as, in Frank O'Connor's words, the nineteenth-century novel was the "normal medium of humanitarian sentiment."[9] But the most cursory examination reveals that a book such as *Little Dorrit* is not a *normal* medium for anything.

It is possible to generalize with confidence as to the reasons that lay behind the writing of the social novels of the 1840's, those of Disraeli and Mrs. Gaskell, for example. Self-interest

[8] See chap. 1 "The Problem of Form."
[9] *The Mirror in the Roadway* (London: 1957), p. 14.

and the advancement of the Tory party were Disraeli's principal motives, while Mrs. Gaskell was moved by a genuine pity
for the poor and oppressed. But the house of fiction, although
it may have many rooms, is a difficult place to enter, and despite
their differences, these writers are united in using the novel for
a limited, and limiting, purpose. This is not too damaging to
Disraeli, for his books contain only a few moments of raw truth
surrounded by wads of melodrama and garish high life. Mrs.
Gaskell, who deserves infinitely more serious treatment, pursues
an objective that runs counter to the true nature of her talent,
and in *North and South*, for example, we can see how a noble
purpose causes the book to fall apart. The love story of Margaret Hale, the representative of a middle-class gentility that
is genuinely civilized, and Thornton, the northern industrialist,
is obviously the center of the book's imaginative interest: "And
she shrank and shuddered as under the fascination of some
great power, repugnant to her whole previous life. She crept
away, and hid from his idea. . . . She disliked him the more
for having mastered her inner will. How dared he say that he
would love her still, even though she shook him off with contempt" (XXV). Compared with this, the passages of social
concern are irritating as well as disunifying. The tone of these
scenes, in one of which Margaret intervenes to prevent strikers
from attacking Thornton, is summed up in her ringing cry:
"Let them insult my maiden pride as they will—I walk pure
before God!" (XXIV). Lack of unity is a characteristic of
Dickens' early novels, and although it arises from other causes
(being more a matter of imaginative vitality and the absence
of a disciplining literary heritage), he displays a similar failure
of understanding in the treatment of some of his social themes.
After the pristine freshness of Mr. Pickwick, as I have shown,
his benefactors go into a decline the main cause of which lies
in his inability to conceive of a humanly viable method of dispensing charity.

One of the principal aims of this book has been to show
how Dickens did achieve the social awareness that differentiates him so markedly from his contemporaries. But the point
I want to make here is that there was nothing divisive in the
union of didacticism and creativity in Dickens; the very reverse, in fact. The strength of his genius lies in a faculty that
is unique in Victorian fiction: it is the seemingly limited social
aim, the didactic purpose, the polemical point, which not
merely sparks Dickens' satirical talent, but, in his best work,

taps the deepest sources of his creative imagination. What Dickens himself thought of Mrs. Gamp is irrelevant, although interesting. If, in conceiving her, a part of his mind had to be concerned with improving the sanitary conditions of the poor, this was only because such a public theme was the necessary starting place for his creative process. It is only such a commitment to the social world which can account for the conception of a novel such as *Bleak House*. Its achievement is extraordinary in the precedence it gives to the institution over the individual, and although, as I have said, this limits its greatness, it is still deeply interesting as an exploration of society.

The release of Dickens' imagination by the public theme can be explained, I think, by reference to another important aim that I have tried to keep in the forefront of my discussion: the notion of Dickens as *the* significant man and novelist of his time. I have traced how in the blacking-factory episode and the Maria Beadnell affair he was made the victim of pressures that reflected some of the determining forces of his age. Dickens suffered much, but he did not suffer alone. His personal drama was a microcosm of the drama of thousands. Dickens had lived the facts of the nineteenth century, and had endured the suffering they imposed before he was capable of fully understanding them; from this he derived the power to chart the depths and the shallows of his epoch. The "intensity of this felt experience"[10] together with an unceasing involvement in the life of his times is the source of Dickens' ability to combine didacticism and creative autonomy.

The nature of Dickens' personal experience determined the direction in which his imagination flowed most readily, and this, in its turn, demanded a form that could encompass the public and private, the didactic and poetic. A major justification of *Bleak House* is that it opened the way to the achievement of *Little Dorrit* and *Great Expectations*. In it, Dickens discovered how to embody his social insights in a satisfactory fictional form. Having mastered that art, he could then move on to combine the institutional and the personal in *Little Dorrit* with a complexity of general theme and a richness of particularity that make it his greatest, because his most finely typical, work, and to achieve a rendering of the social through the personal in *Great Expectations* which is almost as great. It is, finally, in these works that Dickens elaborates what I have

[10] See p. 85.

called his myth of society. They are fictional worlds in which, as I try to show in the next section, the ideal takes precedence over the real (although the real is always the initiating force), and where the created universe exists apart from, although parallel to, the society that has given it birth. It is this quality of self-sufficiency and internal consistency that give to these novelistic worlds their mythic status.

Radicalism and Pessimism

The artistic effort of the novelists of the 1840's was directed toward social amelioration. They attempted to bridge a gap in their middle-class contemporaries' knowledge of society and so bring about a change in their attitude to the poor. This change was to be effected by transforming the minds and hearts, especially the hearts, of their readers. In the final analysis, this kind of personal transformation may be the only one worth having, but it remains true that the social-problem writers gave too little weight to the importance of external pressures, stemming from the nature of capitalist civilization, in forming personal character. They did not understand clearly enough how the processes of capitalism were at work in the world around them, and were unable, therefore, to render this in their novels. It was beyond their range to chart the moral degenera- tion wrought in Pip by his desire for gentility, or even to show a much less interesting breakdown, such as that of Rick in *Bleak House*. With these examples before us, it is impossible to regard Dickens as an untaught genius warbling his native wood- notes wild. Mr. Dombey's pride, William Dorrit's vacillations of character, Bradley Headstone's social insecurity—all show Dickens' understanding of what the structure of society can do to the individual. It often seems as if the earlier Victorian novel is a social form conceived by writers who do not really understand society.

Of course, there were enormous difficulties facing the Vic- torian novelist in his attempt to understand, delineate, and criticize society, because that society was changing at the very moments he was trying to grapple with it. I hope I have shown by now that Dickens was capable of doing all three with amaz- ing success. Particularly remarkable was his ability to realize the deepest meanings of social movements as they came to the surface; in his concentration on money as the key to gentility, for example, and in his exploration of the problems of the newly educated in *Our Mutual Friend*. What none of these writers seemed able to do was to appreciate that changes in the structure of society itself might be necessary before their ideal worlds could come into existence. Perhaps only Dickens and George Eliot, the one by means of his social insight and the other by her force of intellect, would have been capable of this task, but the economic, political, and social analysis of Victorian civilization was in too rudimentary a state throughout most of their careers for them to borrow fruitfully from the work of others. I have said enough in the course of this book to indicate certain resemblances between the thinking of Marx and, say, Carlyle, especially on the subject of alienation. This is, however, a matter not of direct influence—David Thomson points out that although John Stuart Mill became an "undoctrinaire" socialist, he "never mentions, and does not even seem to have heard of, Karl Marx"[11]—but of the amazing unanimity of reaction, in very different minds, to the historical processes of the nineteenth century. Both Dickens and George Eliot were too deeply committed to the concept of individuality ever to have subscribed to a theory of such blind impersonalism as that of Marx, but awareness of an analysis such as his might have modified their views on the possibility of social change. In any event, their main creative energies, especially those of Dickens, were given to the task of forming the fictional structures by means of which they passed judgment on the world of reality. And this is a salutary reminder. It does not lie within the intentions of most imaginative writers to give a detailed picture of the kind of society they would like to see come into existence. They are, rightly, too concerned with present complexities and problems to think profoundly about the future. To ask more of a *Middlemarch* or a *Little Dorrit* would be to display impertinence, as well as a lack of understanding of the nature of fiction. A work such as *Little Dorrit*, in fact, develops its positives from its critical onslaughts, as well as from the more obvious virtues of its "good" characters.

If, however, we can allow ourselves to absorb what I take to be the insistent meaning of Dickens' last novels, the question of social change is seen to be fundamentally irrelevant, for they are characterized by what sets Dickens apart most completely from his contemporaries: a willingness to countenance the utter rejection of society. Victorian individualism and laissez-faire

[11] *England in the Nineteenth Century* (Penguin Books, 1950), p. 51.

were never, in theory at least, meant to be anarchic. For the Victorians they were the means of securing the greatest social as well as personal well-being, and social criteria, in the best and worst sense, were always the touchstones of individual morality. In such a world, the rejection of society represented by Pip's adherence to Magwitch, the criminal outcast, and by the despairing romanticism of the marriage of Eugene Wrayburn and Lizzie Hexam, is complete. The meaning of such actions makes it clear that the word "radical" must be applied to Dickens with great care. He was, as he always claimed to be, radical in some limited political sense, but to pigeonhole him in this way would be peculiarly damaging. Whatever utopian hopes for the future may have guided his earlier work, the hopelessness with which he eventually viewed his society and the path it was taking is unmistakable both in his letters and his novels. *Great Expectations* is radical, as I have observed earlier, in the "sense of being out of sympathy with its time," and with Eugene and Lizzie "pessimism not radicalism is the operative word."

This opposition of radicalism and pessimism, and where the stress should be placed, is illuminated by Dickens' treatment of trade unions and Ragged Schools. His harshness toward them has troubled many critics, especially those who have sought to give his work a radical bias of a narrowly political kind. It brings home to us, despite the important interconnections between them, the ultimate discreteness of Dickens' life and work. He was capable of describing those who attended public dinners as "slobbering cattle," but he himself continued to attend them because people had to be helped and this was a good way of doing so. Dickens never rejected humanity along with society, and he supported any cause or organization that he thought capable of improving the lot of the poor. But to give philanthropy, the unions, or Ragged Schools his unqualified approval in the ideal world of art was another matter. A comparison of life and art can be as instructive here as it was in the American scenes of *Martin Chuzzlewit*. Nothing reveals more clearly the despair of Dickens' final social vision than the cruel humor in the chapter "Of An Educational Character" in *Our Mutual Friend*, especially when this objectively artistic view of Ragged Schools is compared with his personal sentiments. These are expressed in a wonderful letter of 1843 to Miss Coutts, the philanthropist.

The Masters are extremely quiet, honest, good men. You may suppose they are, to be there at all. It is enough to break one's heart to get at the place: to say nothing of getting at the children's minds afterwards. . . . To impress them, even with the idea of God, when their own condition is so desolate, becomes a monstrous task. . . . the Masters think it most important to impress them at first with some distinction . . . between right and wrong, and I quite agree with them. . . . The moral courage of the teachers is beyond praise. They are surrounded by every possible adversity, and every disheartening circumstance that can be imagined. Their office is worthy of the apostles. . . . Whether this effort will succeed, it is quite impossible to say. But that it is a great one, beginning at the right end, among thousands of immortal creatures, who cannot, in their present state, be held accountable for what they do, it is *as* impossible to doubt.[12]

The attitude of Dickens the artist is more reserved and ironic.

The school at which young Charley Hexam had first learned from a book . . . was a miserable loft in an unsavoury yard . . . half the pupils dropped asleep, or fell into a state of waking stupefaction; the other half kept them in either condition by maintaining a monotonous droning noise, as if they were performing, out of time and tune, on a ruder sort of bagpipe. The teachers, animated solely by good intentions, had no idea of execution, and a lamentable jumble was the upshot of their kind endeavours. . . . all the place was pervaded by a grimly ludicrous pretence that every pupil was childish and innocent. This . . . led to the ghastliest absurdities. Young women old in the vices of the commonest and worst life, were expected to profess themselves enthralled by the good child's book, the Adventures of Little Margery, who resided in the village cottage by the mill; severely reproved and morally squashed the miller, when she was five and he was fifty . . . denied herself a new nankeen bonnet, on the ground that the turnips did not wear nankeen bonnets, neither did the sheep who ate them; who plaited straw and delivered the dreariest orations to all comers, at all sorts of unseasonable times. (Bk.2, I)

The mythic quality of Dickens' novels is relevant here. It stems in large part from the fact that he is not dealing in reportage or a simple social realism, but in the fullest kind of imaginative creation. These are worlds in which unions and Ragged Schools exist, but in which their ultimate rather than their limited function is being questioned. And it is in this,

[12] Edgar Johnson, *Charles Dickens: His Tragedy and Triumph*, I, 461–463.

as well as in the width of their scope, that their epic force resides. They examine the entire range of values of modern society. In his life, Dickens gave full approval to men such as
Headstone and Hexam who had struggled up from the depths
of degradation. Their achievement was far from negligible, and
it had made a qualitative difference in their lives. In a limited
sense, any education is better than none at all. But, to use my
own words once again, "Dickens is not concerned here with
short-term ends: Headstone and Charley Hexam are being
weighed, and found wanting, on a much more important scale
than that of mere utilitarianism."[13] Through them, and in all
the great novels of his last period, Dickens is bringing the
entire nineteenth century to the bar of a rigorous moral and
spiritual judgment.

Money and the Novel Form

The whole intention of this book has been to disprove statements such as those made by H. V. Routh in his *Money, Morals
and Manners*; for him, most of Dickens' novels are "concerned
with special and departmental abuses, for instance workhouses,
debtors' prisons, and law's delays—and do not penetrate to
the subsoil in which such growths can survive."[14] In *The
Dickens World*, which despite its interest seems to me misguided in the most fundamental way in its determination to
treat Dickens "as if he were a journalist more than a creative
artist,"[15] Humphry House reaches a somewhat similar conclusion in his discussion of the over-discussed question of Dickens'
direct social influence in his own day. House's argument for this
not only adds another reason to the causes of Dickens' darkening vision of society; it also seems to contradict his earlier
view that Dickens was never in advance of the public in his
social criticism, but that he "was often even rather behind the
times."[16]

For the most impressive thing about "Reform" between 1832 and
1870 was its sloth. No genuine attempt to meet his objections to the
Poor Law was made till the appointment of the Royal Commission of
1905. Private persons were still imprisoned for debts over £20
until 1861, and imprisonment for debt was not formally abolished

13 See p. 184.
14 (London: Nicholson and Watson, 1935), p. 54.
15 (London: Oxford Paperbacks, 1960), p. 215.
16 *Ibid.*, p. 42.

before 1869. Effective compulsion on local authorities about Public
Health only began in 1866 after still another epidemic of cholera, and
the Local Government Board was only set up in the year after Dickens' death. The Civil Service was thoroughly reorganized only in
1870, and the foundations of a national system of education were
delayed till the same year.[17]

Even if one were to argue only from Dickens' attack on "special
and departmental abuses," there is a comprehensiveness in this
never-satisfied grappling with social evil which seems to justify
Bagehot's hostile comment that Dickens spoke "in a tone of
objection to the necessary constitution of human society."[18]

As I have shown, however, Dickens was fully aware of the
"subsoil" from which these weeds drew their nourishment.
Direct personal experience and a generalizing social insight
gave him the ability to understand and portray the determining forces of his age. It was this that conditioned his vision of
English society which I described earlier in this book as "a
series of interlocking systems . . . each bent on maintaining its
power and privilege: Parliament, the law, the church, the civil
service, manufacturers and merchants, financiers, doctors, philanthropists, all pursuing their self-contained and limited aims,
but all finally forming into a vast complex of social, political
and economic oppression. Beneath this structure lies the mass
of unorganized men and women on whom it battens."[19] In a
factual way, this seems to approximate to our impression of the
vastly complex, panoramic sweep of the worlds of *Bleak House*
and *Little Dorrit*. Their darkness is such that even the sun's
rays appear as bars imprisoning the universe, and the monotonous rain that imperceptibly rots Chesney Wold is devoid of
life-giving power. Laughter is never forsaken, but it echoes
strangely in the chambers of Chancery and the cells of
the Marshalsea; the joyful confidence of Mr. Micawber has
crumbled into the fluttering helplessness of William Dorrit;
figures whose capacity for love is their only defense against the
indifference of an inhuman world flit alone through a city black
with a decay symbolic of its evil and heavy with the weight of
man's suffering, their moments of personal contact pathetically
isolated against the teeming menace of their setting. These

[17] *Ibid.*, pp. 222–223.
[18] Walter Bagehot, "Charles Dickens," in *Literary Studies* (London:
Everyman's Library, 1927), II, 191.
[19] See p. 138.

novels form a continual embodiment of one of capitalism's basic
paradoxes, the isolation of individuals who are yet indissolubly
bound to each other by the invisible bonds of economic interdependence. In purely literary terms, they are at the furthest
possible remove from the picaresque form in which characters
and events are unified only by the presence of the hero. It
would be ingenuous to express surprise at how a Pancks, a
Clennam, a Merdle, and a Little Dorrit can be brought into
a relationship not of melodramatic coincidence but of real
significance, and yet this remains an extraordinary fictional
achievement. I hope it is clear by now how it was attained.

The structure of Dickens' early novels was compounded of
elements of the eighteenth-century picaresque and the devices
of melodrama, especially that of coincidence, which were so
widespread in the popular art of his own day. The picaresque
was eventually abandoned in favor of a more unified form, but
this was not something completely new. Dickens displayed the
genius of the great popular artist in taking the given aspects
of his creative world and investing them with a meaning related
to the new subject matter that they had to embody. Mr. Snagsby
may complain of the mysteries by which he is surrounded in
Bleak House, but we do not feel inclined to join in his complaint because we realize that, at their best, these mysteries
are no longer merely gratuitous. The solution of the puzzle as
to the source of Pip's expectations is inextricably bound up
with the most serious levels of the book's meaning; in fact,
in a sense it *is* the meaning. The revelation that Magwitch is
the source of his wealth, and Pip's reaction to this fact, involve us in the economic expectations of a whole society and
their humanly degrading effects. Similarly, the parent and child
relationship between Estella and Magwitch is no part of the
Dickens' problem, a something to be explained away. It is,
brilliantly, a further revelation of the falsity of Pip's desires in
the inescapable link it establishes between Pip's wish for gentility and his love for Estella; both are tainted at the same source.
Mystification, coincidence, dream, fantasy, violence, the unexpected relationship—these are not things of which we should
complain in Dickens at his best. Melodrama is a perfectly suitable medium for the delineation of the irrationalities of capitalist society. A system of communal living which is based
neither on spiritual sanctions nor on the known idiosyncrasy of
valid human contact, but on the amorphous yet highly concrete power of money, seems peculiarly liable to the escape

into delusion, the outburst of violence. We find both in the Pancks of *Little Dorrit*. After a lifetime of "fag and grind," it is surely only the conventional response, to life as well as art, which finds his sudden shearing of the Patriarch's locks unbelievable. And for him to admit that Clennam's involvement with Merdle was a "speculation" instead of an "investment" would mean the destruction of his sense of himself. The calculations that prove that, "regarded as a question of figures," Clennam should have made a fortune "were destined to afford him consolation to the end of his days" (Bk. 2, XXX).

It is now, perhaps, permissable to come full circle and reassert the unity of Dickens' social insight and creative power. He saw beneath the anarchic, shapeless surface of his civilization to what seemed to him the controlling principle, the role of money. This alone formed the cement of a society no longer held together by human bonds. And so, in the formation of those fictional worlds that constitute a comprehensive critique of nineteenth-century life, we find money as the force that unites their disparate elements. The details of plot, character, and action which make up the complex structures of Dickens' later novels reflect the web of financial interdependence that holds individuals and classes in modern society in a grasp as isolating as it is inescapable.

Index